The

ALLOTMENT
handbook

The
ALLOTMENT
handbook

Caroline Foley

NEW
HOLLAND

For Max and Bill

First published in 2004 by
New Holland Publishers (UK) Ltd
London · Cape Town · Sydney · Auckland

Garfield House, 86–88 Edgware Road, London W2 2EA, United Kingdom
www.newhollandpublishers.com

80 McKenzie Street, Cape Town 8001, South Africa

Level 1, Unit 4, 14 Aquatic Drive, Frenchs Forest, NSW 2086, Australia

218 Lake Road, Northcote, Auckland, New Zealand

ISBN 1 84330 583 6

Senior Editor: Clare Sayer
Production: Hazel Kirkman
Design: Casebourne Rose Design Associates
Illustrations: Coral Mula and Sue Rose
Editorial Direction: Rosemary Wilkinson

10 9 8 7 6 5 4

Reproduction by Modern Age Repro, Hong Kong
Printed and bound by Kyodo Printing, Singapore

Acknowledgements: I feel very privileged to have met so many wonderful people in the course of writing this book. My thanks particularly go to Dave Fox, Paul Archer, Derek Humphries, Bernard Coote, June Brandon and Eddie Campbell who generously gave me an unforgettable day showing me around. I am indebted to many others who shed the light – especially Judy Wilkinson from SAGS, Sally Smith at HDRA, Bethan Stagg from ARI, Geoff Stokes and Shirley Fleetwood from NSALG and Abigail Burridge, Agenda 21 Officer. Above all my thanks go to Dr. Richard Wiltshire for setting me off in the right direction for the second time, also to Rosemary Wilkinson and Clare Sayer from New Holland Publishers with whom it is always the greatest pleasure to work.

CONTENTS

INTRODUCTION

There could not be a better time for allotments. After more than half a century of neglect and decline, they are on the brink of a great revival.

In this traditionally cloth-cap, male preserve, there has been a remarkable new uptake by women, young couples and professional people. Food scares have made growing organic food in season seem ever more attractive. Gardening has become all the rage. It is good exercise, it's creative and therapeutic. There is something about nurturing plants and pottering in the fresh air that is immensely soothing to the spirit.

The Earth Summit in Rio in 1992 had an energizing effect. Along with 179 nations, Britain signed 'Agenda 21'. They pledged to promote 'sustainability' – or to make every effort to find ways to improve the quality of life in the 21st century while protecting the environment. One result is that Local Agenda 21 officers have been attached to councils across the land. Part of their programme is to promote community spirit, boost wildlife and encourage local food production. Allotments are tailor-made for all these projects.

An all-party inquiry, 'The Future for Allotments', followed in 1998. It was a wake-up call for local authorities. It recognized the value of allotments for health, for communities and as green space while making recommendations on how to secure their future. 'The Good Practice Guide', in 2001, laid out the ways and means. As a result, allotment files are no longer gathering dust on the back shelf – at least not among the more go-ahead councils.

Now that allotments have a higher profile, charities have stepped in to offer grants. With money to spend they are being transformed. Seen as 'green corridors' through towns and cities, unused plots are being turned into nature reserves. Schools, universities, the elderly, the disabled, refugees and minority groups are being sought out to take plots. There are dozens of imaginative schemes.

Allotments are a hard-earned part of our heritage. They sprung from the dire need of the 'labouring poor' in rural areas in the late 18th century. By then, the common land – long regarded as a right – had been systematically removed by the Enclosure Acts. On the 'commons' labourers had been able to keep a few livestock, gather firewood and grow crops to eke out a living in hard times. When mechanization came in, there was widespread unemployment.

There were sporadic peasant revolts. In 1649 Gerrard Winstanley and the 'Diggers' ('those who had the right to dig') camped on former common land at St. George's Hill, Walton-on-Thames in Surrey. The landowner called on the army to drive them out, rip out their crops and burn their huts to the ground. The Riot Act of 1715 gave landowners the right to 'cut down' any protesters who didn't withdraw once the Act had been read out to them.

The Captain Swing Riots of 1830 – 31, marked the tail end nearly two centuries later. The Captain was a myth and the name was ironically coined. Large groups of workers moved from farm to farm, smashing machinery. The riots were brutally suppressed. Most of the ringleaders were transported. However, the government did pass the first legislation to provide allotments.

It was hoped that allotments would reduce the cost of poor relief. Added to this was a high moral stance, that virtuous and honest industry would 'encourage domes-ticity'★ and keep the workers out of the alehouses. Some landowners made the condition that allotments would be forfeited should a crime be committed (like poaching), while the clergy demanded regular church attendance.

Victorian philanthropists furthered the cause. They believed that allotments would give labourers some self-respect and a greater degree of independence. For this reason, it was felt that a small rent should be charged to avoid any whiff of 'charity'. Federations were formed. The most powerful was the Labourers' Friend Society. With influential supporters, it set out to promote allotments in a monthly magazine aimed at landowners and the clergy. It also sent out 'travelling agents' to spread the missionary word.

Allotments were introduced into the cities for people living in closely-packed housing at the height of the Industrial Revolution. Through the World Wars, 'Dig for Victory' Campaigns meant that every spare inch of land was used for growing food. It was a remarkable effort with 1,500,000 plots producing one fifth of the nation's food. Legislation was passed to make them open to all, not just the 'labouring poor'.

Visiting allotments in different parts of the country for this book has been a real joy. They are magical places, small worlds of their own. They make a patchwork of welcome greenness and peace through towns and cities for the world weary. Deeply traditional in some ways, allotment people hold the values that many others are just discovering. While measuring in anachro-nistic rods, poles and perches, they have always taken great pride in recycling, impro-vising and making do. They have bypassed the consumer society. Bound by an enjoy-ment of gardening, they welcome people from all walks of life. Everyone can share plants, seeds, knowledge and jokes — let alone trials and tribulations.

It is my view that allotments set an example to the world.

★ 'The Allotment Movement in England, 1793 – 1873' by Jeremy Burchardt.

chapter 1

GETTING STARTED

FINDING A PLOT

Most people are surprised to discover that there is an allotment plot holder living in every sixteenth house throughout England and Wales. The only allotments they have noticed are the few on view from the train along the railway sidings. But these are just the tip of the iceberg, a tiny proportion of the thousands discreetly tucked away the length and breadth of the British Isles. Many allotments are almost invisible as they are often enclosed by housing and reached only by narrow alleyways or rustic paths. They form a secret green belt threaded through cities, towns and villages unseen by the world at large.

In cities, allotments can have waiting lists of several years while in the suburbs you can take your pick. Wherever you live, study every option while looking for a plot to suit you. The nearest may not be the best. Many local libraries keep a full record, and most parish councils have a full- or part-time allotment officer who can put you in the

Tip

If you live in an area where there are no allotments, and can find five other people on the electoral role who want one as well, the council is obliged to provide. Inner London is an exception to this as there is not enough green space to go around.

picture. Some say that it is worth cultivating allotment people over a pint at their local to get the inside story.

The perfect site

While you may be lured by a peaceful setting or a pastoral view, consider the practicalities:

✦ Distance from your home is a big consideration. If you take the bus or cycle, and are carrying tools, will you get there after a hard day at work?

WHO OWNS ALLOTMENTS?

Local authorities own 87 per cent of allotments. These are the 'statutory' allotments protected by law. They cannot be closed down without permission from the Secretary of State for Transport, Local Government and the Regions. They are therefore comparatively safe from developers, especially if they are in full use. To close them down, the council must prove that the site has fallen into disuse, or find an alternative site within three-quarters of a mile. Councils do vary from place to place. The best councils advertise vacant plots as they come up, prepare them for newcomers and will even put on courses for beginners.

Other allotments are rented by local authorities on a temporary basis and may well be destined for other purposes. A further 8 per cent are privately owned and have little protection against closure.

- A mains water supply in the form of tanks and standpipes is vital and not always on offer.
- In some parts of the country vandalism, including arson, is an all-too-familiar problem.
- A first-class site will have a clubhouse and a trading shed. Though not common as yet, they might even stretch to a lavatory in the form of a 'tree bog', a 'compost toilet' or a 'leaching bed; system.
- Many councils provide sheds. On the other hand, you might inherit a rickety structure made from bits found in skips, or find yourself hanging up your tools in a corrugated mess hut.

Site management

About two-thirds of allotment sites are run by the Local Authority, while the rest have various degrees of self-management. Devolved government seems to work well. By taking responsibility for the site into their own hands, plot holders generally develop a greater sense of community and become more committed to making things work.

Good leadership can make a huge difference. The committee or site manager may buy goods in bulk to sell cheaply to the plot holders, bring in manure from local stables, wood shavings from the Parks Department, old carpet for smothering weeds and discarded pallets for making compost bins.

They might raise money to hire or buy machinery – rotavators, shredders and mowers, for example – and even get hold of an old shipping container to store them. The best sites will involve the local community, have open days and a public right of way. They might have a stall at the local farmer's market or drop in leaflets door-to-door to advertise vacant plots and keep the site fully used.

The National Society

Roughly one-quarter of all allotments are members of the National Society of Allotments and Leisure Gardeners (NSALG). Established in 1926, it is an independent, self-financing body providing a powerful legal lobby for allotments under threat, on occasion taking cases to the House of Lords. Members can call on them for advice, use their insurance scheme and buy a wide range of seed at around half the normal price. Their magazine, *The Allotment and Leisure Gardener,* covers local, national and international allotment news. They can put you in touch with local federations.

ASSESSING A SITE

Check the rules. Some allotments are run on near-military lines, with penalties inflicted for such crimes as late payment of rent or for neglecting the plot. Others are strict about what you may and may not grow. Following the Allotments Act of 1922 to the letter, some insist on mostly vegetables. Many outlaw trees altogether to avoid shading other plots, while others will allow trees only if trained low or on dwarf stock. Hosepipe bans are common.

The majority are more liberal and will allow you to grow more or less whatever you like as long as you keep your plot well tended and don't upset your neighbours. The most honed-down version I have come across is at Ashley Vale Allotments in Bristol. They only have one rule: 'Use it, don't abuse it'.

Check the policy The truly organic allotment site is catching on slowly.

CASE STUDY

"At Trumpington in Cambridge, a 20-pole allotment has been strimmed and raked to establish a chalk grassland sward. Management of existing hedges is actively being undertaken by the allotment society under the guidance of the City Greenways Project. A new hedge is planned to provide habitat simultaneously with improved site security." – *Allotments: local habitat action for Cambridgeshire and Peterborough.*

Generally, committees resign themselves to discouraging chemicals rather than banning them. In line with Local Agenda 21, some allotment sites set aside plots to encourage native flora and fauna and make 'green corridors' through our cities. This is very helpful for organic growers as it brings in friendly predators to deal with pests and develops biodiversity on the allotment.

Digging the local dirt As you wander round, talk to the neighbouring plot holders about the pros and cons of the site. They should be able to tell you about any problems. Ask them about the soil, the weeds, the wind and the weather.

Full or half plot? Allotments are generally 10 poles – 250 sq m (303 sq yd). This is considered the right size to supply a family of four with vegetables all year round. A half, or even a quarter, plot is recommended by many site managers for the newcomer. If your allotment committee doesn't let out half plots it might be worth sharing a whole plot with a friend.

Check out the land Examine the individual plot available to you. Work out the orientation. If you plan to grow vegetables, the ideal site would face south for maximum sun. It would be flat or gently sloping. Large trees within your plot or on neighbouring plots are not helpful; they will cast shade and drip onto the plants beneath.

Find out about the prevailing winds You may need to plan for a shelter belt or other wind break if the plot is in a windy or exposed position.

Study the neighbours' plots You could be facing a losing battle if you are next to a weedy site which will seed all over yours or, by contrast, a person who sprays chemicals everywhere.

MAKING A PLAN

Having found the site that suits you and chosen your plot, don't rush at it. Spend a little time making a plan.

Make a rough sketch

Even if you are not going to stick to it, making a sketch of your ideal plot will concentrate the mind. If you are planning to grow annual flowers and vegetables, allocate them the sunniest and most sheltered position. You will need at least four big areas to rotate the vegetables *(see page 29)*. Room must also be found for compost bins, water butts and a manure heap. A shed is invaluable for storing tools, getting out of the rain and making cups of tea. The roof can be used for catching water to be siphoned off

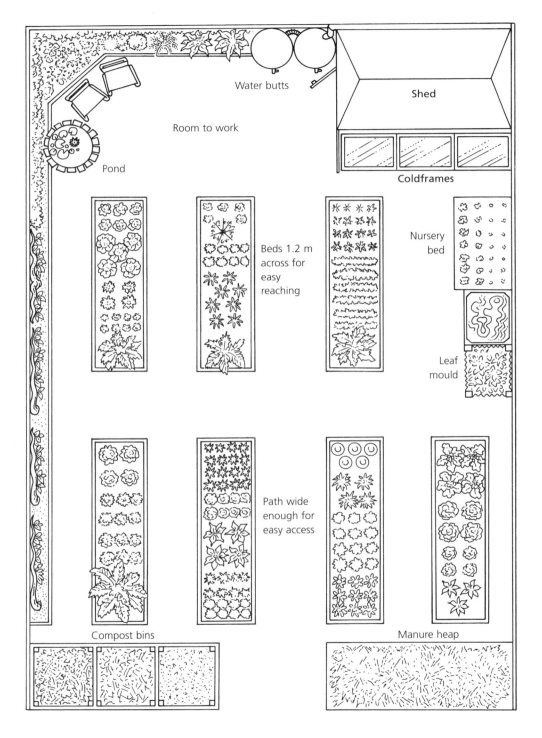

Water butts

Room to work

Shed

Pond

Coldframes

Beds 1.2 m
across for
easy
reaching

Nursery
bed

Leaf
mould

Path wide
enough for
easy access

Compost bins

Manure heap

Layout for an allotment plot

into water butts below. You cannot have too many of these. The south-facing side of a shed makes a handy sheltered position for seedbeds and cold frames.

Sketch out the paths

Paths need to follow the most direct route from A to B – otherwise, in practice, they won't be used. Work out how you will get from the shed to the water butt, from the compost heap to the flower beds, and so on. The main paths should to be at least wide enough to push a wheelbarrow through with ease and without brushing the plants. Treading on the beds will lead to compacted soil, so plan a network of paths – some need only be wide enough for you to get behind the plants to tend them. A grid pattern is probably the most practical solution.

Beds for annual plants

A standard plan that works well is four or more main central beds for annual vegetables and flowers on the rotation plan *(see page 29)*. Ideally, each bed should be no more than 1.2 m (4 ft) across so that you can reach into the middle without having to tread on the soil. You might need several of these, with narrow paths in between. These beds will be cleared of the main crop at the end of each season. If possible, plant the rows north-south so that the plants don't shade each other.

Beds for perennials

The perennials – asparagus, artichoke, rhubarb, and perennial flowers – can go in borders around the edge of the plot along with perennial herbs such as rosemary, thyme and fennel. A comfrey bed is also a good idea for a free supply of fertilizer.

WHAT KIND OF PATHS?

Paths can be made from trampled earth. If the soil is soggy or infested with weeds, you can make temporary paths from strips of old hessian-backed carpet, straw, newspaper or polythene weighed down with wood shavings or grass cuttings. Mown grass makes attractive paths but needs constant upkeep – some allotment sites have a rota system for path mowing. Paving slabs are the best solution for the main paths. If you have some, lay them down without setting them in until you are sure of your plan.

Boundaries

The boundaries of the plot can be made from espaliered fruit trees (where allowed) or trained soft fruit. Other plants can be used to make a screen for privacy. Jerusalem artichokes make a magnificent tall leafy summer screen.

Other features

If you are going to have a seat, plan it to face south for daylong sun, east for morning sun, or west to catch the last rays of the evening. If you have a shed, position seedbeds and cold frames on the south-facing side. At the furthest point from where you plan to sit, leave room for at least three large compost bins, a manure heap and leaf-mould container. Arrange them near the main path so that you can load and unload a wheelbarrow with ease. If you are on a slope, have the heap at the high end so you go downhill when it is loaded.

TOOLS

You will need a few simple tools before getting down to work. A good spade, fork, hoe, rake, trowel, and a pair of secateurs will take you a long way.

Tool handles

The best handles are the Y shape (the ash is split, steam bent and a wooden cross piece is attached with a steel cap), and the D shape. The simple T handle suits people who wear thick gloves. Try different handles and weights to see what feels comfortable. Make sure that it's the right height for you. Standard lengths are rather like trouser sizes, from 70–80 cm (28–32 in).

Spades A spade, sharp enough to split open a compost bag, is a precision instrument. At the same time it needs to be strong enough to take your whole weight when digging. With it you can cut straight edges, make trenches and take off spits of turf cleanly. The back is used for breaking down clods of earth or banging in stakes.

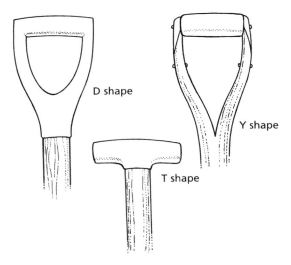

Types of tool handles.

Forks A garden fork's sharp individual tines can penetrate hard ground. It is useful for sifting stones, breaking up clay soils and for harvesting potatoes and root crops. For heavy work, the English garden fork with its chiselled tines is hard to beat. The small border fork is a niftier tool for lighter work.

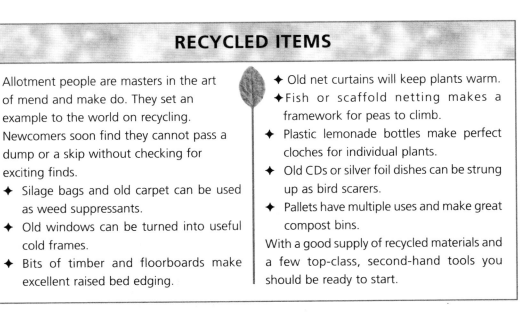

RECYCLED ITEMS

Allotment people are masters in the art of mend and make do. They set an example to the world on recycling. Newcomers soon find they cannot pass a dump or a skip without checking for exciting finds.

✦ Silage bags and old carpet can be used as weed suppressants.

✦ Old windows can be turned into useful cold frames.

✦ Bits of timber and floorboards make excellent raised bed edging.

✦ Old net curtains will keep plants warm.

✦ Fish or scaffold netting makes a framework for peas to climb.

✦ Plastic lemonade bottles make perfect cloches for individual plants.

✦ Old CDs or silver foil dishes can be strung up as bird scarers.

✦ Pallets have multiple uses and make great compost bins.

With a good supply of recycled materials and a few top-class, second-hand tools you should be ready to start.

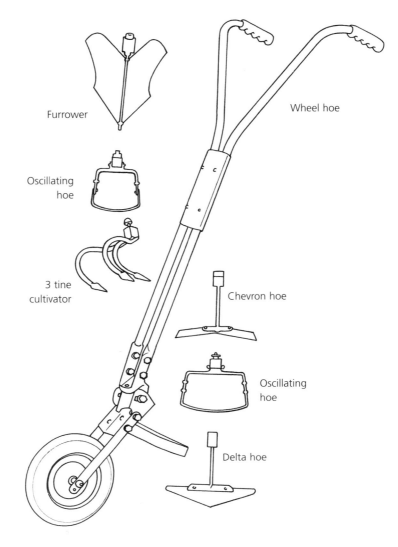

Furrower

Oscillating hoe

3 tine cultivator

Wheel hoe

Chevron hoe

Oscillating hoe

Delta hoe

Diverse hoes

Hoes People can become passionate – almost obsessive – about their hoes, when they find one that suits them perfectly. Throughout the growing season it will be used almost daily. A certain weight in the handle helps.

✦ Draw hoes are generally recommended for cutting off the tops of light weeds. You have more control over them than with a push (or Dutch) hoe. If you choose a swan-necked type, soil won't build up behind it.

✦ The small, heart-shaped warren hoe is used for tickling out weeds between plants. Choose one with a broader blade if you have much ground to cover. The warren hoe, with its narrow triangular or heart-shaped blade, is designed to

Tip

As long as you don't go for the expensive stainless steel varieties, good tools needn't be expensive. Old British tools are the best in the world and can be bought at boot sales and second-hand shops. Look for rolled carbon steel blades and ash shafts with strong fittings.

make sowing drills and is good for hooking out weeds with tap roots.

✦ The wheel hoe (invented by Jethro Tull) makes weeding and cultivating down straight lines between rows on light soil as effortless as pushing a pram.

Trowels are indispensable for planting and transplanting, for making small planting holes and digging out weed roots. The tip of the trowel is useful for scooping spoonfuls of fertilizer or breaking up the soil surface. The deeper bowled trowels can carry more compost while the narrow ones are better for precision work.

Rakes With a good flathead rake and a little practice you can transform a rough patch of ground into a beautifully flat seedbed. Drag stones and debris out on the pull and level on the push. Turn the rake over and you can make a flat track. The bowhead rake is very handy for making straight wide rows, following a line marked out with pegs and string, and for dragging out stones as it does so. In autumn you may need a springbok rake, the most efficient tool for gathering up leaves.

Secateurs are invaluable. You will never be without them. In my view, it is worth buying a pair of new professional-quality secateurs. Good secateurs should last you a lifetime. They should feel very comfortable in the hand, the spring should work smoothly, and the safety catch and the blades should slide together like a well-oiled machine. A holster will guarantee that they are always to hand.

When pruning always use tools that are more than capable of the job in hand. When you have heavy pruning to do, you will need to upgrade from secateurs to loppers or a pruning saw, which you could borrow or hire as when you need them.

chapter 2

GETTING THE LAND INTO SHAPE

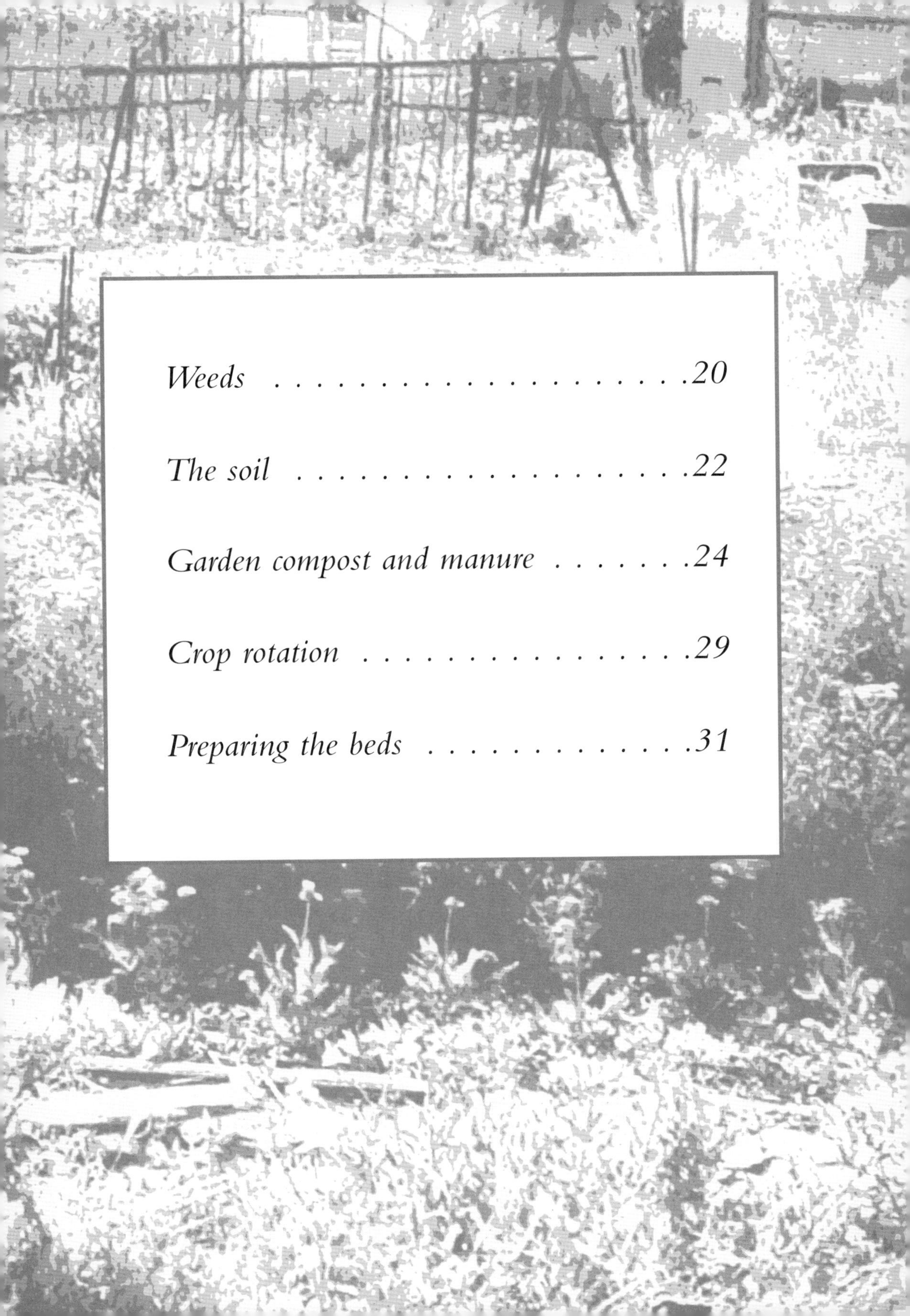

WEEDS

While most people who take on an allotment look forward to a stimulating experience, with plenty of fresh air, exercise and challenges along the way, they may not realise that the first hurdle is usually the worst. The classic scenario on taking over a plot is to be faced with ten poles of weeds! Generally plots are neglected for months before being vacated and during this time the weeds will have really taken hold. Unless you are superhuman, the best approach is to deal with the land in small sections, patiently, step-by-step, over a year or two.

Weeds are great survivors, breed prolifically and have the knack of finding the particular conditions they need to carry on. It is unrealistic to think you can get rid of them entirely, especially on an allotment where seed can be blowing in from all sides. Indeed, it is a good idea to keep a few of those weeds that attract bees and butterflies and make good composting material in odd corners. Nettles make good liquid manure *(see page 51)* and, in a sunny spot, will attract red admiral and tortoiseshell butterflies. The aim is control rather than elimination. You don't want them, good or bad, where you are going to sow seed or among your crops. They will compete for nutrients, water, light and space. The first step is to identify weeds by type. They divide into annuals and perennials.

Annual weeds

Annual weeds are those that grow, flower, seed and die in the course of one season. They propagate themselves by producing great quantities of seed, sometimes many thousands per plant. To get on top of them

Tip

If you don't plan to use all the allotment at once and you have a problem with perennial weeds, consider digging and hand-weeding some areas for immediate use, and smothering the weeds in others.

it is vital to prevent them from flowering and setting seed. If you are really stuck for time, be sure to deadhead the weeds before they can set seed.

Annual weed control

✦ As they generally live in the top layer of the soil, annual weeds can be kept down by hoeing and hand-pulling. Through the growing season, keep your hoe nearby so you can catch them young, before they make much root. This saves a lot of bother later on.

✦ If you feel you are losing the battle, give your plants a headstart against the competition by transplanting, using pre-germinated or chitted seed, or by fluid sowing *(see page 37)*.

✦ Weed seeds lurk dormant in the soil. When you disturb them and bring them up near the light, they will germinate. Once you have sorted out your plot, you may choose the no-dig system *(see page 33)* for this reason.

✦ Mulching is a godsend. It really does help by excluding light and smothering weed seeds. A 5 cm (2 in) layer of organic mulch between plants will dispose of most annual weeds. As the mulch is loose, any rogue seedlings can be pulled out with ease.

✦ A good cover of crops will also shade them out. Aim to keep the ground covered one way or the other.

The stale seedbed

One way to get ahead of annual weeds is to make a stale seedbed. Prepare the bed for planting and let the resulting weed seeds germinate. Hoe them off before sowing your seed and, with luck, your plants should be up before any more weeds appear. If the weather is cold, warm the soil by covering it with polythene or fleece for a couple of weeks to encourage the weeds to show themselves first.

Perennial weeds

These go on from year to year, and are a more serious proposition. On a piece of ground the size of an allotment, you need to take sweeping measures if you have a serious problem with perennial weeds. Most can spread from their roots as well as from seed. Dock and cow parsley grow massive taproots. Couch grass, ground elder, and willow herb make a tangled underground network, while the roots of coltsfoot, horse-tail, creeping thistle and bindweed have very deep storage roots. The roots of bindweed have been found at the bottom of wells. All are difficult to dig out cleanly and will sprout from the tiniest section of root left in the ground.

Trying to rotavate perennial weeds will only make things worse as it chops the roots up along with the gardener's best friend – the worms. Another disadvantage is that it can, in certain circumstances, damage the soil structure by creating a hard pan, an impermeable layer which will affect drainage adversely.

Dealing with perennial weeds

Excluding light No plant can live without light. If you have tall weeds, scythe or strim them down. Cover the area with heavy black plastic buried at the edges and weighed down with stones or bricks. The length of time you need to keep the ground covered depends on the particular weed. Some will die out after a year, while the most persistent can take three years. If you make slits in the plastic to allow in water or use porous horticultural plastic, the land needn't be wasted. You can plant through the plastic by making cross slits; it is best to

CASE STUDY

"Part of my allotment was smothered in bindweed and couch grass. I dug the ground over roughly and laid down horticultural black plastic. The first year I planted courgettes and squashes through it, tomatoes the next. The third year I put in brassicas. The brassicas weren't so successful, as snails and slugs had congregated under the plastic. However, at the end of it I'd had two excellent crops out of three and the ground was completely weed free." —*Dave Fox, Trumpington Allotments, Cambridge.*

use plants that are a fair size and quite vigorous by nature.

Although not all sites permit it, hessian-backed carpet is also used to exclude light and works well. Avoid the foam-backed type as it will eventually break down and be difficult and unpleasant to remove. Other possibilities are large sheets of heavy cardboard of the type used by removal, kitchen or bathroom appliance firms.

If your allotment plot is covered in thick grass and weeds, scythe or strim it down and keep it short. Only small 'rosette' weeds, like daisies, will survive constant mowing. When you are ready to plant, take off the turf, bury it upside down about a spit down and cover with the topsoil. It will soon rot down into good loam. Another method is to to make a turf stack. Stack the turfs upside-down and cover with black plastic or hessian-backed carpet to cut out the light. The stack should become friable and crumbly after six months or so.

Flame gunning This method has been used since the 19th century. A flame gun is not designed to burn the weeds, but gives off the right heat for the cell structure to change and rupture the cell walls several hours later. You can tell if the treatment has been effective if you see dark green fingerprints when you press a leaf between finger and thumb.

Weeds are flame gunned at about 71°C (160°F) for a single second. In agriculture, flame gunning is generally used for clearing small weeds in the carefully calculated time between sowing a crop and the seeds emerging. It has the advantage of not disturbing the soil with the consequence of bringing more weed seed up to the light to germinate. Tough perennials may need several treatments of flame gunning. Obviously there are always dangers attached to fire and you may need to get permission to use a flame gun from your site manager.

THE SOIL

The next and most vital step is to find out about your soil. Good soil is bursting with microscopic life – fungi, algae, bacteria, worms, vegetable and animal remains, air and water. It should be a life-giving cocktail. Look after your soil and it will look after the plants.

If you have been dealing with lush stinging nettles, chickweed and dock, you can be fairly sure that the soil is fertile. A thriving worm population is an excellent sign and will tell you that your soil is friable and will be easy to work. Ideally, there should be two or three worms on every spadeful of soil you dig. Healthy soil has a pleasant, earthy smell.

Feel the texture

Sandy soil is gritty, silt is silky, and clay is sticky. Loam – the gardener's dream soil – will contain roughly equal amounts of all three. You can learn quite a bit about the soil by picking up a small handful half an hour after it has rained to see if it will mould into a ball. If it does, it will be silt or clay. Clay goes shiny when rubbed, chalk will slip through your fingers, while peat is dark and crumbly. The addition of generous quantities of organic matter will improve fertility, drainage, water retention and texture on all soil types.

Clay soil is rich in minerals and nutrients. The disadvantages are that it can become waterlogged, is sluggish to warm up in spring, tough to dig, and cakes in the heat.

Brassicas, which like firm planting, do well on clay, however. If you have clay soil, make narrow raised beds which you can reach across, as treading on the soil will compact it, making it airless. Digging it over in the autumn and letting winter weather get at it will help to break it down. Dig in plenty of sharp sand, grit and organic matter to incorporate air and improve drainage – this will turn it into workable, good soil.

Sandy soil is free draining and easy to work, and it warms up quickly in spring. It is a light soil, particularly good for salad crops and legumes. The problem is that it can be so free-draining that nutrients are washed away, or 'leached', by rain. Sandy soils are often low in potash. Adding well-rotted compost or manure will help to bind the particles together and retain nutrients and moisture. Leave any digging until spring and keep it covered through winter to minimize leaching.

Silt is an alluvial soil, typically from river-banks, and lies somewhere between clay and sand. It is easily compacted but holds on quite well to nutrients. Treat as for clay soil.

Chalk is a free-draining, poor soil. It is full of lime, which makes it alkaline and inhospitable to many plants. Organic matter will help to bulk it up and counteract the alkalinity. It is often low in potash.

Peat, which comes from wetland, is light and easy to work, fertile but acid. It retains water when wet but dries fast, when it has a tendency to blow away. Adding lime will make it more alkaline, and organic matter will give it substance and weight.

Test the pH

A simple soil-testing kit will allow you to test the pH – a measure of whether the soil is acid, neutral, or alkaline. The micro-organisms which provide vital nutrients for the plants do not prosper at either extreme. The optimum pH value for most plants is 5.5–7.5.

Collect three of four small samples of soil from different parts of the plot. You can send them off for a full analysis (as advertised in gardening magazines) but a cheap kit from a gardening centre is probably all you need. A pH of 7 is neutral, above 7 alkaline, and below 7 acid.

✦ **If the soil is too acid**, add lime to counteract it. Ground limestone (Calcium carbonate) and dolomitic limestone (Calcium magnesium carbonate) are the organic choices. Do not add it at the same time as manure as it will react against it. The general practice is to lime in autumn and manure in spring.

✦ **If the soil is too alkaline,** garden manure and compost will send it in the right direction. Test every year to see how you are going.

While you can tip the balance and improve the soil, you cannot completely change its character. However, you can choose plants which prefer your particular soil type. Potatoes and rhubarb, for example, prefer acid soil, while legumes prefer alkaline soil.

Soil profile

If you are being thorough, or have worries about drainage, it is worth digging a small hole around 90 cm (3 ft) deep. This will reveal some interesting horizontal bands – the topsoil, the subsoil, broken rock and the bedrock below.

Topsoil The first layer, the topsoil, is

noticeably darker than the rest. This is the layer that feeds the plants. About 45 cm (18 in) of topsoil is right for soft fruit, while most vegetables will be happy with 38 cm (15 in). Fruit trees need about 60 cm (24 in). Have a look at the soil structure. This is the way particles clump together. If you can see plenty of holes and cracks on the exposed face you can be sure that there is plenty of air going through. If not, then you need to open it up by adding organic matter or raising the beds.

Subsoil This is lighter in colour. It contains few plant nutrients but its structure affects drainage. It is important that water can flow away and air can get to the roots. Test it by pouring some water down the hole to see if it runs away. If it doesn't, it could be due to compacted airless topsoil or an impermeable barrier in the subsoil known as a 'hard pan'. This can usually be broken up with a pickaxe, or loosened with a fork, and kept aerated with regular additions of organic matter.

GARDEN COMPOST AND MANURE

"Compost is no miracle worker but it's the perfect food for miracle workers – the soil population."
A. Guest, *Gardening without Digging, 1949.*

Compost

Making compost is a skill well worth mastering. Composting is a speeding up of nature's own recycling process. As animal and vegetable remains rot down, the population of micro-organisms burgeons.

The heap heats up quickly and can reach the ideal temperature of 60°C (140°F) within a matter of days. This amount of heat should kill off weed seeds, pests and diseases.

Tip

It takes time to make good compost – at least a couple of months in summer and quite a few through winter, so start it off at the first possible moment.

As the activity slows down and the heap cools, the micro-organisms are joined by worms and insects. Much feasting takes place!

When the compost is made, its volume will have reduced by half, it will be sweet smelling, dark and crumbly, and the original contents will be unrecognizable. The end result of composting is humus. It enriches the soil for new cycles and generations of microscopic life. It dramatically improves soil texture, structure, water-holding capacity and drainage. You need a good quantity to get the full effect though – around 5 kg (12 lb) per sq m (sq yd), applied on an annual basis.

Compost bins

You can have an open compost heap but it won't heat as well and the contents can blow about. The best plan is to have three compost bins – one ready to use, one rotting down, and one being filled. You need a container without a bottom for the worms to get in and do their work. Small gaps are important for air circulation but you don't want gaping holes as they will let the heat out and dry the compost. You need a lid or cover to keep the rain off and access from the side or top in order turn the compost and get it out. For fast composting, make the bins at least 1 cubic m (9 cubic ft).

What to use

Wood is the best material for compost bins as it has insulation and 'breathes'. Plastic, including recycled types, is commonly used though it doesn't keep the heat as well. An excellent, no-cost compost bin can be made from three pallets nailed together at the corners with a fourth tied on to make a door. Push straw, old sacks or newspaper into the gaps and make a lid from old carpet, heavy plastic or a piece of board.

What to compost

In theory, you can compost anything organic – kitchen scraps, tea bags and coffee, eggshells, wood ash, hair, newspaper and cardboard, natural fabrics, garden prunings and weeds.

If you are not sure that you will achieve maximum heat, it is prudent to leave out perennial weed roots, weed seeds (which might survive the experience), fish and meat (which might attract rodents) and diseased material. The top growth of potatoes often contains potato blight and potatoes may sprout again, so don't take the risk. Brassica roots may have clubroot. Cat and dog faeces should never be used for compost where you are growing vegetables. I would also leave out the prunings of evergreen plants, which are very slow to decompose. They make good mulches for paths if shredded.

How to make compost

The bigger the heap and the more you put in at the same time, the faster and more effective you will be.

Start off the heap with something coarse and twiggy to let in air. Collect and save a good assortment of materials next, aiming for about half green materials to half dry. It is worth filling a few dustbins full of different things before you start. If you are enterprising, you might pick up extra material from outdoor markets and greengrocers. Chop up woody materials into short lengths and crush the tough stalks. Cut fabrics up into small pieces.

Water any dry materials, such as straw, paper, and cloth, and squeeze them out. If you have too much green materials, particularly grass mowings, you will end up with silage. You want moisture, but not sogginess which will make the heap putrefy. Mix your ingredients together. Shovel it in and let it settle by itself.

A couple of turnings at intervals of a few weeks will make the material rot faster and give you the chance to check on progress. Dig out the whole heap onto a plastic sheet and add whatever it seems to lack – more water or green material if it's too dry, more shredded dampened paper, rags or straw if it's too wet. Overall it should be about as damp as a squeezed sponge. Mix it up again, add some more activator and fork it back. To get full value from your compost when it is ready, apply it to the soil in early spring.

Trenching compost

If you don't have enough material to make much difference to the heap, bury kitchen and garden waste about 30 cm (12 in) deep in a trench. Cover with soil and allow it to rot down for a few weeks. Make holes, fill them with potting compost and plant greedy feeders like courgettes through it. Many people put a layer of mowings or

SPEEDING UP THE PROCESS

If you want to speed things up, use a compost activator every 15 cm (6 in) or so through the heap. A little rotted compost from an old heap also works brilliantly to get the process started. Farm manure, human urine, nettles, seaweed meal, poultry or pigeon droppings, comfrey leaves and blood fish and bone are excellent too. Lime helps if the heap smells sour or if you are on acid soil.

a few comfrey leaves in potato trenches before planting.

Sheet composting

This looks unsightly but is another way to make use of small amounts of kitchen and garden waste if you haven't got a compost heap on the go. Lay thin layers of compost between vegetable rows and let it rot down where it lies on the soil.

Animal manure

It is worth every effort to get a good supply of farmyard manure. Chat up the local stables or farmyard and see if they will supply it – the Fulham Palace Allotments get deliveries from the Royal Mews!

Letting it rot down

Never use fresh manure on the soil – it will scorch the plants, rob them of nitrogen and may be full of pathogens, even chemicals such as wormers, or worse still, hormones. Once rotted down, however, it will be transformed into a great soil conditioner.

Manure on straw bedding is the best. The straw is full of nitrogen from the urine and rots down fairly quickly. It should take three to six months to rot, whereas manure on wood shavings will take about a year.

Making a manure heap

The bigger the heap, the better and the more quickly it will rot down. A good-sized heap would be 1.5 m (5 ft) high and wide. You can speed up the process by turning the sides into the middle from time to time. If you build the heap on a layer of heavy polythene, flatten it with a spade and cover the top and sides with polythene, carpet or a tarpaulin, you will create more heat. An extra bonus of covering it entirely is that you will kill off lurking weed seeds.

When ready, the manure will be dark, crumbly and pleasant smelling.

Using manure

For vegetables, it is best to spread the rotted manure thickly on the soil in winter for the frosts to break it down even further. The worms will do your digging for you, dragging it down into the soil. The one exception is if you need to lime the soil in autumn. It will react with the manure and waste the nitrogen. So if this is the case, lime in autumn and spread the manure in spring.

Other organic composts

Spent mushroom compost from commercial growers makes a good soil conditioner and mulch for neutral to acid soils. It is a mixture of horse manure, peat and chalk, which makes it alkaline. It is best to leave it in a stack for a few months to get rid of any chemicals or mushroom pests.

Spent hops are sometimes on offer from

breweries. High in nitrogen and potash, they can be dug in without delay if still moist. They also make a good surface mulch.

Seaweed has an alginate content which binds soil particles together to help the structure. It is rich in trace elements, has much the same nitrogen, phosphorus and potassium as farmyard manure, plus other goodies – vitamins, amino acids, plant hormones and carbohydrates. It really boosts plant health, can be used fresh, and is an excellent addition to the compost heap. The carbohydrates in it decompose fast, causing a proliferation of helpful micro-organisms.

You can collect it from the shore or sea if you find it loose, but not if it's growing on the rocks. Old seaweed that has dried beyond the tide line is too salty to use. You can also buy proprietary seaweed products.

Grass mowings are rich in nitrogen and make a moisture-retaining mulch. Use sparingly as they get slimy when they rot down. They can also be used over newspaper to keep down weeds for short periods.

Fresh bark or wood shavings from factories or the Tree Departments make

Tip

In the North, many allotment holders keep racing pigeons and hens. Their droppings are so high in nitrogen that they are best used as an activator in the compost heap. Rabbit and guinea pig droppings, which come in small quantities, can be used in the same way.

luxuriant, weed-free paths. They are very slow to rot down and take nitrogen out of the soil until they have done so.

Green manures

'The combination of green manures and crop rotation can result in a truly unbeatable vegetable production system.' –Eliot Coleman, The New Organic Grower, 1995.

Green manures are fast-growing agricultural crops put in the ground for six weeks to a year, depending on the type. They are cut down when young and dug in, adding fertility and improving soil structure. They also provide a very good source of composting material.

+ If you have empty beds which you are not ready to plant, a green manure crop will make temporary cover and help to keep the area free of weeds.
+ Some green manures, such as buckwheat and Italian ryegrass, have root systems which break up heavy ground.
+ Green manures are particularly helpful for light soils, as they will prevent it from eroding and being leached by rain.
+ The leguminous ones (clovers, winter beans, trefoil and lupins) store nitrogen in the roots. This is released into the soil as they rot down when dug in.
+ Phacelia, buckwheat and lupins have flowers that attract beneficial insects. Though the crops are usually dug in to the soil before they flower, it might be worth leaving a few in the ground for this reason.
+ Allotment holders often buy their fenugreek seed from Asian greengrocers and dried winter (broad) beans from the supermarket. Test them for viability before sowing *(see page 37).*

LEAFMOULD

Don't waste all the fallen leaves you sweep up in autumn. Leafmould is another invaluable soil conditioner, low in nutrients but great for soil structure. Collect leaves in a cage of chicken wire or in black plastic sacks. Add a little water and make a few holes and then leave it for a season or two. If you shred the leaves by mowing over them first, it will speed up the process. Apart from stamping the pile down as you add more leaves, there is nothing else to do apart from watering it in the dry summer months. Fungi will break the leaves down in time. Parks Departments are a great source of fallen leaves. Specify that you don't want leaves collected off the roads, as they will be polluted.

Types of green manure

Short term These are fast-growing leafy plants which can be slotted in six to eight week gaps when the ground is cleared between crops. These include fenugreek, mustard, phacelia and buckwheat.

Overwintering Winter tare, grazing rye, winter beans and Italian ryegrass are sown in early autumn when many vegetables are lifted. They will be dug in to the soil the following spring.

Long term Alfalfa, red clover and trefoil can be left in the ground for a year but should be clipped occasionally to stop them going woody. These are useful for resting overused soil, improving fertility or to give you a break. Keep in mind crop rotation (see page 29). Other long-term green manures include winter beans and lupins, which are legumes, and mustard and fodder radish, which are brassicas.

Cutting down

Cut down green manures before they flower or when you need the ground. Dig them up, chopping up the foliage with a spade as you go to speed up decomposition. Leave them to wilt for a few days before burying them by single digging. If you are on the no-dig system, leave the residue on the surface to act as a mulch, or compost it. Some of the perennials (clover, trefoil and rye) may grow again and will need to be hoed off or covered with mulch.

Green manure plants

Alfalfa (*Medicago sativa*) is a deep-rooting, hardy perennial that fixes nitrogen and grows to 80 cm (32 in) tall. It is planted for a full season, either spring to autumn, or late summer to spring.

Buckwheat (*Fagopyrum esculentum*) is a tender annual, growing to 90 cm (3 ft). Sow in April to harvest in June. It has deep roots and smothers weeds. It is easy to dig in and copes with poor soil. The flowers attract helpful hoverflies.

Crimson clover (*Trifolium incarnatum*) and Red clover (*Trifolium pratense*) are fairly hardy perennials, growing up to 30 cm (12 in). Clover is a nitrogen fixer and loved by bees, so leave a few to flower. Plant in spring to late summer and grow for two or three months, or leave over winter. It fixes nitrogen, is fairly easy to dig in and prefers light soils. Don't use repeatedly as the land may become 'clover sick'.

Fenugreek (*Trigonella foenum graecum*) is a semi-hardy annual growing up to 60 cm (24 in). It is possibly the best fast grower and nitrogen fixer for summer. The bushy plants have weed-suppressing foliage. Plant in late spring or summer and grow for up to three months in well drained but moisture-retentive soil.

Lupin (*Lupinus angustifolius*) The agricultural variety of lupin is sown in spring for a slow-maturing summer crop. It takes two to three months to get to the digging stage. Seeds are sown rather than broadcast. Deep rooting, they improve soil texture, fix nitrogen and are effective in suppressing weeds. If left to flower, they are very attractive to beneficial predators. A big disadvantage is that they are poisonous, which may well rule them out on the allotment.

Mustard (*Sinapsis alba*) is a tender annual for summer. Rapid growing and weed smothering, it needs moisture but isn't fussy about soil. It is said to reduce soil-borne pests and diseases. Easy to dig in – a good green manure.

Phacelia (*Phacelia tanacetifolia*) is a semi-hardy annual. Growing to 90 cm (3 ft), it has ferny leaves and bright blue flowers attractive to beneficial insects, so leave a few for them. Plant after the danger of frost has passed and grow for a couple of months. It is happy on most soils and easy to dig in.

Ryegrasses – grazing rye (*Secale cereale*) and Italian ryegrass (*Lollium multiflorum*), are hardy annuals used for overwintering, and can take almost any soil. They need a couple of months to rot down and are likely to reshoot. Ryegrasses are not the easiest to dig

up as they have tough fibrous roots. You can save seed for the following year.

Trefoil (*Medicago lupilina*) is a hardy biennial and a summer grower, reaching 30 cm (12 in). Nitrogen fixing, and one of the few that can cope with some shade and drought, it dislikes heavy acid soils.

Winter beans (*Vicia faba*) are field broad beans, are hardy annuals which fix nitrogen. Plant between September and November to overwinter in moist loam. They are moderately easy to dig in; don't forget to leave the nitrogen-rich roots. An excellent green manure that you can harvest and eat. Dry some seed for the following year.

Winter tare (*Vicia sativa*) is a hardy annual growing to 75 cm (30 in). It is as fast-growing as bushy vetch which provides plenty of leaf cover. It dislikes drought and prefers alkaline soils. Plant in summer or autumn to overwinter. It is reasonably easy to dig in. It is a five-star green manure for fixing nitrogen and suppressing weeds.

CROP ROTATION

The benefits of moving members of the same botanical family to fresh ground each year was recognized as far back as Ancient Rome and Greece. Crop rotation, known as 'pots, roots, legs and bras' in certain circles, controls and prevents a build-up of pests and diseases in the soil, including those to be avoided at all costs – clubroot in brassicas, eelworms in potatoes and tomatoes, root rots in peas and beans, and white rot in onions.

The concept is neat and logical. Each vegetable family group has a tendency to the same diseases and attracts the same pests. The most important groups to rotate are potatoes, legumes, brassicas and roots. If you have four areas, each year two are given manure (which is acid) and two are limed to make them alkaline. In alternate years, each plot will receive the other treatment, so the pH should stay in balance.

Below is the rotation sequence for the first of your beds. For the second bed, start on year 2, for the third year 3 and so on, following the sequence in the same order.

Year 1 The soil is manured for the potatoes. They like a rich soil on the acidic side. Potatoes are the traditional clearing crop for bad ground. They are leafy plants so they keep the weeds down. As there is quite a lot of excavation in potato growing, earthing up and harvesting the crop, soil-borne pests are exposed to the birds.

Year 2 The following year, the same soil will have about the right richness for root crops. Roots prefer a light soil on the alkaline side, so add lime if the pH is low.

Year 3 The third year, the same patch is manured again for the legumes (peas and beans). They take nitrogen out of the air and store it in their roots. The roots are left in the soil when the legumes are harvested, and the nitrogen from them will be of great value to the leafy brassicas (the cabbage family) – the last in the succession.

Year 4 Brassicas like to be planted firmly, so let the ground settle over the winter before planting them. Lime the soil once more before planting, if necessary, as their worst enemy – clubroot – doesn't like

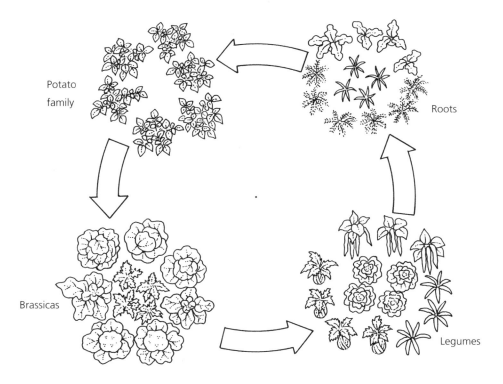

Potato family

Roots

Brassicas

Legumes

Vegetable rotation helps to prevent the build-up of diseases, increases soil fertility and makes cultivation easier.

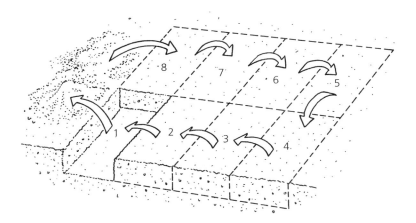

The tried and trusted way to dig is to work step by step in narrow strips

alkaline soil. You don't have to be too strict about rotation for fast-growing brassicas, though it is always good practice.

Other families can join in, too. Good partners are roots, beets and onions, as they don't need rich soil, whereas legumes and cucurbits do. Lettuces and cut-and-come-again crops can be slotted in almost anywhere. The cardoons and artichokes, Good King Henry, rhubarb, seakale and sorrel are perennials so they need a semi-permanent position. Corn salad, New Zealand spinach, purslane and sweetcorn don't belong to the main family groups and can be slotted in where there is space. It is vital to keep records of what is where each year.

Divide your crops into families, as shown in the lists on page 32. There might be some surprises. Who would think that tomatoes are part of the potato family, or that artichokes belong to the lettuce clan?

PREPARING THE BEDS

There are two schools of thought on preparing beds – to dig or not to dig.

Digging

This is the time-honoured way of getting air into the soil, breaking up compaction and burying annual weeds. At the same time, it gives you the opportunity to remove the roots of perennial weeds and to incorporate organic matter.

Single digging is cultivating the topsoil only. Work a narrow strip in sections. Take out one spit of soil (the depth of the spade) to make a trench. Put the soil that you have dug out at the other end of the strip. Dig out a second trench to the same width, get rid of any weeds, mix in organic matter and spade it into the first trench. Carry on in this way. When you get to the end, pile in the soil from the first trench.

Double digging is the same process with the additional work of breaking up the

Pea and bean family

LEGUMES
(PAPILLIONACEAE)

+ Asparagus pea
+ Broad bean (fava bean)
+ French bean
+ Lima or butter bean
+ Peas, mangetout and snowpeas
+ Runner bean

Cabbage family

BRASSICAS (BRASSICACEAE)

+ Brussels sprouts
+ Broccoli
+ Cabbage
+ Calabrese
+ Cauliflower
+ Chinese cabbage and broccoli
+ Kale
+ Kohlrabi
+ Mibuna greens
+ Mizuna greens
+ Mustard greens
+ Pak choi
+ Radish
+ Rocket
+ Seakale
+ Sprouting broccoli
+ Swede
+ Texcel greens
+ Turnip

Potato family

(SOLANACEAE)

+ Aubergine
+ Chilli
+ Pepper
+ Potato
+ Tomato

Carrot family

ROOT VEGETABLES
(APIACEAE)

+ Carrot
+ Celeriac
+ Celery
+ Florence fennel
+ Hamburg parsley
+ Parsley
+ Parsnip

Beet family

(CHENOPODIACEAE)

+ Beetroot
+ Chard
+ Good King Henry
+ Perpetual spinach
+ Red orach
+ Spinach

Lettuce family

(ASTERACEAE)

+ Cardoon
+ Chicory
+ Endive
+ Globe artichoke
+ Jerusalem artichoke
+ Lettuce
+ Salsify
+ Scorzonera

Onion family

(ALLIACEAE)

+ Garlic
+ Japanese bunching onion
+ Leek
+ Onions – globe, pickling, Japanese
+ Shallots
+ Spring onion
+ Welsh onion

Cucumber family

(CUCURBITACEAE)

+ Courgette
+ Cucumber
+ Gherkin
+ Marrow
+ Melon
+ Pumpkin
+ Squash

subsoil as you go, by plunging a fork into it, if necessary up to the hilt. This should drain off compacted soils and help deep-rooting plants to penetrate to lower levels and find water for themselves. Generally, this is only done if there are drainage problems.

The no-dig system

The principle of no-dig gardening is to leave the soil undisturbed. Every year you lay on a thick top layer of well-rotted compost as a mulch. This stimulates the earthworm activity. The worms build up fertility and improve the structure of the soil. As the soil stays moist under the mulch, the micro-organisms, which help to release nutrients to the plants, get an extra boost. The soil is protected from sun, wind, and heavy rain and leaching. Weed seeds are blacked out. No-dig gardening has many adherents and works wonderfully well once you have good drainage and have got rid of any perennial weeds. My own feeling is to excavate the soil thoroughly once if it needs it. Then take up the no-dig system, providing you have enough compost to make it work. The one argument against it is that any soil-borne pests will go unchecked, as they won't be turned over for the birds to eat.

Raised beds

Beds rise up naturally once you start adding organic matter on a regular basis. Though not strictly necessary, it's a good idea to contain them to prevent leaching, define them and separate them from the paths. An edging of old planks is as good as anything. Drive a peg into each corner and nail the planks onto the outside of the pegs. Logs sawn in half lengthways are a good alternative. While untreated hardwood railway sleepers make excellent edgings, those treated with creosote are now considered to be harmful to the garden.

A FEW RULES OF DIGGING

+ Never dig if the soil is frozen or waterlogged. If it sticks to your boots, it's too wet.
+ Dig heavy soils in autumn and leave them in rough clods the size of a fist for the frost to get at them.
+ Dig light soils in spring so the winter rains won't leach out the nutrients.
+ Keep the topsoil and the subsoil separate and put them back in their own layers.
+ Don't over do it – think of your back.

chapter 3

GARDENING TECHNIQUES

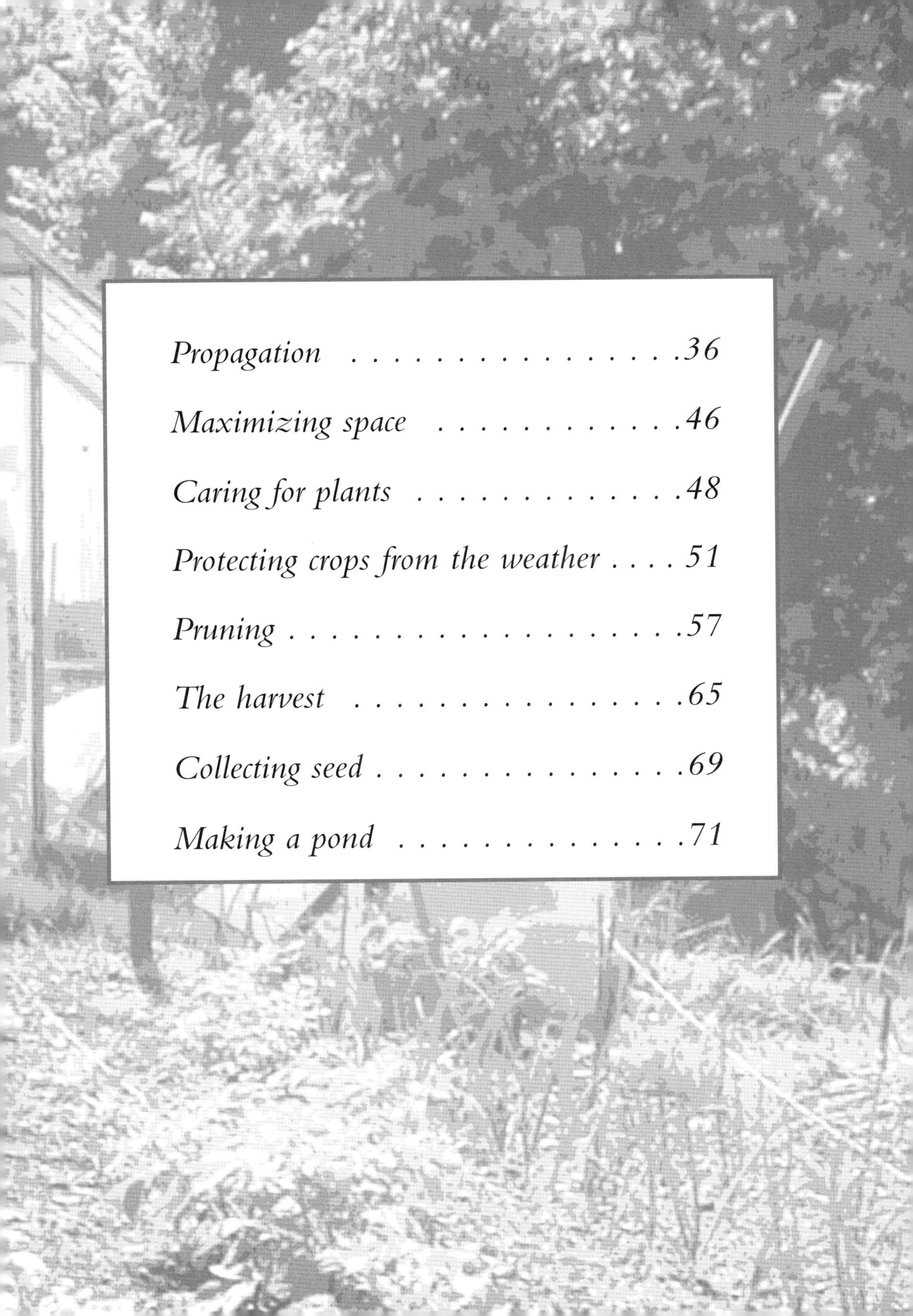

PROPAGATION
How to raise new plants

Seed You are spoilt for choice when it comes to seed. You can try distinguished old breeds, suited to particular areas, which might have been lost forever if heritage seed libraries had not gone to some lengths to preserve them. Equally you can benefit from modern breeding, which has made plants resistant to disease and bred out other weak traits.

Growing from seed is the most practical way to raise most types of vegetables in the quantities needed for an allotment. Once you get a system going, it is really very easy, and the delight of seeing seed spring to life never palls.

Plants that come from warm countries – tomatoes, aubergines, peppers and okra – need three or four months of sunshine to grow to maturity. They have to be started off in a warm greenhouse or in the home early in the year in Britain.

Buying young plants If you only want a few and don't have the time, facilities or patience, it is worth splashing out on a few plants ready to go out in sunny June. Tomatoes are prolific so you don't need many while most people don't want great quantities of peppers, okra or aubergines.

Vegetative methods Most of the perennials can be grown from vegetative cuttings, a fast and free way to increase your stock. Globe artichokes can be grown from offsets or plantlets that they produce naturally. Jerusalem artichokes can just be replanted from your own stock. Rhubarb and asparagus can be divided up to make more plants. Raspberries put out suckers and strawberries make runners. Shrubby herbs can be propagated from cuttings.

Virus-free stock

It is important to buy 'certified virus free' seed potatoes every year. Growing from your own potatoes which you save year to year is too big a risk in terms of diseases. Most of the soft fruits and the first garlic bulb should be bought from a reputable nursery and come with the same guarantee. It is an initial expense. After that you can keep up your own supply of garlic and soft fruit for some years.

Growing from seed

✦ Send off for, or telephone for, the free catalogues provided by seed merchants (*see page 189*). They offer a far more interesting choice of varieties than the garden centres.

✦ For sure-fire results, buy top-quality seed. It saves disappointment and wasting time as both the germination rate and the resulting plants will be better.

✦ Look for disease resistance as it makes life much easier.

✦ Keep an eye out for the RHS Award of Garden Merit (AGM) which is shown on seed packets. The award is given after extensive trials for outstanding excellence, for plants that do not need specialist growing conditions or care, or for plants that have a good constitution and are widely available. This hallmark can be easily recognised whenever you see the AGM trophy symbol. ♈

✦ Where possible, buy organic seed. It is grown without man-made chemicals and on clean land. Most seed companies have an organic range and there are specialist organic seed merchants.

✦ Try some of the heritage varieties from seed libraries – these are often not found

Tip

Have a chat with your allotment neighbours and find out which vegetables and which varieties work best in your area.

commercially. The Plant Varieties and Seed Act (1973) was designed to protect the consumer from fraudulence in the seed business. The downside is that varieties not registered on the UK National List cannot be sold. Heritage libraries give them away free to members.

Types of seed

F1 hybrids are the result of the scientific crossing of two parent lines, resulting in reliable, uniform results. F1 stands for 'first filial generation'. With vegetables they concentrate on vigour, flavour and disease-resistance. The criticisms of F1 seeds are that they are more expensive and that they all mature at the same time – this is good if you are growing for commercial purposes but perhaps not so desirable for the home grower. Of course, you can plant a few at a time to space out the crops. Don't save seed from these plants as there is no guarantee as to how the second generation will turn out.

Pelleted seed has been devised to make sowing fine or irregular-shaped seed easier and more accurate.

Seed tapes are designed for trouble-free, perfect spacing which will avoid thinning. The tapes to which the seeds are attached are biodegradable.

Pre-germinated seed is useful for tricky plants like cucumbers and melons which need Mediterranean warmth.

Primed or sprinter seed has been germinated and then dried, and must be sown within two months. It is usually more successful than untreated seed if you are planting early in the season or in adverse conditions. However, it is easy to pre-germinate them yourself *(see page 43)*. Check that treated seeds have not had chemicals added.

Seed from grocers In allotment circles there is a good success rate in growing from seed that has been dried for cooking, particularly the pulses. It is certainly worth a try if you are willing to take the risk of it not working out. Check that the seeds are alive, or 'viable', before planting as no seed keeps forever. Soak a few in water overnight, then put them on wet kitchen towel in a seed tray (or on a plate) covered with a plastic bag, and keep them at about 20°C (68°F). If all is well, they will start to sprout roots and leaves in about three weeks.

Your own seed Saving your own seed is economical and satisfying *(see page 69)*.

Sowing seed

Work out how many plants you want, and add a failure margin as there might be a few duds. There is a UK statutory minimum germination rate for seeds. This varies from plant to plant. While most have a near 100 per cent rate of viability, others are more unpredictable. Carrots only have to have a 65 per cent success rate, and the tricky parsnip is let off altogether. It is a good idea to have a seed-sharing scheme with your neighbours as there may be far too many seeds in one packet for a single family – 500

37

GENERAL PRINCIPLES OF SOWING FROM SEED

✦ Read the directions on the packet carefully and follow the instructions on the planting depth, sun and shade considerations, cultivation tips and when to sow.

✦ Use common sense on the sowing times – you know your local weather best.

✦ You can often plant more closely than recommended if you want smaller vegetables (see page 47).

✦ Seeds need warmth, moisture and light to germinate. Cold, waterlogged conditions are likely to be fatal.

✦ Avoid planting your seeds too deeply. The seed carries within it all it needs to germinate but only has the power to grow a limited distance. It needs to reach the light before it can grow further and fully develop. A general guide to planting depth is two-and-a-half times the size of the seed. Sow as sparsely as possible to save time thinning the seedlings later.

✦ Decide whether to sow directly outside or to start them off under cover or in a nursery bed and transplant later.

or more quite often. Keep a few back, however, in case of bad luck or foul weather.

Sowing seed under cover

This has many advantages over sowing outside. You can begin earlier and provide the best conditions for a flying start. You can protect seedlings from pests until they have built up strength and vigour. It also means the plants spend less time in the allotment beds, so you can make optimum use of the space. Brassicas, which recover well from being moved, are usually started off in this way.

A propagator, which provides the right level of heat from underneath, is a good investment. If you don't have one, you can manage very well with an airing cupboard or the top of a radiator kept at 20°C (68°F) and a light windowsill out of direct sunlight.

Choosing a container

Almost any container is fine for growing seeds. Old tin cans, ice cream tubs and yogurt pots will do as long they are well scrubbed and have drainage. The traditional 7 cm (3 in) clay and plastic pots, and seed trays work well. Clay is porous and so your seeds are less likely to suffer from overwatering, but it is less hygienic than plastic.

If you are sowing seed big enough to handle and are buying new, go for the module or 'plug' style of planters in which each seed has its own compartment. The great advantage of these is that they more or less eliminate any damage to the roots when transplanting.

If you already have standard seed trays, you can buy small square plastic pots designed to fit neatly into them. Good inventions are biodegradable products made from paper and peat alternatives. When you are ready to transplant, plant them in their pots, thereby avoiding root damage.

You can also get biodegradable tubes, or root trainers, for plants with long roots such as sweet peas and runner beans. The shape of the pot directs the roots downwards to help the plant seek out water low in the soil. The inner cardboard tubes of toilet rolls and kitchen towel can be used in the same way. Polystyrene cell blocks give insulation and are a good idea for seedlings raised in a cold greenhouse. They usually come with a presser board to pop out individual plugs. Old polystyrene cups are the DIY version for seed warmth.

Composts

Don't take shortcuts. Use new seed and potting compost or multipurpose compost. They contain everything that seedlings need – the right texture for moisture-retention, aeration and nutrients. They are also sterile – free from weeds, pests and diseases.

How to sow

With a few exceptions, seeds germinate best in the dark. Fill your container with compost, leaving space at the top for watering. Shake it from side to side to get a flat surface and firm it down gently. A firming board, or piece of timber cut to the size of the tray with a handle on the top, is useful for this. If you are using pots, press down with the bottom of another. Either water the compost thoroughly before sowing, or sit the tray in water afterwards and the compost will soak it up. You shouldn't need to water again until the seeds have germinated. While rainwater is generally best for plants, it is safer to use sterile tap water for seedlings.

If the seeds are big enough to pick up by hand, make holes with a dibber (a pencil or chopstick will do the trick) to the right depth and drop them in. Fine seed should be scattered – carefully to achieve an even distribution – on the top of the compost. The easiest way to do this is to have some in the palm of one hand and take a pinch at a time with the other. Mixing fine seed with a little silver sand as a spreading agent helps to distribute the seed more evenly. Sieve a thin layer of compost over the seed you have sown.

Cover the tray or container with polythene or a sheet of glass and put it in a warm, dark place. Ideal temperatures for germination vary, but few seeds like it hotter than 20°C (68°F).

Check every day for signs of life. As soon as the first seedling makes its appearance, put the seedlings in a light place but out of direct sunlight and take off the cover.

Looking after seedlings

Watering The most common problem with seedlings is damping off, a fungal problem caused by excess moisture or poor hygiene. Keep the seedlings just moist. Water slowly to avoid disturbing them or simply let them soak up water from below.
Light If you are growing them on a windowsill, they need to be turned every day to get even light all round. An alternative is to put them in a box with the back lined with kitchen foil to reflect light.
Air Seedlings need good air circulation, but keep them out of drafts.

Thinning

If they become overcrowded, seedlings need to be thinned out. Growing them too close together leads to competition for water and nutrients, and can cause weak growth or even disease. Water the compost well before you start, then pull or ease out the surplus seedlings, leaving the strongest ones in place (an ice lolly stick is an effective tool). If they are entangled, pinch them out at the base.

Pricking out and potting on

When seedlings grow too big for their container, or if they are ready but the weather is not, you will need to prick out and pot on. This is best done when the plants have two true leaves. The first set that look like leaves are part of the seed. Water well ahead of time and, using a dibber, gently ease out the seedlings, taking as much compost with them as you can to avoid disturbing the roots, and replant in pots or trays with more space for them to develop. If you need to support the plant, hold it by the leaves, not the stem which is easily damaged. If you have grown them singly in modules, just tip them out and plant in bigger pots to the same depth.

Hardening off

Acclimatize your young plants to the outside world in stages. Start by keeping them under cloches or in the cold frame, lifting off the cover by day and putting it back at night. Protect them from fluctuations in temperature until they are tough enough to cope.

Transplanting

The danger with transplanting is that young plants can get checked or suffer from transplanting shock due to root damage and drying out. To avoid this:

✦ Where possible, grow seedlings in plugs or modules.
✦ Work at a steady pace. Have the land raked to a fine tilth, watered and lined up for planting before you start. Roots dry out extremely fast out of the soil.

✦ Move them in the cool of evening or on a dull day.
✦ Water them well the day before and keep them well watered after until they have perked up after being transplanted.

Sowing seed outdoors

Once the soil is warm, most plants can be sown outside which saves time and bother. Some plants – notably root vegetables, cucumbers and sweetcorn – don't transplant well and are generally sown where they are going to grow. Onions usually go straight out as they don't take up much space. The seeds of the hardiest plants – most brassicas, Oriental greens, peas, broad beans and radishes – can be sown outside when the soil temperature at night has reached a constant 5°C (41°F) for a week. Tender vegetables, like French and runner beans, sweetcorn and tomatoes, need a minimum of 12°C (52°F) which is unlikely until June in most places. Most vegetables require conditions between the two. Err on the cautious side, however. It is wiser to plant late and grow fast.

Having a seed bed in top condition will save the effort of bringing the whole allotment up to scratch. The seedling vegetables can then be transplanted to their permanent positions when they are ready and there is a gap in which to plant them.

Preparing a seed bed

If you have heavy, wet clay soil it is worth making a raised bed for good drainage into which you can sow seed successfully. Ideally, the bed should be partially prepared the autumn before by digging and mixing in plenty of organic matter. Leave it to settle through winter.

Tip

Use cloches and the cold frame for early sowings. They will extend the growing season considerably and get your plants off to a good, early start resulting in an earlier harvest.

A couple of weeks before you are ready to sow in spring, warm the soil with clear polythene. This will encourage any dormant weeds to germinate so you can dispose of them before you start. If the bed is prepared in spring, you may need to flatten the surface by walking up and down on it. Do this when the soil is reasonably dry and don't stamp. You are aiming for a flat and reasonably firm surface, not a compacted one.

Break up lumps of soil by bashing them with the back of a spade and rake the bed until you have a fine tilth – crumbly soil in small particles that seeds can push through effortlessly. The way to do this is to keep the rake as near parallel to the soil as possible and patiently use a forward and backward movement from different directions. Sprinkle on some general-purpose fertilizer if necessary.

Hot beds

If you have access to fresh stable manure, you could try a hot bed. It is an adaptation of the cold frame, with the advantage of providing bottom heat like an outdoor propagator. Victorian gardeners made great use of them on large estates for out-of-season crops and early delicacies for the house. It is a great idea for the allotment, especially for those who don't have

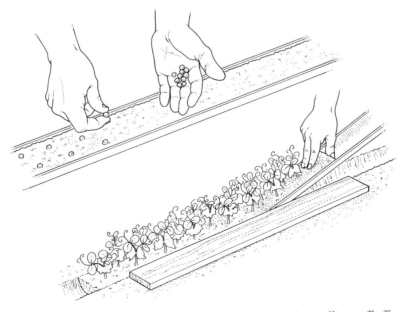

If you sow your peas in a piece of plastic guttering, you can slide the seedlings off effortlessly into a prepared furrow outside without disturbing the roots.

the luxury of a greenhouse or propagator. It makes an interesting challenge, is free (unless you pay for the manure), low-tech and energy saving.

What you will need

You need a cold frame lid with glass or plastic windows. It could be made up from old window frames. The other essential is a good heap of stable or farmyard manure with straw in it – so fresh that it steams in the cold. If you find you haven't got enough, mix it with up to an equal quantity of newly collected leaves. Victorian writers recommend oak or beech, but almost any will do.

The bigger the heap, the higher the temperature you will achieve. To get a hothouse temperature of 27°C (80°F) you would need about 1.2–1.5 m (4–5 ft) square once it has settled down. However, you can get useful warmth from a hotbed half that size.

Turn the manure and straw at least once (some say twice or three times) each day, shaking the fork to break it up and get it well mixed. After about week it will be ready for making a hotbed.

Making the hotbed

Decide whether you want to dig a pit or build the hot bed on the ground. A pit will keep things tidier and give some insulation. If you have cold, wet soil though it's better to make it on the surface.

If you decide on the pit method, dig a hole about 30 cm (12 in) deep, reserving the topsoil. If you are building it on the surface, just remove the topsoil and make a flat base. The dimensions of the heap will depend not only on how much manure you

have, but on the size of the frame. Allow for a good border, about 30 cm (12 in) around the frame for stability.

Pile the manure into the pit, beating it down so that it will stay firm and flat. Make a neat heap, aiming for a compact, squared-off pile. Leave for a few more days for the steam to escape and for the heap to settle. Add a 10 cm (4 in) layer of the reserved top soil. Check the soil temperature – if it is over 27°C (80°F) wait a few days until it cools down.

Cover the heap with the cold frame, leaving a little chink for gases to escape. Make holes for potting compost and sow your seed in it. Cucumbers and melons will really love it.

An adaptation of this idea is to use your existing compost heap. Square it off, add a layer of potting compost and cover with a coldframe.

Sowing seeds in their permanent positions

Prepare the area for planting in the same way as a seed bed, clearing weeds, taking out all stones, raking to a fine tilth, adding fertilizer and watering if needed before you sow. Watering afterwards may make the soil cap, or form a crust, making it difficult for seeds to push through.

Mark out the space so that you will know where exactly your plants will be. Planting in rows or in a geometric pattern helps you to discern what is weed and what is seedling. Define each row (even if it is a straight line in a pattern) with a gardener's line, or string with pegs at each end, to make sure that it is perfectly straight.

Choose a hoe of the desired width (or use a corner) to mark out the rows or drills

SOWING TECHNIQUES

Parallel drills are practical for beans, peas and other climbers that need support. If they run north-south they won't shade each other. Climbers can be grown up strings attached to a central pole, though there will be more of a shade problem.

Blocks or squares are suitable for low-growing plants. As the plants grow their leaves will grow together, shading out weeds and keeping in moisture. They will be easier to manage when netting. Still being in a pattern, it is just as easy to see where your plants are.

Station sowing is used for vegetables that will be some distance apart. Usually three or four seeds are planted together. After germination, choose the strongest seedling and thin out the remainder. If carefully done, they can sometimes be transplanted.

If you are planting large seeds (marrow, peas or broad beans) quite far apart, the simplest method is to make individual holes with a dibber and pop the seeds in them. For safety's sake, sow two or three for thinning later.

---

to the right depth for the particular seeds. For smaller seeds, a stick will do the job. Use a measuring stick to get equal spacing. Avoid windy days if you are planting fine seed – it can easily blow away.

Broadcasting seed

If you are planting in blocks with fine seed like carrot you can broadcast it for speed, then rake it carefully (so as not to bury it) in both directions. Outside you can use a little fine dry soil as a spreading agent to bulk up the seed.

Fluid sowing

This is a modern commercial technique which gives surprisingly rapid and even results. It is particularly effective for tricky customers (like parsnips) and for getting a crop going (like sweetcorn) when the soil is a little too cold for it. The seeds are germinated without compost. Then they are mixed into a gluey carrier gel and squeezed out like toothpaste onto prepared ground.

The home method is to line a plastic container with a few layers of wet (but not sopping) kitchen towel, lay the seeds evenly on it, put on the lid and keep it at 21°C (70°F). Check for progress regularly as you want to catch them at the stage when they have just germinated, still look embryonic and before the roots get too long. For the majority of vegetables, the roots should only be about 5 mm (¼ in) long. Rinse them carefully off the paper towel into a fine meshed sieve.

Mix some fungicide-free wallpaper paste at half strength, or some water-retaining granules (sold for container gardening), with water. When the mixture has thickened, add a few seeds, taking care how you handle them. Use tweezers or the tip of a plant label. If they sink, the paste isn't thick enough. When you are satisfied with the viscosity, stir them in. Put the mixture into a plastic carrier bag and snip off one corner.

Ooze them out evenly along the prepared drill (rather like icing a cake) and cover with compost in the normal way. Don't let the mixture dry out.

Vegetative propagation

Many perennials can be increased by taking pieces off the parent plant – by separating the roots, snipping off offsets, cutting up tubers or taking cuttings. The results are faster, and it is less work than growing from seed.

Dividing rootstocks works well for rhubarb and asparagus, perennial herbs and ornamentals, once the plants are three or four years old. This will give the plant a new lease of life, as well as providing you with new plants. Lift the plant when dormant in autumn, late winter or just stirring in early spring. Divide up the roots so that each piece has a few buds and roots.

Asparagus usually pulls apart quite easily, or you can use a sharp knife. Rhubarb is a tougher proposition. It can be divided by plunging two forks among the roots, back to back, and levering them against each other to separate the clump. If the centre of the root clump looks woody, cut it out and discard it. Replant the divisions.

Removing offsets Globe artichokes produce baby plants next to the rootstock. When they show themselves and have grown some roots in spring, carefully scrape away some soil and detach them with a clean sharp knife. Trim off the leaves, bar one or two, and replant firmly, making sure that the tip is above soil level. Keep well watered and warm until they establish.

Dividing tubers Jerusalem artichokes can be divided up to make more plants. Dig them up and cut up the larger tubers at the joints with a clean sharp knife, making sure

Tip

An alternative to semi-ripe cuttings is to tear off little side shoots ('heels') from where they emerge from the branches. Cut off the rough edge with a sharp knife and proceed as for semi-ripe cuttings (see opposite).

there are healthy buds on each section before replanting.

Root cuttings are usually used to propagate seakale. Mark the spot where a healthy and mature seakale plant is growing before it dies down for winter. During its dormant period, dig it up, taking care not to damage the roots. Cut off a few of the roots from the outside and divide these into 7.5–10 cm (3–4 in) lengths. Note which end is which – make a straight cut at the top end of the piece of root (the one nearest to the plant), and an angled cut at the bottom. Tie into bundles of five or six of equal length and bury them in moist sand up to the neck.

In spring they should begin to sprout. Don't delay – carefully lift them and remove all but one bud from each piece of root. Plant them upright using a dibber. The tops should be buried about 2.5 cm (1 in) below the soil surface. Keep moist and remove the flower buds as they develop.

Taking cuttings

Semi-ripe cuttings are the easiest to do. They are taken from woody plants when the current year's growth is just toughening at the base. It is ideal for increasing your stock of shrubby herbs such as rosemary or

RUNNERS

Strawberries put out runners, complete with mini roots searching for the soil. All you need to do with these is to plant them while still attached to the parent in the same way as layering. Even better, plant them in small pots arranged around the parent plant. Sever the new plants from the parent when they begin to establish. Choose healthy parent specimens and restrict each to no more than four runners. If you can spare a few strawberries, it is good practice to remove the flowers of the plants you choose to propagate.

lavender. Choose a vigorous, non-flowering shoot. Cut it off just below a leaf node or a joint with a sharp knife. Strip off the leaves, all except the top two or three. Cuttings can rot off if they are kept too wet so mix some grit, sand or perlite in equal quantities with multipurpose compost and use it to fill some pots. Plunge the cuttings in up to their necks, leaving the few leaves at the top poking out. Water the compost.

The next step is to cover the cuttings to create condensation. A sawn-off plastic bottle will do. If you are using polythene, don't let it touch the plants – rig up a frame out of wire or sticks before covering them. Keep the cuttings out of direct sunlight until they have rooted, usually 4–6 weeks later. Plant them out the following spring after you have hardened them off.

Softwood cuttings of fresh new growth are taken in the same way, but earlier in year, from spring to summer. They will need to go into a propagator to root.

Hardwood cuttings are taken in the same way in autumn. This is the usual method of propagating many soft fruits – blackcurrants, redcurrants, whitecurrants and gooseberries. The cuttings are put in very free-draining compost and kept nearly dry to tick over in a cold frame or cold greenhouse over the winter.

With blackberries, take off all the leaves but leave the buds as they will grow into branches. If you want a clear stem for redcurrants, whitecurrants or gooseberries, take off the lower buds leaving two poking out of the soil. Alternatively, you can plant hardy types out in a slit trench with sand mixed into the soil and a cloche over them for protection. Hardwood cuttings can take a year to get going.

Layering

Rosemary, sage, bay, blackberries, raspberries and many evergreens will develop roots on their stems when they come into contact with the soil. Cultivate the soil a little where you plan to layer, adding sand or grit if you have heavy soil. Choose a vigorous young stem and strip off the leaves and side shoots.

Slightly wound the stem by scraping it with a knife where you want the roots to grow and bury it about 15 cm (6 in) deep, holding it down with hairpins of wire. The tip of the stem should stick up at right angles to the soil. Secure it further by

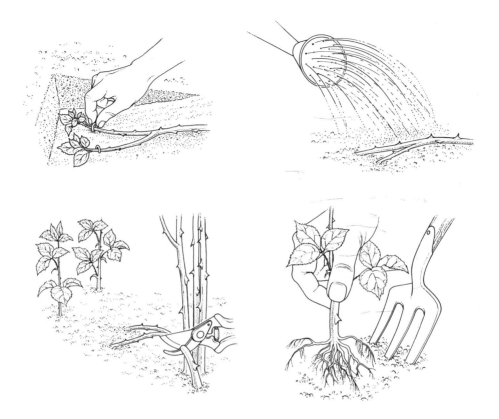

Layering. Propagating blackberries by burying a young, vigorous stem, secured in place with a hairpin of wire. Keep watered until there is some growth and it is ready to be severed.

putting a stone on top. It is usually done in early spring and the new plant should be ready to remove by autumn. If not, leave it for another year. When you see an upsurge of growth, the new plant can be severed from the parent plant. Blackberries need little encouragement to layer. In late summer, bury the tip (tip layering) rather than the stem.

Lifting suckers

Raspberries put out suckers which can be dug up, with some root attached, and transplanted to create new plants. Only use the healthiest young stock.

MAXIMIZING SPACE
Catch cropping

Once you are familiar with the growing times and particular needs of your crops, there are many ways that you can get more from your most fertile beds.

There are some fast growers that can be slotted into empty space between main plantings. It makes good use of your best beds and keeps up weed-suppressing cover. You may find you have a gap of a couple of months between harvesting winter crops and planting tender ones in summer.

Successional sowing The speediest growers are baby carrots, beetroot, radishes

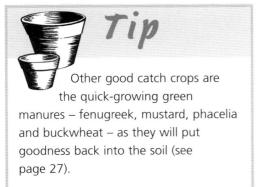

Tip

Other good catch crops are the quick-growing green manures – fenugreek, mustard, phacelia and buckwheat – as they will put goodness back into the soil (see page 27).

and the cut-and-come-again crops – the gourmet baby salad leaves which cost a fortune to buy. Salad Bowl lettuce, cutting lettuce, leaf and seedling radish, curly endive, spinach, sugar loaf chicory, corn salad, the Orientals (particularly mizuna and mibuna greens) all grow fast.

The idea is to plant little and often. When the first sowing has germinated, sow a few more seeds. In this way you can keep a constant fresh supply in the amounts you can realistically use.

When you harvest cut-and-come-again crops, always leave the lowest pair of leaves to resprout. The best time to grow them is in the cool of spring and autumn when they are less likely to bolt. Make sure the bed is completely free of weeds before sowing or you could find yourself eating weeds! If you are using the land to this level of intensity, it is important to keep it well fertilized and in top condition.

Intercropping makes use of the gaps between slow-growing plants which are spaced for the size the will become at maturity. Cauliflowers, Brussels sprouts, celeriac, parsnips, Hamburg parsley, salsify, scorzonera and purple sprouting broccoli will eventually take up a lot of space. Until they do, there is room between them for speedy crops.

Don't let them overlap too much and compete with the main crop, however.

Undercropping is making use of the space under tall vegetables. Sweetcorn, garlic, Brussels sprouts and the climbers – beans, cucumbers, tomatoes or squashes grown up canes – are ideal for the purpose.

Strip cropping is an economic and labour-saving method of growing vegetables. You grow plants in parallel beds that need cloche protection at different times of the year. Through winter you could have hardy vegetables under the cloches. In late spring these would be left uncovered and spring sowings would be planted in the next row under the same cloches. By summer the spring sowings would prefer to be out in the fresh air and the cloches could be used for tender vegetables such as tomatoes, aubergines or peppers.

Spacing

When you buy seed, you are given recommended planting distances. However, in many cases the distances can be manipulated depending on whether you want large or small vegetables. If you want small onions for pickling, baby carrots or miniature cauliflowers, plant them closer together than recommended by the seed company.

The Institute of Horticultural Research has run tests on different planting distances. They discovered that if Brussels sprouts are allowed to grow to full height and treated as a cut-and-come-again crop, the recommended planting distance of 90 x 90 cm (3 x 3 ft) is about right, allowing access for picking and room for hoeing. However, if you want a bulk supply of small sprouts for freezing, plant them closer at 50 x 50 cm (20 x 20 in) as commercial growers do.

CONSERVING WATER

+ Maximize the water-holding capacity of the soil by adding lots of well-rotted organic matter on an annual basis.
+ Eliminate the competition for water by keeping weeds down.
+ Mulch after a good rainfall.
+ Conserve water by making a shallow moat or reservoir around plants.
+ Collect as much as you can in water butts. If you have a shed, make guttering and down pipes to collect it from the roof. Keep the butts covered to prevent evaporation and stop them getting clogged with leaves.
+ Sink a flower pot or section of pipe into the ground to get water down to the roots of thirsty plants, like courgettes or cucumbers.
+ Water in the cool of the evening to avoid rapid evaporation. There is a school of thought that it is better still to water in the morning, but to get the benefits it has to be done by sunrise.

Remove the growing point and small leaves of the plant when the biggest sprouts are the size of your little fingernail. Then a single harvest is taken when the bottom sprouts are just past their best.

CARING FOR PLANTS
Watering

On an allotment, watering is a time-consuming business, generally done by hand from a standpipe or water butt. Quite apart from conservation issues, you will want to keep watering to a minimum.

You can manipulate the performance of plants both by the timing and the quantity of water you give them. The National Vegetable Research Station has made a study on the moisture-sensitive stage of growth. The general response to watering is leaf growth – exactly what you want for leafy vegetables. However, it is not what you want for peas and beans. It is better to keep them on the dry side until they flower. At this point the root activity slows down and the plant could do with a boost. A thorough watering at this stage will produce more flowers, hence more peas and beans.

Watering tips

+ As a rough guide, all plants need sufficient water when young until their roots establish.
+ Vegetables grown for their leaves should never be allowed to dry out.

Tip

Check the moisture content of the soil by digging a hole with a trowel. If it is damp 23–30 cm (9–12 in) deep then the roots of established plants will have access to moisture. This doesn't apply to seedlings, obviously.

✦ Fast-growing plants, like courgettes and marrows, need plenty of water right through their short growing season.

✦ Overwatering can produce a lot of soft growth attractive to pests, and make plants susceptible to cold or rotting off.

✦ Edibles grown for their roots, pods and fruits need steady but not excessive water until the flowers, fruits or roots start to form.

✦ Potatoes profit from a good dousing when the tubers are the size of marbles.

✦ When watering make it thorough – at least 11 litres per sq m or 2 gallons per sq yd. The water should soak to the lower depths of the soil to encourage the roots to grow down. If you just sprinkle water, the roots will look no further and can dry out as soon as you turn your back.

✦ Water brassicas at the base to avoid the damp conditions on the leaves that can encourage fungal disease.

✦ For plants sensitive to cold (such as tomatoes and aubergines), use water from the water butt.

Watering seeds

The best policy is to dribble water into the seed drill before planting. Watering from overhead can make the soil 'cap', or form a crust, making it difficult for the seeds to push through. If you need to water after the seedlings emerge, use the finest rose on the watering can.

Watering transplants

Transplants are particularly vulnerable and need nursing until they establish. Water before and after transplanting. This is the one occasion when you should water little and often (every day or even twice a day in dry weather) and carefully at the base of the plant.

Feeding

With high soil fertility you shouldn't need to feed much, as long as you keep up the regime of digging in, or laying on, a good quantity of well-rotted manure or compost on an annual basis. The organic organization, Henry Doubleday Research Association, says that best practice is to use no fertilizer – it is a supplement, not a replacement, for bulky organic materials. This is something to aim for over the years.

Meanwhile, you may need to add fertilizers to boost the major elements for plant growth – nitrogen, phosphorus and potassium, otherwise known as NPK. Occasionally, trace elements or minerals may be lacking. Iron deficiency on very alkaline soils and phosphorus deficiency on very acid soils is not uncommon. If you are concerned, it is best to send off for a full soil analysis to pinpoint the problem.

Other reasons for fertilizing are when your crops need a boost – hungry ones like tomatoes which are still indoors because of bad weather, or those that have overwintered outside and are looking a bit ragged. The exact amount and which type of feed depends on the plants, whether you want to improve the fruit and flower, or put on leaf growth.

The standard practice, used until the soil is fully fertile, is to apply a top dressing of an all-round fertilizer like blood, fish and bone or seaweed meal prior to planting. Liquid fertilizers are used to perk up plants in containers where nutrients may be running out, or for a quick boost for failing specimens. Organic fertilizers come from

MAJOR ELEMENTS (MACRONUTRIENTS)

 Nitrogen (N) encourages leaf and shoot growth. A component of chlorophyll, it gives plants their greenness. Too little and the plants will be stunted and the leaves pale. Too much will produce sappy growth which will attract pests and collapse at the first sign of frost.

Phosphorus (P), or phosphate, encourages healthy growth throughout the plant, especially the roots. Only small quantities are needed. A deficiency will show as stunted growth and a purple or red discoloration on the older leaves first.

Potassium (K), or potash, is associated with the size and quality of flowers and fruit. It toughens up the plants to protect them against pests and diseases. A deficiency will show up as small fruit and flowers, and yellowing or browning of the leaves.

Magnesium (Mg) is also a constituent of chlorophyll, the greening agent. A deficiency is usually a sign of insufficient organic matter in the soil. Magnesium deficiency causes chlorosis; the symptom is yellowing of the leaves starting between the veins of the leaves.

Calcium (Ca) helps in the manufacture of protein.

Sulphur (S) is part of plant protein and also helps to form chlorophyll. It is unusual to find it missing in places where plenty of organic matter is added. The same goes for the trace elements.

plant, animal and mineral origin found naturally. They will not harm the soil or the populations of micro-organisms within it, whereas many of the man-made alternatives can.

Dried fertilizers

✦ **Bone meal** is rich in phosphate for root growth and is useful when planting shrubs and trees.

✦ **Blood, fish and bone meal** is a balanced NPK all-round fertilizer.

✦ **Blood meal** provides nitrogen and is used for a quick tonic for overwintered crops in spring.

✦ **Dried manures** have all the trace elements but are low on NPK.

✦ **Epsom salts** are a soluble form of magnesium alone.

✦ **Fish meal** contains nitrogen and phosphate.

✦ **Hoof and horn** is rich in nitrogen and works on a slow release. It needs to break down, so apply it to the soil a week or so before planting.

✦ **Rock phosphate** is a good alternative to bone meal for dog owners. It promotes rooting, particularly for shrubs and trees.

✦ **Rock potash** is a useful source of potash alone – a benefit to poor and light soils. It works on slow release which is particularly good for fruit vegetables.

✦ **Seaweed meal** is a good slow-release, all-round tonic with all the trace elements. It contains cytokinins, hormones which promote photosynthesis and protein production, apart from

TRACE ELEMENTS (MICRONUTRIENTS)

Manganese (Mn) is another player in the formation of chlorophyll and protein. A deficiency will show as stunting and yellowing of the younger leaves.

Iron (Fe) plays much the same role as magnesium, though it's only needed in tiny quantities. A deficiency is more common in alkaline soils.

Copper (Cu) and **Zinc** (Zn) activate enzymes.

Boron (B) is an important element throughout the growing tissue. A lack can cause corkiness in fruit and root crops.

Molybdenum (Mb) helps to produce protein.

Oxygen, carbon and hydrogen are taken up from the air, sunlight and water.

---

helping to create humus in the soil.

✦ **Wood ash** from your own bonfire (if allowed) is high in potassium and has some phosphate though quantities of each depend on the type of timber.

Liquid fertilizers

Liquid fertilizers don't stay long in the soil. Seaweed extract is an excellent all-round tonic for promoting strong growth, and supplies the full range of trace elements. It is easy to make your own first-class liquid fertilizers out of comfrey or nettles. Tie up a bunch of leaves in a hessian sack and leave it to steep in a barrel of water over a couple of weeks. Sheep, cow, horse or goat manure can be treated in the same way.

✦ **Comfrey** is a superb all-round fertilizer, but some people can't stand it as it gives off a foul smell. The leaves can be used as an activator on the compost heap, thrown down into a potato trench or laid as a mulch. It is alkaline, so do not use it on chalky soils. Its long roots draw up potassium from the subsoil.

✦ **Nettles** make a good general tonic, though they provide less phosphate.

They are not suitable for alkaline soils. Nettles gathered in spring are the richest in nutrients.

✦ **Well-rotted manures** can be treated in the same way. Sheep manure is the highest in phosphates. Linton Carby, from Uplands Allotments, Birmingham, makes liquid feed from his own compost.

PROTECTING CROPS FROM THE WEATHER
Windbreaks

These are a good idea if you are situated on a blustery, chilly site. While plants need plenty of air circulation, they suffer badly in strong cold winds.

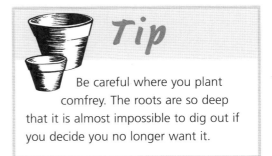

Tip

Be careful where you plant comfrey. The roots are so deep that it is almost impossible to dig out if you decide you no longer want it.

GROWING COMFREY

Site it where it can stay for twenty years or more, or persuade your committee to plant a patch. The less-invasive type is Russian comfrey (*Symphytum* x *uplandicum* Bocking 14). As it rarely sets seed, the best way to start off is to buy some root offsets or get some off a neighbour. Plant in spring, or early autumn, though any time will do except deepest winter when it is dormant. Incorporate some well-rotted compost and clear the weeds, then plant 60–90 cm (24–36 in) apart. Plant with the growing tips just below the surface.

Don't harvest in the first year, but remove the flowering stems and go easy in the second year while the plants build up strength. After this, comfrey can be cut back three or four times a year with shears when the leaves are about 60 cm (24 in) high.

A good windbreak will work on a diminishing scale, for a distance up to ten times its height, cutting down the wind by 50 per cent or more. So a 1.5 m (5 ft) high windbreak would cover the area 15 m (50 ft) in front of it.

To protect the whole of a full-sized allotment, therefore, you might need two or three going down in scale towards the hardier plants.

The most effective windbreaks filter the wind. It is fruitless to try to block it with a solid structure. If wind meets a dead end it will turn into turbulence, creating icy eddies.

Choosing a windbreak

A good deciduous (or mixed evergreen and deciduous) hedge is very effective and has the additional bonus of providing habitats for wildlife. Remember to plant your crops well away from it as it will take up nutrients. Wooden fences with gaps, lathe and wattle, or wire or plastic netting stretched across stout posts work well and give you a structure for climbing plants. Keep the more vulnerable plants at the end of the allotment near a tall windbreak, with lower localized windbreaks on the windward side of crops with sacking, mesh or fleece stretched across low stakes.

A solid windbreak creates turbulence. A permeable one filters the wind and can cut its force by half.

Localized protection

Developments in plastics have proved highly efficient for bringing on and protecting plants from cold, wind and pests. Polytunnels, plastic cloches, floating mulches of polythene, horticultural fleece and mesh have transformed the gardening scene.

Cool-climate crops – cabbages, cauliflowers, radishes, sprouts and turnips – will germinate when the temperature has reached a consistent minimum of 5°C (41°F). Carrots and parsnips need a slightly warmer 6°C (43°F). By warming the soil and using protective cover, it is reckoned that you can keep the temperature above 6°C (43°F) for an extra three to four weeks at each end of the season.

The non-porous types of cover, like polythene, come into their own in spring, autumn and winter. They are less good in summer as the atmosphere underneath can get too hot and humid and foster fungal diseases. Plants that have been grown in a protected atmosphere need to be watched, aired and hardened off with extreme care.

The greenhouse

This is an expensive structure and difficult to heat without electricity, though some people do use kerosene heating. Quite a few enthusiastic gardeners have a heated greenhouse at home to raise young plants.

More common on allotments is a cold greenhouse. If you are lucky enough to have one you will find it very useful for extending the season, for propagating out of the rain, for growing tender crops and winter salads.

Cold frames

A cold frame can be made by anyone with basic DIY skills. It is a must for hardening off seedlings, growing early and late salads, for successional quick-growing crops and as a nursery bed for brassicas. In summer, it is a good place to grow tender crops like ridge cucumbers, aubergines, peppers or tomatoes. Generally made with brick or wooden sides, it has a sloping glass or plastic roof which can be removed or lifted up for ventilation.

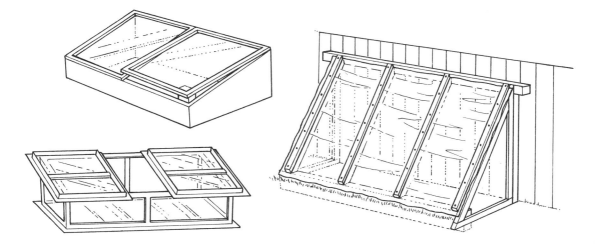

Cold frames can easily be made from old window frames. Keep in mind the final size of the plants.

When making a frame consider the size of the plants that you will want to grow. You don't want your plants to become weak and leggy by over-reaching themselves to get to the light. If you plan to grow tomatoes you would need a tall frame, but for salad crops only a low structure. A selection of sizes would be handy. You can buy kits which are usually made of aluminium, steel or timber frame and rigid see-through PVC or other synthetic materials.

Polytunnels

A walk-in polytunnel is occasionally seen on allotments. It is reckoned to extend the season by six weeks in spring and four in autumn and creates a nearly wind-free environment. It works in much the same way as a cold greenhouse – the temperature and airflow need to be controlled manually.

Cloches

Cloches work in the same way as cold frames but they are portable. They can be used to warm the soil by a vital degree or two if positioned two weeks before planting or sowing. They will protect crops from birds, rabbits and insect pests. They keep hardy crops warm through the worst of winter weather and protect half-hardy plants from passing frost and wind. Herbs

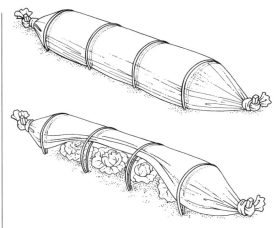

A miniature polytunnel can be made by stretching transparent sheeting over hoops.

and salads are given a longer season into early winter if covered with cloches, and a racing start in spring. Another benefit is that they keep the soil on the dry side, discouraging fungal diseases, slugs and snails. Rainwater, which falls each side, will still find its way to the roots.

Cloches should let in plenty of light, especially in winter. They should be easy to open up for ventilation on hot days and to close to block out wind on cold ones. They need to be stable yet easy to move and assemble.

Choosing a cloche

Cloches come in many shapes and sizes. The simplest is a plastic lemonade bottle with the bottom cut off (a serrated bread knife will slice it off with ease) and the top removed for ventilation. Polytunnel cloches can made from hoops covered in polythene or insect netting, with the edges buried or weighed down with stones. They can be bought in kit form or devised. There are dozens of different proprietory brands and types. Polycarbonate sheeting has more or less taken over from glass and is a safer

> ## *Tip*
> An excellent cold frame can be made from an old wooden drawer, propped up at an angle, with a window frame on top.

option if there are children about. Sheets balanced against each other to form an 'A' shape are handy to cover a row of plants. Keep in mind that cloches need to be lifted for watering, so they shouldn't be too heavy.

Horticultural fleece

This is made of polypropylene, a synthetic fabric so light that plants barely notice that it is there. It provides warmth while letting in light, air and water so crops can be grown to maturity under it while being protected against pests. It can be used to cover up crops throughout their growth. This is known as a floating mulch and speeds up growth quite dramatically. Make sure you've got rid of weeds as they will sprout with equal vigour. When covering the crop, allow a little slackness for growth. The usual method is to bury the edges of the fabric so that you can let it out as the plants grow. If you have raised beds with wooden edging, the fleece can be stapled to the sides.

It is very useful to keep a roll to hand to throw over vulnerable plants if frost threatens. The one disadvantage is that it will eventually get dirty and tear.

Mesh fabrics

Mesh fabrics or perforated transparent film are made of plastic. They don't keep the plants as warm as horticultural fleece but are just as effective against pests and last longer, especially if they are UV treated. As they let in more air than horticultural fleece, diseases are less likely to develop. They can be used like fleece as a floating mulch. Mesh comes in various gauges (the smallest is 0.8 mm which will keep out tiny pests like flea beetle) so get the right size for the particular pest you want to keep out.

Tip

If you don't have any horticultural fleece to hand and a frosty night is imminent, a layer of straw or newspaper can be laid over plants and covered with chicken wire to hold it in place. Even old net curtains will help.

Polythene

This is useful for warming large areas of soil by a degree or two. If you have any farming friends, ask them to let you have their old silage bags.

Polystyrene

A sheet of polystyrene under your seed trays is a good insulator and will help to prevent cold creeping up from below. A box made from polystyrene sheets glued together with a see-through top, can make a cosy environment for plants in a cold greenhouse during the winter months.

Supports for trees

Trees need a short stake which comes about one-third of the way up the trunk. Drive a stout stake into the ground by about 45 cm (18 in) before planting. The tree will need to be attached to the stake to support it. Make sure that the ties won't cut into the trunk as it grows. Either use tree ties which are designed to be let out like a belt, or an old pair of tights or stockings. They stretch with the growth and don't chafe the tree.

Wind the tree ties or tights into a figure of eight between the stake and the trunk. After a couple of years, the stake will no

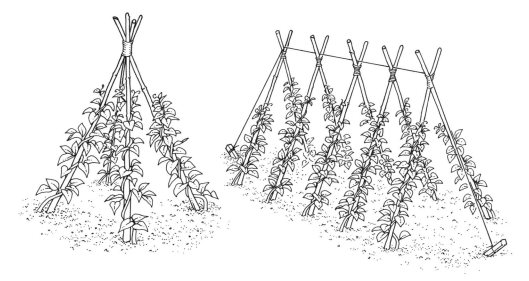

Runner beans are traditionally grown up sturdy poles crossed at the top and secured with taut wire.

longer be needed. Stakes are not used to hold the tree up, but to keep the roots still until they have established.

Some plants – notably fruit trees that are going to be trained flat in cordons, fans or espaliers – will need a permanent framework. If you can find them, use oak or sweet chestnut supports. They will last for 20 years in the soil, whereas pine starts to rot after five. Choose timber which has been pressure-treated with a wood preservative, but avoid preservatives which contain toxic chemicals – not what you want in an organic allotment. For extreme durability,

> ## Tip
>
> Sharp cane tops are a hazard to eyes, so be sure to cover them. Some people swear by small plastic drinks bottles, others by film canisters or old tennis balls.

it might be better to use metal stakes. Wires are then strained between the posts, from the top working downwards.

Supports for climbing vegetables

Climbing vegetables, such as runner beans, can be grown in rows of criss-cross poles or on wigwams. If possible, avoid imported bamboo canes. Some allotments are encouraging a little indigenous forestry in unused corners, both for wildlife and self-sufficiency on bean poles. Hazel is a native tree, needing no attention, and is quite happy to occupy a shady corner. Every six or eight years it can be coppiced (cut to the ground) to supply fine bean poles. All the twiggy bits can be used to support peas and herbaceous plants. Meanwhile, it makes a good habitat for wildlife.

An alternative to hazel is willow which can be bent and twisted into any shape. Strip the bark from the part that will be below soil level to prevent it rooting. You can also grow your own bamboo canes. Chose a tall

CASE STUDY

 Geoffrey Sinclair, a forester in charge of 2,000 acres, was horrified when he came across an allotment in Ipswich where great quantities of bamboo canes were being used. He was so upset that he and some friends took over some disused allotment plots to grow traditional hazel bean poles.

"There could be no better indicator of how remote we have become from our environment than this importing of twigs from China to support runner beans," he says. "Until we can supply our own twigs without going to China or Poland, it is difficult to imagine us ever successfully tackling the bigger sustainability issues."

From this the Local Woodlands Product Initiative was formed to encourage people to grow, use and reuse local wood. They help sites in the area to grow their own poles, provide them with a nature reserve and put on woodcraft workshops and an annual festival. The ultimate aim is to encourage better care of woodland in the UK. Website: www.allotmentforestry.com

---

variety like *Phillostachys nigra* – the black bamboo. It is a handsome plant and should provide you with canes in about three years after planting.

Peas will scramble and cling onto twigs or netting hitched between posts. The net can be any lucky find from an old fisherman's net left on the beach to an old tennis net. Some people use chicken wire and burn off the dried debris at the end of the season to save picking it all out.

PRUNING

In nature, nothing is pruned unless it is eaten or blown away, and plants seem to do very well. However, there are several reasons for pruning:

✦ To improve the health of the plant by removing dead, damaged and diseased growth, or rubbing and crossing branches.

✦ To encourage better fruiting and improved flowering.

✦ To create the desired shape and a strong, healthy structure.

Use tools that are sharp, clean and well within their capacity to do the job. Always cut just above a joint or bud to prevent die back. If taking out a whole branch, cut back to the stem. New growth will shoot in the direction that the bud is facing. Always cut to an outward-facing bud so that the new growth springs outwards and not back towards the centre of the plant.

Training fruit trees

Not many allotments allow large trees on individual plots, but there is potential in training them into shapes that won't cast shade on the neighbours. Training the branches towards the horizontal encourages more fruit, while slowing down growth. So if you find that one side shoot is more vigorous than its partner, lower it to dampen its ardour. Tie the weaker one at a more upward angle until it has caught up.

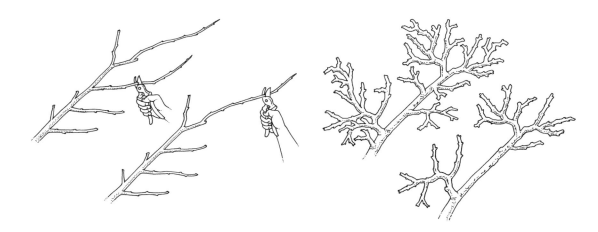

Shorten the secondary growth of fruit trees to three buds through summer to build up a network of short fruit-bearing spurs.

The form you choose depends on the amount of space, the type of fruit and how much time you are willing to spend. Make sure you have the right rootstock *(see page 163)*. You can buy fruit trees already partly trained by the nursery. To train one yourself, is best to start with a one-year-old whip, as it will be highly flexible, or a two- or three-year-old feathered maiden. Choose specimens with strong straight stems and plenty of side shoots.

It will take you a couple of years to make a good framework and longer for complicated forms. Winter pruning encourages fast growth, while summer pruning slows it down. Shortening the secondary growth throughout summer lets in light and air to the flowers and fruits and keeps the shape. Keep your secateurs to hand and trim off unwanted growth regularly. If you are training apples and pears, you need the common spur-bearing types rather than the more unusual 'tip bearers'. The spurs are short shoots that bear flowers and fruits right along the branches rather than in clusters at the tips.

NICKING AND NOTCHING

For perfect symmetry, professional pruners use the techniques of 'nicking' and 'notching'. Nicking is cutting out a tiny section of bark below a bud to check an overly vigorous branch. It cuts down the flow of nutrients and encourages other parts to grow. Notching is same procedure just above a bud to stimulate a new shoot to spring from or beneath it.

Tree shapes

The cordon doesn't take up much space and is particularly suited to apples and pears. The single types are best for the allotment as double and multiple cordons are more secure grown against a wall. Set up a post and wire arrangement or run wires along a fence. Secure canes (or bean poles) top, middle and bottom at an angle of 45° with strong wire. Plant the young trees at the same angle and attach them to the canes. Single cordons are planted 75 cm (30 in) apart and allowed to grow to about 1.8 m (6 ft) high. Cut the leading shoot back by one-third of the current year's growth and snip back all the side shoots at a downward-facing bud to 7 cm (3 in) long. Through the summer, keep the side shoots to the same length and secondary shoots at 2.5 cm (1 in). In winter, prune the leader back by one-third of the current year's growth. Keep going in the same manner over the years until the tree reaches the desired height. Slow its growth in summer by snipping off the leader to a bud.

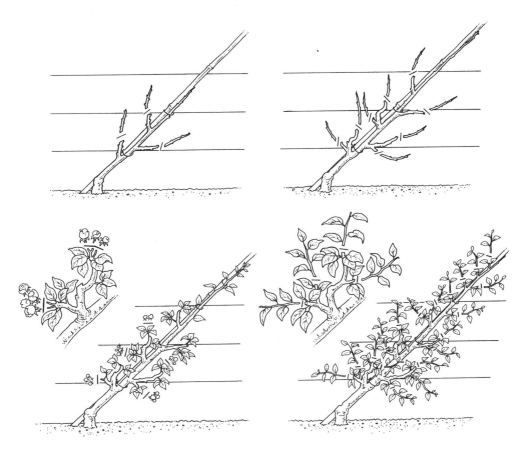

The cordon. Secure a cane against a wire support at a 45° angle, plant and tie in the young tree to it. Cut back the leader by a third and trim the side shoots to some 7 cm (3 in). Through summer keep trimming the side shoots. Carry on over the years until the tree reaches the top of the support.

The stepover is a low, single cordon, usually grown in a series like a hoop edging. Space 60 cm (24 in) posts about 1.5 m (5 ft) apart and stretch a wire between them. Start with a one-year-old whip as it will be flexible. Plant at an angle of 45° and attach the tip to a peg and twine which you will

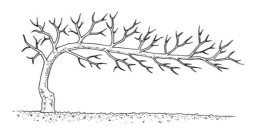

Lower the stem until it is at a right angle.

gradually tighten through summer until the young tree is at an angle of 90°. Shorten the laterals (side branches) to three buds and snip off the leader to a bud when it has grown to the right length.

The espalier is an elegant form suited to apples and pears. As it takes up more space, it needs a strong support. If you can find a feathered maiden with near perfectly spaced side branches, it will give you a head start. Otherwise, get it right from the beginning with a one-year-old whip.

You grow it tier by tier. Every winter, cut back the leader above a pair of buds, making sure there are two buds in the right place to make lateral branches. This encourages the uppermost buds to shoot sideways. Tie in a strong upper shoot to make the new leader. When the new shoots appear tie them to a cane at about 45°. At the end of the growing season, lower them to the horizontal and tie them in. Continue until you achieve the desired height and trim off the leader in summer to slow growth down.

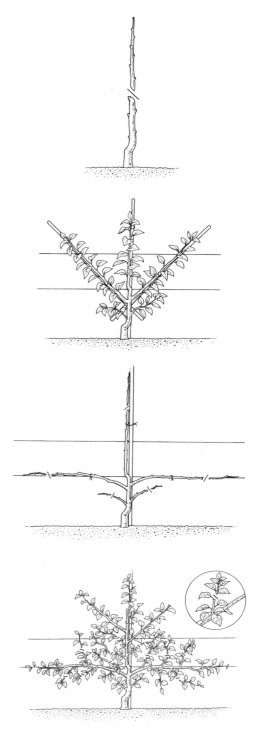

An espalier is grown tier by tier.

The fan is a simpler version of the espalier and it suits stone fruits, such as plums and greengages, particularly well. In an ideal world it should be against a wall, though post and wire is fine in warmer areas. Plant a feathered maiden with two good low side shoots about 25 cm (10 in) from the ground.

In spring, tie these at 45° onto canes strapped to the framework. Cut the leader off above a bud, making sure that the cut is higher than the side shoots. Snip the side shoots back to an underside bud about 40 cm (16 in) from the main stem. These will form the 'arms', the main structure. Trim off any other side shoots from these to two buds.

As summer progresses, encourage well-placed side growth (ribs) on the arms of the tree and tie it in. Remove everything you don't want back to two buds. In the second and third years, shorten the ribs to encourage more branching.

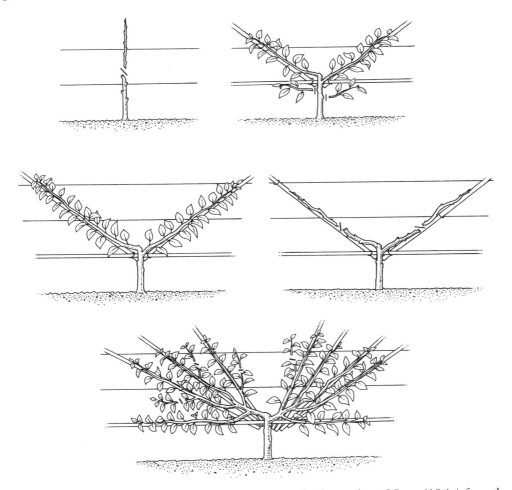

The fan. Choose a feathered maiden with two strong side shoots about 25 cm (10 in) from the ground. Tie onto canes strapped onto the framework at 45°. Cut the leader off slightly higher than the side shoots. Encourage well-placed side growth while trimming back extra shoots to two buds.

Tip

When tying in branches to a supporting framework, use soft twine in a figure of eight between branches and supports.

Pruning soft fruits

Pruning cane and bush fruits will encourage strong growth, fruitfulness and – in the case of the prickly ones – will make picking a bit easier. As soft fruits are prone to viruses, have a solution of disinfectant to hand in which to dip your secateurs before moving from plant to plant. Except for autumn raspberries, they all bear their fruit on old wood (stems that were produced before the current year).

Blackberries and hybrid berries are vigorous and need stout supports – post and wire, or a good fence about 1.8 m (6 ft) high. Plant out one-year-old 'rooted tips' in early winter or spring. Cut them down to about 25 cm (10 in) to encourage growth from the bottom. In the summer, cut the original canes right out.

The prickly cane fruits can get into a real tangle if they are not organized. The aim is to separate the woody canes that will fruit the current year from the supple new growth that will fruit in the next year. One way to do this is to tie in the fruiting canes on one side and the new shoots on the other. Another is to tie the fruiting canes to the lower wires and let the new growth shoot up the middle. When the fruit is picked, the old canes are cut down to the ground. So by autumn all you have left are the canes ready for the next season's fruit and these can be rearranged into whatever pattern you have chosen. Cut out any weak stems and suckers as they appear. In early spring, tip prune the canes by 15 cm (6 in) or, if there has been frost damage, cut further back to healthy growth.

Summer raspberries are bought as single canes and are planted out between autumn and spring. They need a strong support system as they stand out through winter. Post and rail is generally recommended as it allows a good circulation of air. Snip back in early spring to a few leaves to encourage fresh growth. Space out the new shoots and tie them in as they grow.

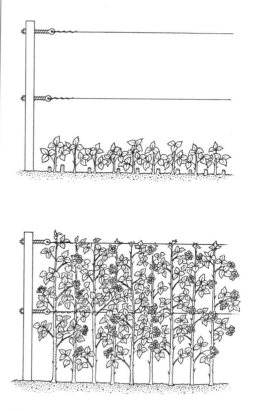

Plant young raspberries in the dormant season against a strong post and wire support.

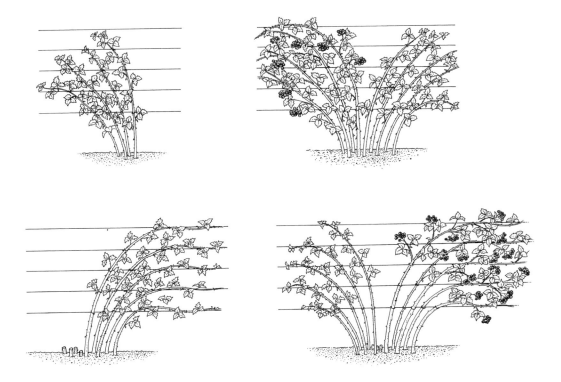

Blackberries and hybrids. The new canes are tied in along the wires on one side of the support. After fruiting, they are cut right down while the new canes for next year are trained along the other side.

You may need to help them when they are small by looping string around the lowest wire. Remove any flowers in the first year. The next summer, cut down the fruiting canes as they go over and tie in the new growth. You can keep old and new separate, in the same way as for blackberries.

Autumn raspberries are bought and planted in the same way as the summer ones. They don't need support, except in windy places. In late winter or early spring before new canes start to shoot, cut all of them down to the ground. New canes will appear and fruit in the first year. Simply carry on in this way. Don't tip prune them as they bear fruit on the tips. Autumn raspberries are easier than summer ones.

Blackcurrants are bought as small two-year-old bushes. Plant a little deeper than they were in their pots to stimulate the plants to produce new shoots. Cut back all the shoots to two buds to encourage strong growth the following year. In the second winter, remove weak shoots leaving the stronger ones to fruit the following summer. Once the plant has borne fruit, it can be pruned to let in light and air, or you can wait until winter.

Remove the oldest branches in favour of the younger ones. Keep in mind the shape of the bush, the balance and proportion. Trim off the lowest shoots at the base of the plant so the fruit doesn't touch the soil.

Redcurrants and whitecurrants can be grown as bushes or trained as cordons or fans *(see page 61)*. They are quite easy to cultivate once you have built up a good framework. They don't fruit until the third year. Choose a one-year-old bush on a short stem, about 10 cm (4 in), with some healthy shoots. Plant it in late autumn or winter. If there are any buds on the stem, rub them off. Prune the shoots back by half to an outward-facing bud. Allow it to grow on through the summer.

The second winter, cut back the new growth by half and shorten five or six strong shoots of the older growth in the same way. Your aim is to achieve a perma-nent framework in an open goblet shape for air circulation and balance. In the following winters, all shoots that come off the main framework are cut back to one bud. This will make the plant produce more short fruiting shoots or spurs.

Gooseberries are lethally barbed (with a few exceptions among modern cultivars), so it is a good idea to grow them as cordons or espaliers. However, they are generally grown as quite big bushes – up to 1.8 m (6 ft) tall – so they need quite a lot of space. Some cultivars have a pendent habit, others an upright. As with redcurrants, buy a one-year-old plant with a short stem and some well-placed, strong branches. Plant in autumn or winter. When the plant is dormant, cut back the branches by three-quarters. If it is a pendent type, cut to an upward-facing bud. Through the summer, plenty of side shoots should develop.

The following winter, select about ten of these to make a well-balanced framework and cut out the rest. Shorten the side shoots to four buds. The fruit will come in the summer. If you continue to shorten the side shoots each winter on the permanent framework you have created, you will get fewer but bigger fruits. The alternative is to cut out a few older branches entirely each year for more but smaller fruits. If you thin the fruits by half in spring, the remaining ones will be bigger and the thinnings can be used for cooking.

Blueberries are usually sold as two-year-old plants. Plant in winter and allow the plant to grow on, removing misplaced or weak growth and encouraging a well-formed open shape. Trim away unwanted growth at ground level. Once it has estab-lished, cut out a proportion of less productive wood every winter, reducing the plant by no more than one-third. You can differentiate the fruit buds from the growth ones as they are noticeably plumper.

Blanching and forcing

Forcing is a way to get your own out-of-season crops. Chicory, rhubarb and seakale can be forced for winter eating. Blanching removes bitterness by excluding light.

✦ **Chicory** Dig up the 'chicons' in autumn, trim off the outside leaves and replant in a container (or box) in peat substitute. Keep them in a warm, dark place. They should grow to some 20 cm (8 in) and be ready to eat in a few weeks. To force outside in autumn, cover the plants with a flower pot, raised a little on crocks or tiles to let the air in, and block the hole at the top. The 'Witloof' varieties are the best for forcing.

✦ **Radiccio** can have the bitterness removed by placing a saucer or plate over the heart of the plant to blanch it for about a week before harvesting. Make sure there are no slugs inside first.

✦ **Rhubarb** needs a period of cold before it can be forced, so wait until midwinter. The plants can be brought indoors like chicory but they are big plants to move. It is much easier to cover the entire plant where it grows with a bin, bucket or forcing pot wrapped in straw to keep it warm. You will get tender shoots about three weeks early. Let the plant recuperate afterwards until the following year.

✦ **Seakale** Tidy up the plant once it has died back in early winter by removing the old leaves, put on a layer of straw for warmth and cover it in the same way as rhubarb. Allow about 40 cm (16 in) of space for growth. It will be ready in two or three months.

✦ **Leeks** can be blanched, either by earthing up, or placing small sections of plastic pipe over the bases of the stems.

✦ **Celery** can be treated in the same way, but tying newspaper around the lower stems will have the same effect without the problem of washing off the mud.

THE HARVEST

Gathering in the fruits of your labours is deeply satisfying. Through the height of summer, harvesting the crops, particularly catching the prolific fruiters such as runner and French beans, tomatoes and courgettes at their peak, becomes a daily task. On every visit there will be the outer leaves of the cut-and-come-again crops to collect and something new to take home for supper. Harvesting becomes a race against the plants becoming coarse or bolting. Turn your back in June, July or August and the crops will become overblown and your courgettes will have turned into giant marrows. If you are going away, get a neighbour to pick for you.

As autumn approaches, make a plan for the remaining produce. All frost-tender fruit and vegetables need to be brought in and stored in one way or another. Good kitchen gardeners need to be talented cooks to get full value from the allotment. Ripe tomatoes can be sun dried, juiced, made into pasta sauces or ratatouille with the remaining courgettes and aubergines. Those that haven't ripened as the days shorten make good green chutney. In the same way, other vegetables and fruits can be dried, bottled, pickled, preserved or frozen.

It is as well to get organized before you start the big autumn harvest, laying in storage jars, freezer containers, crates, sacks, sand and whatever else you will need. Produce begins to deteriorate as soon as it comes out of the ground or off the bush or tree, so aim to be fast and efficient.

The golden rules for harvesting

Avoid damage Only perfect specimens can be stored. Broken tissue invites fungus and bacteria, and rough handling can lead to bruising.

Use a clean sharp knife for trimming. A clean cut will repair fast.

Cool down the crops straight after lifting The ideal time to harvest is early in the morning on a cool day. Move the crops from the ground to the shade of a tree, to the shed or refrigerator with due speed.

Once stored check regularly If any stored fruits or vegetables start to rot, remove them immediately to save the rest of the crop.

Storing carrots, parsnips, beetroot, swedes and turnips

Avoid overhandling. If you choose a dry day and the soil falls off the vegetables, you won't need to wash them. If you have heavy clay that sticks to crops or you suspect damage or disease. washing is a good idea. Twist off the tops, leaving a small topknot. Take care not to damage the crown, particularly of beetroot which 'bleeds' at the slightest injury. Lay the vegetables in crates, in layers, putting sand in between. The sand will help to insulate one from the other should any start to rot, and will let air circulate. Store in a cool, frost-free place.

Storing potatoes

Potatoes are not hardy and are lifted before the frosts. When the leaves die down on the main crop, they are ready to harvest. Choose a dry day and dig carefully from the outside, working inwards, to avoid piercing them with your fork. If the potatoes come out wet, you need to air off surface moisture before storing them.

CASE STUDY

"An old gardener told me that he used to store new potatoes harvested in June for Christmas. He'd pack them in a sealed biscuit box in dry compost and bury them. I was intrigued and I thought I'd try it. I put some in a plastic container in sand and, believe it or not, they came out six months later perfect. You could even scrape them." — *Shirley Fleetwood, Robin Hood Allotment, Nottingham.*

CASE STUDY

"You can get free potato sacks from greengrocers, but you may have to lie a bit. I told the truth to the first one I went to, and said that I wanted them for my own potatoes. 'Oh, you do, do you?' he replied rather menacingly. 'Why don't you buy from me?' After that I went to several and gave them a tall story. It worked." —*Stephen Butler, Circuit Lane Allotment, Reading.*

Pick out any damaged ones for eating straight away and store the rest in double-thickness brown paper sacks. They are made for the purpose and completely cut out the light, while allowing air circulation. Hessian sacks will also serve as long you make sure that no light gets in, causing poisonous green patches. Tie the neck and store in a cool, frost-free place. Alternatively, you can store them in a clamp.

The clamp

A time-honoured way to store root vegetables is in a clamp. It is practical for the allotment as there is usually more room outside in winter than in the shed. A clamp will keep the vegetables fresher for longer than storing them in sacks or crates.

First decide whether to make a cone or a narrow rectangular shape like a roof ridge. If you will want to raid it bit by bit, a long thin clamp is more practical than a cone as you can seal it up as you go without fear of it collapsing.

Making a clamp

Make a base layer of sand or sandy soil with some wood ash or bran around the edge to deter slugs. Choose a fine day to lift the vegetables. Prepare them as before, drying them off and twisting off the tops. Sorting through to remove damaged or diseased roots is vital as one bad specimen could wreck your entire precious cache.

Build a 'castle' of the vegetables, with the largest at the bottom and the smallest at the top, aiming for a pitch of 45°. Cover it generously with vertical layers of straw, dried grass or reeds. Wheat straw is the easiest to work with as it is straight and rigid. The straw keeps soil off the vegetables and protects them from frost. Tie it at the top to make a top knot. It will poke out of the finished clamp like a chimney and act as an air vent. For a long thin clamp you will need several of these, spaced a few feet apart. Pack a 15–20 cm (6–8 in) layer of soil around the structure, patting it down firmly with your hands. Work from the bottom, tier by tier, pushing soil into cracks and hollows. End by compacting it with the back of a spade.

Removing the produce

When you want to get your vegetables out of the clamp, make a door by chipping away at one side near the base. If there are any signs of structural damage, pack in more soil. Don't open the clamp in frosty weather. Potatoes are particularly sensitive to frost, so if you want a good supply for the New Year, get enough out to see you through. If the weather becomes icy, close up the chimney but don't forget to open it again as soon as possible. As long as the soil layer is thick enough, you shouldn't have any problem with rodents. However, if you do, cover the clamp with galvanized wire mesh.

Storing onions

Onions, with their many layers of papery skin, are natural storers. The sign for harvesting is when the leaves droop and start to die back. The onions should be lifted carefully to avoid bruising and left to dry in the sun on a rack in a single layer. If the weather is wet, they will have to come under cover into the warm. After a week or two, when the skins are brown and papery, they will be ready to store. Take out any damaged ones and any that show signs of sprouting. They need to be kept dry and have plenty of air circulation. If they get wet they will start to grow again. Onions can be stored in nets or made into ropes by plaiting the dried leaves, and hung up in an airy spot. Alternatively, they can be laid out in vegetable trays in a single layer and left in a cool shed.

Storing fruits

Apples ripen at different times according to variety and their whereabouts on the tree. Those on the sunny side will ripen first. Early varieties don't store well and should be eaten soon after picking, mid-season ones will keep for a couple of months, and the best of the late apples for up to a year. The most reliable way to see if the fruits are ready to pick is to cup a fruit in one hand and twist. If ripe, it will come off easily with its stalk. Harvest them in the same way, keeping the stalks on and laying them carefully in a lined basket as apples bruise easily. The traditional fruit tray with slats and corner posts for stacking works well, allowing for circulation of air at the sides

WILL THEY BE BETTER OFF IN THE GROUND?

Most root vegetables – carrots, parsnips, beetroot, swede, turnips and leeks – stay freshest where they grow. Growth slows down in cold weather to a gentle ticking over and they will have the benefits of natural free refrigeration. Give extra protection against frost by earthing them up, putting on cloches or covering them thickly with straw or leaves. Don't do this until the last minute (December in most places) as the additional warmth could encourage growth.

Choose winter types as they grow more slowly and tend to cope better with the cold. Carrots and parsnips will generally survive the winter well. Parsnips become sweeter for the experience. Beetroot, swedes and turnips are usually dug up and stored or eaten before the end of winter as, if left too long, they can become coarse and fibrous.

However, if you have a pest problem, or if the soil temperature in your allotment is likely to drop below freezing, it would be wise to lift and store them in autumn.

and from the top. Keep apples in a dark place like a cellar or shed that will get no cooler than 7°C (46°F). Though not essential, wrapping them in paper individually will help to keep them moist.

Pears are picked when they are hard, and are ripened indoors. If left until they are completely ripe the chances are they will be spoilt and have gone brown inside. The test for the picking time is the same as for

Tip

"When picking blackcurrants, cut off entire branches for autumn pruning. Retire with them to a comfortable seat or take them home to get the job shared." – *Derek Humphries, NSALG Representative for Yorkshire.*

apples, when, with a small twist, they part easily from the branch. Taking care not to bruise them, lay them in single layers, unwrapped, and keep them in the cool. If you only have a few, the bottom shelf of the refrigerator is as good a place as any. They only keep for a matter of weeks. Bring them into the warmth of a room to ripen as you want them.

Soft fruits are picked when still firm if they are to be used for jam or freezing. Berries are generally picked individually, whereas currants are picked in clusters, or 'strigs'. The blueberry bears fruit in clusters like currants but the berries need to picked individually as they ripen at different times. You can tell they are ready when they soften and turn bluish–black with a waxy bloom.

Storing herbs

Herbs are no exception to the rule that you can't beat fresh. Get a few extra weeks in autumn by putting cloches over culinary herbs like mint, parsley and basil. Alternatively, pot some up and bring them to the kitchen windowsill.

Herbs for storage should be picked at their peak before they come into flower. Freezing is perhaps the best method of storage, particularly for parsley, basil, chives and mint as they don't hold much flavour when dried. Just chop them up and freeze in ice cube trays with a few drops of water. Transfer them to plastic bags in the freezer for handy use through winter.

Drying

The secret of drying herbs is speed. Shake off any insects and wipe them dry. Don't wash them as this will slow up the process. Lay them out in trays and leave them in a warm kitchen or airing cupboard, aiming for a temperature of 27°C (80°F) and plenty of air circulation. When the herbs are bone-dry, store them in airtight jars in a dark cupboard.

Herb oils and vinegars

Except for garlic oils, which don't keep, you can make flavoured oils and vinegars for the taste of summer in winter. Steep the fresh herbs in them for a few days (vinegars are quicker), straining off and repeating until you get the right flavour.

COLLECTING SEED

Collecting and growing from your own seed makes you feel like a real professional. It saves money, conserves rare breeds and encourages local diversity. Peas, French beans and tomatoes are good ones to start with, being generally easy and reliable. With many others there are a few things to take into account. They may need to be isolated or covered so they don't cross with the wrong plant.

You need to know about the individual plant's biological clock and its particular requirements for setting seed. Many common vegetables, such as carrots, parsnips, main crop onions and Brussels sprouts, are biennials. This means that they won't flower until the following year and you will have to keep them through winter. Beetroot and carrots are frost tender and would need to come out of the cold to survive until the following year. Some plants need a period of cold before they can set seed. Generally, perennials are best sown from fresh seed and not dried or stored.

Pure breeds

Plants are divided into self-pollinators and cross-pollinators. The self-pollinators are fairly certain to come out pure, exactly like the parent plants. They fertilize themselves before the flowers open so they should come out true to type.

The cross-pollinators, like kale, cabbage, broad beans and leeks, are pollinated by insects. Sweetcorn, beetroot and spinach are pollinated by wind. If they are crossed with

Tip

If you plan to save seed, select a few of your best specimens. For safety's sake remove any nearby plants that look less than healthy and any other varieties of the same species.

a different variety or a different member of the same species (it could be a weed), you will end up with an interesting mongrel – a cross of celery and celeriac, or sugar beet with beetroot, for example.

Hand pollination

You can prevent insects reaching the flowers and pollinating them by netting the entire plant or individual flowers. The perforated cellophane bags on supermarket loaves of bread are ideal for this. Horticultural fleece or fine net curtain are alternatives. Put it loosely over both male and female flowers, possibly ten per plant, when they are on the verge of opening. Tape it to make sure that no insects can creep in. When the flowers open, take off the bag and carefully pull off the petals to get to the pollen on the male flower. With a small paintbrush, tickle out some pollen and take the bag off the female plant. Brush the pollen onto the stigma of the female flower. Another method is to cut off the male flowers, pull off the petals and brush the anthers onto the female stigma. Cover without delay before any insects arrive. Repeat this over the plant and any others of the same species and variety nearby. You want a good cross-section to avoid inbreeding. The pollen from one male flower will pollinate quite a few female ones. When the flowers wilt, take the bag off and wait to see if the fruit will form.

Harvesting seed

Most vegetables are dry seeded or soft fruiting.

Dry seeded vegetables When seed in seedheads, pods or capsules is ripe, it is usually so dry that it rattles. It is best to let nature choose the moment. Tie brown paper bags over the heads when you deem them to be nearly ripe. If the weather turns and the seeds have already gone brown, cut down or dig up the whole plant and hang it upside-down in a dry shed.

Soft-fruiting vegetables The seeds of tomatoes, melons, squashes and cucumbers are harvested when the fruits are perfectly ripe for eating. You can store them a little longer to ripen further. Give them a good wash to get rid of the pulp and the gel on tomatoes. If you are being thorough, soak them in water with a teaspoon of washing soda. You can tell that the gel is off when you see it floating on the top. Rinse and spread them out to dry quickly before they start to germinate or go mouldy. Put them in a warm place, out of direct sunshine, and turn them over every so often. You could speed things up by using a cool hair dryer.

Separating the seed from the chaff

Most seed can be cleaned by hand. For fine seed, like carrot, work over a colander (possibly several going down in size) so that the seed falls through. Heavy seed can be separated by winnowing with a hair dryer. If you have a lot you can thresh it by putting the seeds in a sack or bag and treading on it.

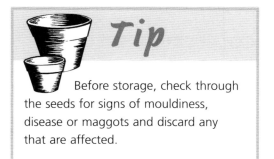

Tip Before storage, check through the seeds for signs of mouldiness, disease or maggots and discard any that are affected.

Drying

A little further drying will give your seeds greater shelf life. Spread them out on a tray and put them in the airing cupboard or on a windowsill at a maximum temperature of 30°C (86°F). They are ready to store when so dry that they shatter if hit with a hammer.

Storing seed

Seed deteriorates quickly if not stored well. Keep commercial seed sealed in the original packets or your own in paper bags in an airtight jar in the refrigerator or a chilly cellar. Buy some silica gel from the chemist and put this in the jar to keep them bone dry. Test that they are still alive, or 'viable', when you are ready to sow the following year. Lay some out on wet kitchen towel and keep in a warm place. They should sprout leaves and roots within three weeks. Keeping in mind that less will germinate outside than in, you really want a minimum 60 per cent viability to make it worthwhile sowing them.

MAKING A POND

A pond is invaluable on an allotment. Even a tiny pond, no bigger than a washing-up bowl, will bring in useful predators to keep down the levels of troublesome pests on your crops. Frogs and birds are wonderful slug eaters and will be attracted by the water.

Site a pond away from trees so it doesn't fill with leaves. An old bath, basin or cattle trough sunk into the ground will make a perfectly good pond. A better plan is to excavate a hole. It should be 60 cm (24 in) deep at some point to guard against freezing, and have a shallow plateau in another for birds and other creatures to bathe in, wade in and drink. Remove any sharp stones, line the hole with sand or old carpet and lay in a butyl liner with a good overlap. Throw a little subsoil into the bottom and fill with water. If possible, add some pond water to kick-start the ecology.

When the pond is full, weigh down the liner around the edges with heavy stones and trim off any excess. Fill the gaps with soil to disguise the liner. Frogs quite often find the pond by themselves but otherwise add a little frogspawn. If there are small children about, cover the pond with mesh.

chapter 4

MONTH-BY-MONTH GUIDE

January • February • March

April • May • June

July • August • September

October • November • December

January

January is usually bitterly cold. It is the most likely month for gales and snow. The sharp frosts that come with them have their advantages though. They kill bugs, sterilize the ground and break down heavy soils. They give you the opportunity to see where the frost pockets are. The coldest air settles on the lowest points and in corners blighted by easterly winds. Make note to avoid these areas for tender plants and fruit.

Allotment people tend to keep quite a low profile in January. They make their way there to pick overwintering vegetables, check that nothing has blown down or is likely to get frozen to a crisp and return home to browse through the seed catalogues by the fire. If you are starting off a plot, it is an excellent month to make plans, draw up your design, lay paths, build a shed or put up a fence on good days. Start off on a positive note by shredding the Christmas tree.

GENERAL MAINTENANCE

- ✦ Keep an eye on vulnerable trees and shrubs.
- ✦ Make sure that mulches and covers put on in autumn stay securely in place.
- ✦ Check stakes and ties.
- ✦ Shake snow off branches.
- ✦ Hoe out winter weeds like chickweed and groundsel while at the seedling stage as they can harbour disease. Put healthy annual weeds on the compost heap and throw out perennials.
- ✦ It's a good month for a bonfire, if allowed, but watch out for dormant hedgehogs.
- ✦ Clear decaying leaves, taking particular care to expose the crowns of herbaceous perennials and asparagus as they can rot in damp conditions.
- ✦ Compost leaves to make leafmould.
- ✦ Take advantage of icy conditions to make piles of organic matter at strategic points ready to spread later. The wheelbarrow should move effortlessly over hard frozen ground.
- ✦ Mend, repair and clean tools ready for the growing season. Scrape off any dried mud with a stiff brush. Fill a

WEATHER

SUNSHINE: Edinburgh 48.4 hours, Durham 54.1 hours, Nottingham 45.8 hours, Lowestoft 46 hours, London 42.3 hours, Cardiff 52.7 hours, Exeter 51.8 hours.

RAIN: Edinburgh 11.4 days, Durham 11.4 days, Nottingham 12.4 days, Lowestoft 12.3 days, London 10.7 days, Cardiff 15.2 days, Exeter 13 days.

AIR FROST: Edinburgh 11.1 days, Durham 13.4 days, Nottingham 12.5 days, Lowestoft 9.8 days, London 8.9 days, Cardiff 9 days, Exeter 10.2 days.

MAXIMUM TEMPERATURE: Edinburgh 6.4°C, Durham 5.8°C, Nottingham 5.9°C, Lowestoft 6.1°C, London 7.2°C, Cardiff 7.4°C, Exeter 8°C.

MINIMUM TEMPERATURE: Edinburgh 0.9°C, Durham 0.2°C, Nottingham 0.6°C, Lowestoft 1.4°C, London 1.9°C, Greenwich 1.9°C, Cardiff 2°C, Exeter 2°C.

capacious bucket with coarse sand and mix in a small amount of vegetable oil. Dip the tool heads into this several times. They should come out transformed. Sand off any remaining rust and wipe with an oily rag before hanging them up. To keep your tools in tip-top condition, it's good practice to do this at the end of the day every time they are used.

- ✦ Shred prunings. If you can get a few neighbours, or your committee,

TROUBLE-SHOOTING

Most pests are dormant at this time of year. Fungal disease in the greenhouse, particularly grey mould (botrytis), is common however. The spores are carried in the air and, in the unventilated conditions of winter, it can spread. On sunny days, get some air into the greenhouse but close it up by evening. Scrub it with a garden disinfectant, getting into corners where pests are inclined to hibernate. Protect fruit trees with grease bands to trap the female winter moths and other insects that crawl up to lay their eggs.

to share the cost it is worth hiring a shredder. Go for the biggest and best model you can afford as the cheaper models are a real bone-shakers. Petrol shredders are more powerful than electric ones. Remember to wear goggles and protective clothing. The shredded prunings make a luxuriant carpet for paths.

✦ Make new beds. If you got behind preparing new beds last year, you can start now if conditions are right. Never work on frozen or waterlogged soil, however, as you will do more harm than good. If the mud sticks to your boots, it's too wet to work.

✦ Make sure the birds have a source of food and water.

✦ Check your stores and remove anything that is less than perfect.

VEGETABLES

Although January is traditionally known as the 'hungry gap' it is possible to have a wide selection of fresh vegetables on the allotment. You could be harvesting Jerusalem artichokes, leaf beet, perpetual spinach, Brussels sprouts, sprouting broccoli, winter cabbage, winter cauliflower, celeriac, corn salad, kale, komatsuna, leeks, protected winter lettuce, mibuna and mizuna greens, Oriental mustards and saladini, pak choi, parsnip, winter radish, rocket, salsify, scorzonera, Swiss chard and sorrel.

✦ Force chicory. If you planted chicory outside last May you can force it for winter salads or cooking. Lift the plant with its tap roots and pot it up in compost. Cover with a large flower pot and block the drainage holes. Keep at a temperature of 10–13°C (50–55°F), and moist but not wet. It should be ready to eat in three to four weeks. Seakale can be forced in the same way under a big flowerpot with the hole blocked.

✦ Order new potatoes to plant outside in late February or March from a garden centre or by mail order. Set them in egg boxes or wooden crates from the end of January in mild areas, February in cold ones. Put the end with the most 'eyes' facing upwards in a cool frost-free place – the shed or an unheated room. When they have sprouted, choose three of the healthiest shoots on each potato and rub out the rest.

✦ Order seeds. It makes sense to order for up to three months ahead as the seed merchants can sell out of the more interesting stock. Quite often they will give a reduction for quantity. Get onto your committee or neighbours and order in bulk.

- ✦ Start onion and shallot sets in the unheated greenhouse. Also sow broad beans, early carrots, leeks and lettuce under cover.
- ✦ Sow radishes and hardy salad lettuces like 'Tom Thumb' in the cold frames for early crops. Even better, make a small hotbed for them in the cold greenhouse. Build a flat-topped mound of fresh horse manure about 60 cm (24 in) high in a box and trample it down. It can be mixed with leaves if you don't have enough. Top it with 15 cm (6 in) of garden compost or fine soil and cover with a frame (either bought or made from an old window frame). Wait a week or so until the fermentation period is over and soil is warm, but not hot, and ready for sowing.
- ✦ Bend the leaves over cauliflowers to protect the developing curds. If you don't have enough to reach over, snap off a few outer leaves and tie them around with string.

FRUIT

- ✦ Force rhubarb for early tender young stems. You need a big healthy clump at least three years old. Clear away dead foliage, pack straw around the clump and cover the plant with a bucket or dustbin with some holes for ventilation. It should be kept in total darkness. The bin may need to be weighted down. The tender blanched stems should be ready to eat by March.
- ✦ Plant fruit trees and soft fruit, ordered in autumn, if they arrive now. They may appear at any time from November onwards. If the weather is not right for planting, heel them in or cover with wet sacking and keep in the shed. Plant as soon as possible.
- ✦ Winter-prune apples and pears, black-currants, redcurrants and whitecurrants, blackberries and hybrids, raspberries and gooseberries on days without hard frost. Don't touch the stone fruits yet – they are best pruned in summer to avoid silver leaf disease.

HERBS

- ✦ Check that French tarragon, young sage and rosemary are well protected against the frosts with straw and leafmould around the base.
- ✦ Continue to grow chervil, parsley and chives inside in cold areas and outside under cloches in warmer ones.

February

Temperatures in February can be even lower than in January with hard frosts and occasional thick snow. There are fewer gales, however, the days are getting longer and there is more sunshine. Don't be deceived by the odd sunny day as the weather is likely to be treacherous for many weeks to come. Soft fruits will need your attention this month. Finish winter pruning and protect any early flower buds from frost and birds.

Preparing the beds is a good task to undertake on fine days and is also invigorating exercise. There are always plenty of DIY jobs to be getting on with. A certain amount of friendly rivalry as to who wins the race for the first new potato can make some allotment holders risk planting a few at the end of this month. In mild areas, you can sow a few vegetables outside under cloches, in the cold greenhouse, or more in the warmth at home.

GENERAL MAINTENANCE

✦ Continue to protect plants against cold weather.

✦ Clear decaying leaves and other debris.

✦ Check stakes and ties.

✦ Hoe off weeds when the soil is dry enough.

✦ Check the pH of your soil before the growing season. Add either manure or lime (never both together), depending on the planned crop and the pH of the soil. Lime should be added at least two months ahead ready for planting out in May. Choose a still day and wear goggles and a mask.

✦ On finer days finish digging and making new borders ready for spring planting. Keep in mind that you will do more harm than good working on soggy or frozen soil. Turning over freezing soil moves the cold soil from top to bottom so that it will take longer to warm up in spring.

✦ Prepare the seed bed. It will be in full use over the next few months. Rake to a fine tilth. Cover it with polythene to warm the soil a few weeks ahead of planting time.

✦ Make a bean trench. Dig out a trench

WEATHER

SUNSHINE: Edinburgh 69.8 hours, Durham 65.6 hours, Nottingham 55.3 hours, Lowestoft 64.9 hours, London 62 hours, Cardiff 70.6 hours, Exeter 67.4 hours.

RAIN: Edinburgh 8.7 days, Durham 8.9 days, Nottingham 10.2 days, Lowestoft 8.8 days, London 7.2 days, Cardiff 10.6 days, Exeter 10.3 days.

AIR FROST: Edinburgh 10.5 days, Durham 11.8 days, Nottingham 12 days, Lowestoft 8.1 days, London 7.8 days, Cardiff 8.2 days, Exeter 8.6 days.

MAXIMUM TEMPERATURE: Edinburgh 6.6°C, Durham 6°C, Nottingham 6°C, Lowestoft 6.2°C, Greenwich 7.5°C, Cardiff 7.6°C, Exeter 8°C.

MINIMUM TEMPERATURE: Edinburgh 0.8°C, Durham 0.3°C, Nottingham 0.5°C, Lowestoft 1.4°C, London 1.8°C, Cardiff 1.7°C, Exeter 2°C.

about 45 cm (18 in) wide and the depth of a spade for runner beans. If you want to grow them up a wigwam, make it circular, and if you want a double row make it twice as wide. Pile in plenty of good organic matter and fork it in. Leave the trench open until you are ready to sow or plant at the end of May or in June.

✦ Prepare the asparagus bed. It will last for twenty years so don't stint. Get rid of every trace of perennial weeds, dig really well and mix in plenty of top-quality manure or garden compost.

✦ Warm the prepared beds with polythene, cloches or little polytunnels for planting next month.

✦ Check soil temperatures with a soil thermometer. Though not expensive, this would be a good item for the committee to buy for general use. Push it 5–10 cm (2–4 in) into the soil to take a reading. The rule of thumb is that the soil should be above 7°C (46°F) consistently for a week before sowing the seeds of the hardiest plants under cloches.

✦ Check newly planted trees. Young trees and shrubs planted in autumn will not have had much chance to get their roots down. The freezing and thawing action of icy conditions causes shrinkage and expansion and the roots can get pushed out of the ground. Firm the soil around the rootball with your boot.

✦ Feed the birds. Put up nesting boxes so that they become familiar with them before the breeding season.

✦ Check stores.

VEGETABLES

✦ Start sowing. In mild areas sow summer cabbage, spinach, early carrots (like 'Amsterdam Forcing'), the hardiest broad beans (Longpods) and radishes in the cold greenhouse or on warmed soil under cloches.

✦ Seakale can be sown from seed now under cover but is more easily grown from offsets next month.

✦ Early peas like 'Kelvenden Wonder', 'Little Marvel' or 'Early Onward' can be started off sown in sections of guttering in the greenhouse or cold frame to give

them a head start. Slide the entire contents into shallow trenches outside when they are ready to transplant.

✦ Sow tomatoes in a propagator in gentle heat of 18°C (64°F) and aubergine seed at 21°C (70°F).

✦ Bulb onions and shallots can also be sown from seed at home in February though they are more easily grown from 'sets' later on. They need a minimum temperature of 10°C (50°F) in order to germinate.

✦ Hardy green manures can be sown at any time starting in February.

✦ Jerusalem artichokes can be planted out in warmer places.

FRUIT

✦ Plant rhubarb.

✦ Plant new fruit trees and bushes. There are advantages to planting now rather than in autumn. Spring is around the corner which means that they don't need to sit in cold wet soil throughout winter. Mark out a circle with a stick. It needs to be big enough for the roots of the grown tree to settle comfortably – at least 1.2 m (4 ft) in diameter. If the area is grassed, take off the turf. Dig out the topsoil and stab at the subsoil to improve drainage. Bang in a short stake off-centre. Break up the turfs and drop them upside down into the hole or put in some leaf mould. Mix some well-rotted organic matter into the topsoil wiht bone meal or seaweed extract for rooting. Put a stick across the hole so you judge the depth and put the tree in, making sure that it will be planted to the same depth as before. Spread the roots. Backfill with the topsoil mixture, shaking the tree from time to time. Attach to the stake. Stamp down when the hole is filled. Give the tree a pull to make sure it is firmly planted. Water to clear any air locks, mulch well and keep well watered in their first summer.

✦ Protect flowers of soft fruit (which will be emerging now or will be soon) from frost by covering with horticultural fleece or netting on cold nights.

✦ Hand–pollinate fruit trees if necessary.

✦ Spray with seaweed.

✦ Weed and mulch the beds regularly.

✦ Cut down autumn raspberries to the ground.

✦ Tidy up outdoor strawberries and cover with cloches for an early crop.

HERBS

✦ Sow parsley and chervil in biodegradable modules (they have tap roots and hate being transplanted) and grow with heat. Alternatively, wait until next month to sow in the cold greenhouse.

✦ Divide mint. To get a good supply, dig up existing plants. They propagate themselves by rooted runners. Cut the runner into sections, making sure that each has some healthy root and shoot. Mint is invasive and thuggish, so plant the root cuttings in an old bucket with drainage holes plunged into the soil. Keep a few potted up in the house for daily use.

✦ Divide chives. Dig up, pull apart the clumps and replant.

TROUBLE-SHOOTING

Check for big bud mite (blackcurrant gall mite) on currants. You will spot it by the unnaturally swollen buds in blackcurrants and the withered ones in redcurrants and whitecurrants. Pick off infected buds. Deal with slugs and snails as you come across them to reduce problems later.

March

In March, the north-south divide is at its widest. It may be spring in Cornwall, while still winter in the Highlands. March weather is erratic, with fresh bright days followed by wintry showers and frosts at night. Listen to the local forecasts as the weather is critical now.

Many vegetables are sown or planted to emerge when the frosts are over, which requires careful timing. This is always a guessing game. Warming the soil with polythene will give you a head start, not least because the soil will stay fairly dry and easy to work to a fine tilth.

Cover all outdoor sowings with fleece or cloches to give them frost protection. Check the temperature of the soil before going ahead with sowings. The hardiest vegetable seeds need a minimum and consistent soil temperature of 7°C (46°F) before they will germinate. It won't help them to be sitting around doing nothing in cold wet soil. When in doubt, it is safer to wait.

GENERAL MAINTENANCE

✦ Move covers and cloches off plants outside on sunny days but replace them at night.

✦ Keep a hoe handy to catch germinating annual weeds. Throw them on the compost heap. Dig out perennial weeds while young and burn or bin them.

✦ Mulch beds with organic matter after a good rain to retain moisture. A good mulch will also improve the soil and black out weeds.

✦ Warm areas of soil by covering with polythene for plantings in April.

✦ Make 'stale seedbeds' to induce weeds to show themselves so you can hoe them off before sowing or planting your crops next month.

✦ Put carpet or black polythene over beds that are not ready to plant, to deal with bad perennial weeds.

✦ Clear up any remaining debris.

✦ Feed overwintered crops with general organic fertilizer between plants if

WEATHER

SUNSHINE: Edinburgh 106.4 hours, Durham 105.5 hours, Nottingham 93 hours, Lowestoft 110.7 hours, London 102.4 hours, Cardiff 114.7 hours, Exeter 109.8 hours.

RAIN: Edinburgh 9.7 days, Durham 10.2 days, Nottingham 11.3 days, Lowestoft 10.1 days, London 9.4 days, Cardiff 11.8 days, Exeter 10.9 days.

AIR FROST: Edinburgh 6.8 days, Durham 8.3 days, Nottingham 7.9 days, Lowestoft 4.8 days, London 3.9 days, Cardiff 5.6 days, Exeter 6.3 days.

MAXIMUM TEMPERATURE: Edinburgh 8.7°C, Durham 8.3°C, Nottingham 8.8°C, Lowestoft 8.6°C, Greenwich 10.3°C, Cardiff 10°C, Exeter 10.2°C.

MINIMUM TEMPERATURE: Edinburgh 2.2°C, Durham 1.6°C, Nottingham 1.8°C, Lowestoft 2.5°C, London 3.2°C, Cardiff 3°C, Exeter 2.9°C.

needed. Feed and water plants when they need it regularly as they will be growing well now.

✦ A spray with seaweed, comfrey or nettle liquid feed or has a magical effect on plants that look tired after the winter. Seaweed is known to improve the growth and health of plants – though quite how remains a mystery. Scientists refer to it as a 'bio-stimulant'. It is known to stimulate the micro-organisms in the soil, leading to a notable increase in root

TROUBLE-SHOOTING

Pests will be on the move now after your young vegetables. Aphids will begin multiplying. Start inspections and patrols. Cut off infested shoots early to prevent problems later. Wage war on snails and slugs by putting out beer traps. Check that grease bands put on through winter around the trunks of fruit trees are intact to prevent winter moths crawling up now and laying their eggs.

growth. Vigorous roots enable the plant to take up more moisture and nutrients. For roots it is best applied on planting and then four weeks later. On leaves it encourages the production of chlorophyll – the greening agent responsible for photosynthesis. Plants sprayed with seaweed extract are less attractive to aphids. It has no insecticidal properties but appears to improve the defence system.

✦ Put in stakes in readiness for young plants to grow up.

✦ Keep the windows of the greenhouse clean for maximum light. Open the doors and windows on bright days.

✦ Feed the birds.

✦ Check your stores of vegetables and fruits and discard any that are rotting.

VEGETABLES

✦ Plant early, second early and maincrop potatoes chitted in January or February.

✦ Sow early cultivars of Brussels sprouts (like 'Peter Gynt') for autumn eating. Protect with fleece or cloches.

✦ Sow summer cabbage, salsify, scorzonera, spinach, spinach beet and chard. Protect with fleece or cloches.

✦ Sow maincrop broad beans, calabrese, early carrots, swedes and leeks. Protect with fleece or cloches.

✦ Sow early and second early peas. Protect with fleece or cloches.

✦ Sow celery, globe onions and pickling onions if you can keep them at 10–15°C (50–59°F), either indoors or outside with cover.

✦ Sow seed of aubergine at 21°C (70°F) and tomatoes in heat at home. They need a temperature of 18–20°C (64–68°F). Alternatively, wait and buy young plants to go straight out in June.

✦ Plant asparagus crowns and Jerusalem artichokes.

✦ Start to make successional sowings of Japanese bunching onions, kohlrabi, radishes, early carrots, and salad leaves.

✦ Shade young seedlings under glass on bright days with newspaper.

✦ Thin seedlings planted in February before they become overcrowded.

✦ Prick out and pot on cuttings, seedlings and young plants as they outgrow their containers.

✦ Harden off young vegetables and annuals for planting outside. Err on the cautious side as March weather is unpredictable.

✦ Sow green manures on empty beds. Crimson clover is a nitrogen fixer only grown for two to three months.

✦ If you are planning to grow trenching celery, dig a trench a spade's depth and half-fill it with organic matter.

✦ Plant onion and shallot sets.

✦ Plant one-year-old crowns of asparagus.

If you haven't prepared the asparagus bed there is still time.

✦ Plant seakale offsets, garlic and Jerusalem artichokes.

✦ Keep going with successional crops – lettuce, rocket, mizuna greens and oriental saladini, spinach, spring onions and red orach under the cover of cloches or mini polytunnels on warmed soil.

✦ Sow Hamburg parsley and texcel greens either in modules for transplanting or in the seed bed with cover from the middle of the month.

✦ Sow hardy peas in guttering to go out next month.

✦ Forced chicory and seakale will be ready this month.

✦ Harvest the last of the winter brassicas. Clear winter crops as they go over. Put healthy debris on the compost heap.

✦ Plant out salads and other crops sown earlier under cover and protect with cloches.

✦ Feed the birds.

✦ Continue to check stores.

FRUIT

✦ Finish winter-pruning on soft fruit, apples and pears. Leave stone fruit trees until later in the year.

✦ Clear weeds and give soft fruit a dressing of wood ash from the bonfire (potash) to help fruiting, finishing with a good mulch of rotted manure or garden compost. Spray with seaweed if they look battered.

Last Chance...

❋ Very last opportunity to plant bare-rooted trees and fruit bushes. Once the leaves come through the trees will dehydrate quickly if they are kept out of the soil. Pinch out any flowers so the plants can concentrate on getting their roots down.

❋ Winter-prune cane and bush fruits.

❋ Plant garlic as it needs a period of cold to get started.

✦ Continue to prevent frost damage by covering fruit trees and bushes when it threatens.

✦ Hand-pollinate flowers if they come before the insects.

✦ Prune away any winter damage and tie in soft fruits as they grow, before they get into a tangle.

✦ Forced rhubarb should be ready to harvest.

HERBS

✦ Lift and divide chives, marjoram and mint.

✦ Sow dill, chervil, chives, summer savory, parsley and sorrel outside under cloches, in the cold greenhouse or cold frame.

April

The combination of bright sunshine and April's sweet showers make everything grow at once this month, including the weeds. There's definitely a positive spring feeling in the air and as many people take advantage of spring holidays at this time, allotment gardeners will be out and about in number.

In spite of the approach of warmer weather, there still can be frosty nights, the odd snow shower in the north and gale-force winds along the coast. In the cooler north, the March plan should work for April. In the south, there is much raising from seed to do and planting out. If you didn't have time to propagate under cover in last month, don't worry – you can sow most hardy plants straight out into the allotment this month with cloche cover. More tender subjects – runner beans and courgettes – must wait awhile.

GENERAL MAINTENANCE

+ Remove cloches from hardy vegetables planted last month if conditions are right. They will be needed for the next batch of plantings.
+ Water regularly when the weather is dry.
+ Chase after weeds with regular hoeing and mulching.
+ Thin out seedlings. If you thin carefully without harming the roots, sometimes you can transplant the seedlings. They will crop a little later than the rest having been 'checked'. If that doesn't work you can eat the thinnings in salads.
+ Put up sturdy supports for climbing peas and beans.
+ Feed the birds.
+ Check your stores.

VEGETABLES

+ Finish planting early, second early and maincrop potatoes, or earth-up potatoes planted last month.
+ Sow the last summer cabbages and start sowing winter cabbage in the seedbed along with sprouting broccoli and perennial broccoli.

WEATHER

SUNSHINE: Edinburgh 139 hours, Durham 133.1 hours, Nottingham 119.2 hours, Lowestoft 151.4 hours, London 139.2 hours, Cardiff 159 hours, Exeter 152.6 hours.

RAIN: Edinburgh 39 mm, Durham 147 mm, Nottingham 53 mm, Lowestoft 45 mm, London 45 mm, Cardiff 62 mm, Exeter 50 mm.

AIR FROST: Edinburgh 3.4 days, Durham 4.2 days, Nottingham 3.1 days, Lowestoft 1.6 days, London 1.4 days, Cardiff 2.3 days, Exeter 2.7 days.

MAXIMUM TEMPERATURE: Edinburgh 10.9°C, Durham 11°C, Nottingham 11.6°C, Lowestoft 10.6°C, London 12.9°C, Cardiff 12.9°C, Exeter 12.7°C.

MINIMUM TEMPERATURE: Edinburgh 3.6°C, Durham 3.1°C, Nottingham 3.6°C, Lowestoft 4.4°C, London 4.8°C, Cardiff 4.6°C, Exeter 4.4°C.

+ Start sowing calabrese in bio-degradable modules as it resents root disturbance.
+ Move from sowing early to sowing late sprouts (like 'Braveheart') for eating in the New Year.
+ Start sowing maincrop broad beans for summer eating.
+ Sow autumn and mini-cauliflowers in mid-April to early May when the soil temperature has reached at least 7°C (46°F).

TROUBLE-SHOOTING

Watch for vine weevil, a non-flying blackish insect with yellow spots, which eats irregular holes around the edges of leaves. The larvae, which hatch out in spring, do the most damage having fed on the plant roots all winter.

Put up carrot fly netting. A barrier of plastic sheeting or fleece 60 cm (24 in) high attached to stakes effectively thwarts carrot fly.

Watch out for slugs and snails. Rake up debris where they are inclined to lurk. Top up beer traps and encourage their predators – hedgehogs, frogs, toads and thrushes.

Aphids – catch them early. Rub them off or shower with water as soon as you see them. Sow plenty of annual flowers like nasturtiums, marigolds and the poached egg plant to attract friendly predators. Flea beetles are active between April and midsummer. Watch for sawfly caterpillars on gooseberry bushes and pick them off.

✦ Sow celeriac, kohlrabi, Hamburg parsley, leeks, mizuna greens, seakale, salsify, scorzonera, spinach, spinach beet, Swiss chard and early bunching turnips.

✦ Sow fenugreek and good King Henry.

✦ Continue small sowings of hardy peas like 'Early Onward'.

✦ Carry on with successional crops of mizuna and mibuna greens, kohlrabi, carrots, lettuce and salad leaves, radish, spring onions and Japanese onions.

✦ Sow rocket, komatsuna, Florence fennel, radicchio and sugar loaf chicories, texcel greens and red orach.

✦ Sow celery under cover in gentle heat, timing it eight or nine weeks before the last frosts.

✦ Finish planting Jerusalem and globe artichokes, onion and shallot sets and asparagus crowns.

✦ Harden off and transplant last month's vegetables sown from seed that are ready to go out to their final positions. Remember to put collars round brassicas, or plant through a mulching sheet or membrane to deter the cabbage root fly from laying its eggs at the base of the plants.

✦ Under glass, with heat or at home, (you need a minimum temperature 16°C or 61°F), sow French and runner beans, chillies, aubergine, sweetcorn and tomatoes. Remember that you can sow tender beans outside next month and buy tomatoes, aubergines and sweetcorn as plants ready to go out.

✦ Shade young plants indoors with newspaper against bright sunlight.

FRUIT

✦ Control weeds around cane fruit and give them a good mulch of well-rotted farmyard manure.

✦ Protect fruit against the birds with netting. If you use a gauge of about 2 cm (¾ in) the bees will have access to pollinate. Give frost protection when necessary.

✦ Pick off the flowers of newly planted early and late varieties of strawberry to hold them back for a bumper crop next year.

✦ Prune stone fruits if weather allows.

✦ If you have missed out on bare-rooted fruit trees, container-grown plants will be available from now onwards.

HERBS

✦ Sow basil indoors for planting out after the frosts. Pinch out the tip when there are three sets of leaves. Stop the bush from sprawling by trimming off the side branches. Feed once a week and water in the daytime so that the leaves are dry by nightfall.

✦ Sow fennel in well-drained loamy soil in the cold greenhouse. Alternatively, plant a piece of root from an established plant. Don't plant it near coriander or dill as it will cross-pollinate with them.

✦ Sow summer savory in the cold frame.

✦ Sow winter savory, take softwood cuttings or dig up and divide. Plant in poor soil in sun with cloche cover.

✦ Sow parsley seed in good deep soil outside with plenty of organic matter added to the soil.

✦ Divide established chives and replant in rich moist soil in a sunny spot. They make a pretty edging around vegetable beds, as does parsley.

✦ Take softwood cuttings from rosemary, sage and thyme.

✦ Divide creeping thymes.

✦ Dig up a plant of French tarragon and pull the roots apart. Pot up or replant in a spot with good drainage and plenty of sun. It's a spreader, so plant it in a bottomless bucket buried in the ground or a container. Keep it frost free.

✦ Split mint from now or at any time through the growing season and plant in the same way as French tarragon. It has a rampant tendency.

✦ Cut back lavender bushes to stop them sprawling and becoming sparse. Cut off weak and damaged shoots on other established herbs.

✦ In warm climates the Mediterranean herbs are pruned after flowering but in the UK it is safer to wait until spring. Trim lavender back to a few inches of the new growth. Lavender and rosemary don't spring easily from old wood so avoid cutting into it. Let rosemaries grow freely but cut away lanky and damaged growth completely. Usually the plants are replaced every four years or so. However, if you have an old lanky specimen you can try radical action. Cut back half the shoots to half the length and next year tackle the other half. Sprawling old sage plants can be rejuvenated by cutting almost to the base. Many plants get a new lease of life from this treatment – tarragon among them.

May

In May there will be beautiful days, although the nights can still be chilly. Everything is growing fast and you can enjoy the first spring crops of the season, including asparagus and early peas. With the end of the frosts just a few weeks away, this is a busy time for propagating plants.

May is a bright month full of the promise of summer, though there is still the chance of freak frosts. Fruit growers live on tenterhooks as this is the time when most fruit trees are in blossom and a sharp frost could destroy the crops. Keep fleece to hand for emergencies and remain wary of planting out too soon.

There should be plenty of delicacies to harvest from the allotment in May. The early peas, young broad beans, salads, fresh radishes and asparagus should all be ready for picking. Everything will be growing fast but there is still plenty of seed sowing to do. This month you move from early to late varieties of broad bean, carrots and cabbage for autumn and winter eating. Make sure your precious seedlings are thoroughly hardened off before they go out into the big wide world. If you have missed out on sowing seed or need more plants, you'll find starter packs of vegetables in the garden centres now.

GENERAL MAINTENANCE

✦ Keep on hoeing.
✦ Thin seedlings as they grow.
✦ Keep potting on, hardening off and transplanting.
✦ Warm the soil ready for new sowings next month.

Last Chance...

❈ Plant out onion sets for autumn.
❈ Plant potatoes.
❈ Sow spinach now or wait until late summer.

WEATHER

SUNSHINE: Edinburgh 174.3 hours, Durham 169.4 hours, Nottingham 170.3 hours, Lowestoft 204.8 hours, London 185.7 hours, Cardiff 195.3 hours, Exeter 186 hours.

RAIN: Edinburgh 9.8 days, Durham 9.9 days, Nottingham 10.4 days, Lowestoft 8.8 days London, 8.8 days, Cardiff 10.7 days, Exeter 9.5 days.

AIR FROST: Edinburgh 0.5 days, Durham 0.8 days, Nottingham 0.3 days, Lowestoft none, London 0.1 days, Cardiff 0.3 days, Exeter 0.4 days.

MAXIMUM TEMPERATURE: Edinburgh 14.1 °C, Durham 14.3°C, Nottingham 15.6°C, Lowestoft 14.2°C, London 16.8°C, Cardiff 16.2°C, Exeter 15.8°C.

MINIMUM TEMPERATURE: Edinburgh 6.2°C, Durham 5.6°C, Nottingham 6.4°C, Lowestoft 7.6°C, London 7.8°C, Cardiff 7.5°C, Exeter 7.1°C.

✦ Make stale seedbeds to get ahead of the weeds.
✦ Water young plants regularly.
✦ Feed plants when necessary. Seedlings growing in proprietary compost will have everything they need.
✦ Feed the birds – they may need it for their young.
✦ Check fruit and vegetable stores.
✦ It is not too late to sow sweet peas outside in May. They will need supports. The fast growing French or English

TROUBLE-SHOOTING

Watch for every kind of pest and set up regular vigils. Battle on with getting rid of aphids, slugs and snails. If you have had trouble previously from the codling moth maggots boring holes in apples and pears, put up pheromone traps. Check broad beans for black fly and pinch out the flowering tops where they congregate. Check for signs of mildew. Pick off any sawfly caterpillars.

Watch for capsid bugs and scab. Put up a screen of fine netting or cover completely to protect carrots from carrot fly. Check for vine weevil maggots in the roots of any plants in pots.

marigolds (*Calendula* and *Tagetes*), the poached egg plant (*Limnanthes douglasii*) and many other annuals will brighten up your plot, provide flowers for the house and bring in friendly predators. They may seed themselves around every year but are no trouble to pull up if you don't want them.

VEGETABLES

✦ Sweetcorn, French beans and runner beans can be sown outside at the end of the month in mild areas. By the time the seeds have germinated, the threat of frost should be over.

✦ Keep earthing-up potatoes. Never let the tubers get near the light or they will develop poisonous green patches. This is the last month to plant them.

✦ If you have been raising tomatoes, peppers and aubergines under cover and the weather is not warm enough for them to go out, they may need to go into bigger pots.

✦ Harden off and transplant seedlings sown last month. Water well before and after transplanting and over the next few days to come.

✦ Outside sow maincrop beetroot, winter cabbage, sprouting broccoli and perennial broccoli, kale and swedes.

✦ Sow autumn and late winter/early spring cauliflowers.

✦ Sow the last of the early and maincrop leeks.

✦ Switch from early varieties to maincrop types of broad bean and carrot seed.

✦ Sow parsnips in situ outside. Try pre-germinating them and fluid sowing.

✦ Carry on sowing salsify, scorzonera, and Swiss chard.

✦ Sow autumn and mini cauliflowers.

✦ Amaranthus and fenugreek can be sown outside when the soil temperature is above 10°C (50°F).

✦ Under cover, sow the tender asparagus pea this month.

✦ Plant offsets or 'thongs' of seakale.

✦ Plant sweet potatoes from 'slips', if the soil is at least 12°C (52°F).

✦ Add early bunching turnips to your successional plantings, and carry on with the others.

✦ Plant globe artichokes, either bought as small plants or which have been grown from seed under cover.

✦ Courgettes, marrows, squashes, pumpkins and outdoor cucumbers can be sown either outdoors on warmed soil under cloches in mild areas or – safer and faster – under cover in modules for planting out next month.

✦ Transplant self-blanching celery at the end of the month. To make maximum use of the space, interplant with sowings of fast crops – beetroot, early carrots, salad onions, lettuce, radishes and early bunching turnips.

FRUIT

✦ Net developing fruits to protect them from birds.

✦ Remove blossom from new trees to give them every chance to establish before bearing fruit.

✦ Tuck straw under your strawberries to prevent rain splash and slugs. Fluff it up to let in air. Barley straw is the best if you can get it. Remove runners so the plants put all their energy into the fruits. Pin down a few runners for new plants next year. Keep young plants well watered but avoid wetting the fruits. Water from the bottom in the morning so that any splashes or spills will be dry by night. Slugs are partial to strawberries so set out beer traps or cover with cloches.

✦ Prune out any unwanted shoots of raspberries to give the fruits good air circulation, get sunshine on the berries and to avoid a tangle later.

✦ Prune and tie-in fans and cordons.

✦ Tie-in canes as they grow on blackberries and their hybrids.

✦ Remove alternate berries on gooseberry bushes for big fruits. These early pickings can be used for cooking.

✦ Prune plums. These were left unpruned through winter to avoid silver leaf disease. Now that the weather is milder, wounds will heal before the disease can start to take hold.

HERBS

✦ There should be plenty of herbs to harvest this month.

✦ Sow chervil in light but moist soil in partial shade. Use seed bought this year from a reputable merchant to make sure that is less than a year old.

✦ Sow coriander seed outside in situ as it doesn't like being moved, and cover thinly with soil.

✦ Divide chives.

✦ Sow seed of marjoram under cover at 16°C (61°F).

✦ Thin out seedlings sown last month.

✦ Layer creeping thyme by burying the runners with hairpins of wire around the parent plant. When the little plants start to grow, cut them free.

✦ Divide established lovage.

✦ Sow dill in a bright sunny place in well-drained soil.

✦ Carry on sowing parsley.

✦ Pot on basil and remove any flowers.

✦ Keep harvesting coriander, chives, fennel and dill to encourage new fresh growth, but always leave two-thirds of the leaves.

June

June is a heavenly month. Allotments are in full swing

and you will start to see the fruits of your labour.

Strawberries and many soft fruits will be ready to pick.

The first new potatoes will be ready. The more tender

vegetables — tomatoes, aubergines and runner beans can be

planted out with confidence now.

In June, it is a joy to be gardening out on the allotment. You can take off covers with confidence as the chance of frost is virtually nil from now until the end of September. Strawberries, early raspberries, early whitecurrants, redcurrants and gooseberries will be ready to eat this month. New potatoes can be harvested – trim your mint to give it a new lease of life in readiness. Summer cabbage, young carrots, cauliflower, spring and Japanese onions, cut-and-come-again salads and the last of the asparagus until next year, could all be on offer. This month you can plant out all the tender vegetables – tomatoes, aubergines, peppers, sweetcorn, courgettes, squashes, sweet potatoes and outdoor cucumbers – to feast on through high summer into autumn.

GENERAL MAINTENANCE

✦ Water plants thoroughly. A good soaking less often is better than frequent light sprinkling.

✦ Conserve moisture. Apply and renew mulches. If using grass cuttings don't spread it deeper than 5 cm (2 in) or it will generate too much heat.

✦ Earth-up maincrop potatoes.

✦ Carry on weeding.

✦ Make sure the birds have water.

✦ Check your stores.

VEGETABLES

✦ Plant tomatoes, aubergines, outdoor cucumbers and peppers (either bought as small plants or grown from seed indoors) in a sunny and sheltered spot outside. Make a little moat around the plants to keep them moist. Feed with a high-potash fertilizer every week.

WEATHER

SUNSHINE: Edinburgh 176 hours, Durham 163.7 hours, Nottingham 175.7 hours, Lowestoft 203.6 hours, London 187.4 hours, Cardiff 198 hours, Exeter 189.5 hours.

RAIN: Edinburgh 8.5 days, Durham 8.9 days, Nottingham 8.9 days, Lowestoft 7.8 days, London 7.4 days, Cardiff 9.4 days, Exeter 7.3 days.

AIR FROST: None

MAXIMUM TEMPERATURE: Edinburgh 17°C, Durham 17.5°C, Nottingham 18.7°C, Lowestoft 17.6°C, London 20.1°C, Cardiff 19.3°C, Exeter 19.1°C.

MINIMUM TEMPERATURE: Edinburgh 9.3°C, Durham 8.6°C, Nottingham 9.4°C, Lowestoft 10.4°C, London 10.9°C, Cardiff 10.5°C, Exeter 10.1°C.

Last Chance...

❈ Plant out tomatoes, runner beans, sweet potatoes and sweetcorn in time to get a really good crop.

❈ Sow winter brassicas.

❈ Sow the last turnips, carrots, summer beetroot, fast-growing peas and radicchio for autumn eating.

TROUBLE-SHOOTING

Keep an eye out for cabbage white butterfly by checking the undersides of leaves for small clusters of yellow eggs. Gooseberry sawfly caterpillar can also be a problem at this time of year. Put up pheromone traps against codling moth – one trap protects five apple trees.

If you detect grey mould (botrytis) on strawberries, remove any infected parts. Make sure there is plenty of air circulation and there is straw or mats underneath the plants so the fungus is not spread by rain.

Look for big bud mite in blackcurrants. You'll spot it by the unnaturally large buds and distortion in the leaves. Pick off anything that looks infected. If it is serious, dig up the bush and burn it.

Tomato cordons will need staking. Remove side shoots from cordon tomatoes, cucumbers and melons.

✦ Fill gaps in beds. Drop in quick-growing vegetables like salad greens and radishes in empty spaces. Throw in a few seeds of annual flowers such as candytuft or marigold to encourage useful predators.

✦ Young sweetcorn plants should be planted now. They are wind-pollinated (the male flowers are the tassels at the top and the female parts are lower down the plant), so for successful pollination plant in blocks.

✦ If you want to try lima (or butter) beans pot up young plants and put them in a hot spot under fleece.

✦ Sow runner beans and climbing French beans outside. Spray the flowers when they form with water every day or so to 'set' them and help to produce pods.

✦ Sow New Zealand spinach.

✦ Continue to sow maincrop carrots like 'Autumn King' for winter storage and fast-growers such as 'Nantes 2' for autumn eating.

✦ Sow main crop 'wrinkled' peas.

✦ Sow Witloof chicory this month for forcing in winter.

✦ Continue to sow salad vegetables every two or three weeks. Lettuce doesn't germinate in high temperatures so find it a fairly shady and moist place in summer. Stop sowing texcel greens and rocket for a few weeks as they bolt in hot weather.

✦ Marrows, courgettes, pumpkins and winter squashes – either grown from seed or bought in the garden centre – will be ready to plant out now. They are greedy feeders and like nothing better than being planted in the manure heap. Make sure they have masses of organic material incorporated in the soil and plunge sections of pipe alongside the plants to get plenty of water to the roots.

✦ Plant sweet potatoes in a hot spot in mild areas under cover. The soil must be at least 12°C (54°F). The soil mustn't be allowed to drop below this throughout their growth. To ensure this, start by warming the soil with black plastic or a cloche for several days before planting. The soil should be deep and sandy, well dug and enriched with rotted manure or compost. Add some fertilizer before planting for good measure. Plant them about 15 cm (6 in) deep and twice the distance apart. For safety's sake grow them under fleece or cloches. Keep them weed-free and well watered for harvesting in September – fingers crossed.

✦ Transplant leeks and late Brussels sprouts, for harvesting from January to March, to their permanent positions.

✦ Stop cropping asparagus at the end of June until next year so the plants can build up strength.

✦ Earth-up potatoes.

FRUIT

✦ Continue to peg down strawberry runners for new plants. Or trim off as they will take energy from the plant. Remove cloches to ripen strawberries for picking.

✦ Pinch out side shoots on trained fruit and tie in the ones you want as they grow.

✦ Thin gooseberries for larger fruits.

✦ Thin apples and pears so the fruits won't touch each other when fully grown.

✦ Tie-in new canes of blackberries and blackberry hybrids.

HERBS

✦ From now on (after the frosts) sow a few seeds of coriander every few weeks in well-drained soil in full sun. You need quite a few plants to get a good bunch of leaves.

✦ Basil can go out into the allotment now in a sunny place.

✦ Keep chervil, coriander, fennel, dill and parsley well watered in dry spells. Remove their flowers regularly to keep up a supply of leaves, unless you want to take seed.

✦ Give mint a trim to perk it up.

✦ Trim sage after it flowers.

✦ Take softwood cuttings of rosemary and sage if you want more plants.

✦ Make a second sowing of parsley. It will be much happier in partial shade at this time of year.

✦ Build up your collection of shrubby herbs – thymes, sage, rosemary, bay and lavender. The nurseries and garden centres will have a great collection on offer in June.

July

July and August are the hottest months of the year and are usually dry. Watering and keeping up with the harvesting are the most arduous tasks. Enjoy the sunshine while taking stock of your achievements and spend those long summer evenings thinking about sowing and planting for autumn and winter.

You can go at a more leisurely pace this month and enjoy the delicious summer produce that you have grown. Tomatoes, French and runner beans, peas and courgettes need picking almost every day. Shallots and garlic will be ready this month, along with globe artichokes and new potatoes. Summer fruits – late strawberries, raspberries, redcurrants and whitecurrants, blackcurrants and gooseberries will be ready or ripening. Sow a few seeds for autumn and winter. Study the allotment now that it is in full swing and make a note of what you might want to change next year – if anything.

GENERAL MAINTENANCE

✦ Keep up regular hoeing and weeding.

✦ Stake and tie in. Keep a ball of string in your pocket.

✦ Deadheading – keep a pair of secateurs to hand.

✦ Conserve water. Only water the plants that need it. Young vegetables like tomatoes and aubergines need watering daily in hot weather. When short of water, many vegetables and herbs are inclined to bolt, or produce seed too early. A light

WEATHER

SUNSHINE: Edinburgh 172.9 hours, Durham 154.8 hours, Nottingham 168 hours, Lowestoft 192.6 hours, London 182 hours, Cardiff 201.5 hours, Exeter 191.3 hours.

RAIN: Edinburgh 9.1 days, Durham 8.1 days, Nottingham 8.2 days, Lowestoft 8.1 days, London 6.9 days, Cardiff 8.2 days, Exeter 6.5 days.

AIR FROST: None

MAXIMUM TEMPERATURE: Edinburgh 18.4°C, Durham 19.2°C, Nottingham 20.4°C, Lowestoft 19.8°C, London 22.2°C, Cardiff 21.2°C, Exeter 21°C.

MINIMUM TEMPERATURE: Edinburgh 11°C, Durham 10.4°C, Nottingham 11.3°C, Lowestoft 12.5°C, London 13°C, Cardiff 12.4°C, Exeter 12°C.

sprinkling achieves little – give them a good soaking less often. Get to the roots of thirsty vegetables (such as courgettes and marrows) by sinking a pipe next to them. Runner beans need plenty of water to form pods and set flowers. Many seasoned gardeners recommend spraying the flowers with water every evening to 'set' the flowers.

✦ Feeding. Plants become tired in high summer. Organic compost and manure applied in spring should see you through but keep an eye on the greedy feeders like melons, courgettes and tomatoes.

Last Chance...

❋ Sow fast-growing carrots now for autumn eating.

❋ Sow runner beans for a good crop this summer.

❋ Sow salad and successional vegetables – beetroot, fast carrots, turnips, spinach and salad onions to see you into autumn.

TROUBLE-SHOOTING

Be especially watchful as the high humidity and heat in July encourages the spread of plant disease. Mildew is common in dry weather; control it by keeping plants well watered. Leaf spot and rust can also be a problem in hot weather especially following a damp spell. Gather and burn all affected leaves and try to improve air circulation.

Tomato problems include blossom end rot (sunken brown patches) caused by a lack of watering and a resulting calcium deficiency. Keep them very well watered. Tomato and potato blight may also appear. Tomatoes must be pulled out and destroyed. Chop off all the leaves on potatoes.

Watch for raspberry beetles which burrow into blackberries as well.

✦ Top up ponds in hot weather.
✦ Make sure the birds have water for drinking and bathing.
✦ Start to collect seed.
✦ If you are planning a holiday, find someone to take over. Ask them to water and harvest to keep up the supplies.

VEGETABLES

✦ Carry on harvesting early and mid–early potatoes. Lift one plant to check that they are ready. Water well once a week now to encourage the tubers to grow.
✦ Lift garlic, onions and shallots carefully with a fork when the leaves turn yellow and lay out in the sun to ripen. Bring them in if you get wet weather and put in a light airy place to dry further. To make an onion plait, tie one firmly to a string attached to the ceiling or a door frame. Tie in the onions either by their necks or with more string, starting from the bottom and working up.
✦ Keep harvesting beans and courgettes while young and tender.
✦ Sow spring cabbage. Make several sowings a couple of weeks apart so they will be big enough to survive the winter. They need to be well established before the first frosts but not too large or they may bolt. A rule of thumb is the last week of July in the north and early August for the south.
✦ Sow maincrop turnips.
✦ This is the best time to sow headed Chinese cabbage.
✦ In cooler areas, sow mustard greens.
✦ Sow autumn and winter salads. Corn salad and rocket, komatsuna, pak choi, winter radish, mizuna and mibuna greens may also be sown.
✦ Sow winter peas, choosing mildew-resistant varieties.
✦ Sow maincrop carrots, winter leeks, late Brussels sprouts, sprouting broccoli and spring broccoli.
✦ Sow fast carrots for an autumn crop.
✦ Sow runner beans in situ until the end of the month.
✦ Give texcel greens and rocket a rest as they are likely to bolt in hot weather.
✦ If you have cordon tomatoes outdoors, pinch out the growing tip and the side shoots when five trusses have set. This will help to set and ripen the fruits. Feed with high potash (tomato) fertilizer.

+ Stop climbing beans when they reach the top of their supports to encourage them to make more side shoots and more beans.
+ Pinch out the tips of the trailing stems of pumpkins and squashes.
+ Earth-up (or put sections of pipe or wrap newspaper round) hearting celery when the stems are 30 cm (12 in) high, leaving the top leaves exposed.
+ Cover cauliflowers over with their leaves to slow down the curds from opening too soon.
+ Blanch endives by covering over with a flower pot with the hole blocked.
+ If you see white roots appearing on cucumbers, cover with a top dressing of well-rotted manure.
+ Continue to spray runner beans with a fine jet of water every evening to help the flowers 'set'.
+ Finish planting out winter brassicas sown in April and May, putting collars or fleece over them to protect against the cabbage root fly laying its eggs.

FRUIT

+ Pick and store summer-fruiting raspberries, blackcurrants, redcurrants and whitecurrants.
+ Prune and train redcurrants and whitecurrants, gooseberries, blackberries and their hybrids and fan-trained fruits.
+ Cut down the old canes of summer raspberries as soon as they have finished fruiting and keep tying in the new.
+ Thin out fruit on apples and pears.
+ Protect the ripening fruit of plums from birds and wasps.

+ Layer blackberries and their hybrids if you want more plants.
+ Shear off old foliage from strawberries once they have finished fruiting. Clear away the straw and hoe around the plants carefully. Dig out strawberries when they are three years old and start anew with the runners, or buy certified virus-free plants from a reputable nursery. The classic method is to have three rows, replacing one each year. A few strawberry cultivars, including perpetual strawberries, don't produce runners but can be propogated by division in autumn. Avoid planting strawberries in the same spot for a minimum of three years (six if possible) and don't plant them where raspberries have been as they are prone to many of the same diseases.

HERBS

+ Make a second sowing of chervil for winter under cloches.
+ Cut lavender, sage, rosemary and thyme and other herbs and flowers for drying. Tie into bunches and hang them in an airy place upside-down or freeze the culinary ones.
+ Take cuttings of sage and thyme. When they root in four to six weeks, pot them up individually.
+ Pick herbs regularly to keep up a supply of young shoots and stop them becoming spindly. If they are looking tired, give the bushy types a light trim all over with shears.
+ Trim sweet marjoram after it flowers.

August

August is generally hot and sultry with the odd thundery shower. The pace slows down with the hot weather. The tender tomatoes, cucumbers, courgettes and peppers will be abundant now. There will be plenty of bush and tree fruit to harvest. If you go on holiday this month, arrange for a neighbour or friend to water and harvest for you.

Having done most of the hard work through autumn and spring, this is a good time to potter and enjoy the sunshine and all the produce. The sweetcorn will be ripening and is absolutely delicious barbequed. All the exotics – tomatoes, cucumbers, aubergines, lima beans and peppers – will be ready to harvest. Beans and courgettes need to be picked nearly every day while young. Stone fruits, apples, pears and the late soft fruits will be ripening. Enjoy the first Brussels sprouts, Hamburg parsley, mini cauliflowers, parsnips and baby leeks. If you are going away, arrange for someone to water and harvest for you.

GENERAL MAINTENANCE
✦ Hoe and weed, watching out for desirable self-sown seedlings while doing so.
✦ Water well in dry spells.
✦ Deadhead unless collecting seed.
✦ Sow green manure crops on vacant ground. Mustard is a good choice for the potato patch as it inhibits eelworm and can be sown now and dug in in autumn. Other overwintering green manures, alfalfa, crimson clover, winter tare,

---

Last Chance...

❋ Plant strawberries so they can get established before winter.
❋ Sow the last batch of spring onions, lettuces, red-leaved chicory, turnips, radishes and parsley in time for autumn eating.
❋ Sow maincrop turnips to establish for winter.

WEATHER

SUNSHINE: Edinburgh 155.9 hours, Durham 155.5 hours, Nottingham 161.7 hours, Lowestoft 190.4 hours, London 179.7 hours, Cardiff 186 hours, Exeter 173.3 hours.

RAIN: Edinburgh 10.6 days, Durham 9.5 days, Nottingham 9.6 days, Lowestoft 8.2 days, London 7.7 days, Cardiff 10.1 days, Exeter 7.7 days.

AIR FROST: None

MAXIMUM TEMPERATURE: Edinburgh 18.3°C, Durham 19.1°C, Nottingham 20.2°C, Lowestoft 20°C, London 21.7°C, Cardiff 20.8°C, Exeter 20.8°C.

MINIMUM TEMPERATURE: Edinburgh 10.9°C, Durham 10.4°C, Nottingham 11.2°C, Lowestoft 12.7°C, London 12.8°C, Cardiff 12.3°C, Exeter 11.7°C.

---

grazing rye, or Italian rye grass can be sown at the end of August through to autumn. Broadcast the seed and level with a rake.
✦ Trim hedges. They won't be growing much after this.
✦ Top up ponds in hot weather.
✦ Provide water for the birds.
✦ Continue to collect seed.

VEGETABLES
✦ Harvest the summer vegetables – cabbages, cauliflowers, carrots, peas, young turnips, beetroot and globe artichokes.

TROUBLE-SHOOTING

Heat and high humidity can cause diseases to spread. Watch for mildew which thrives in warm dry weather. Fungal diseases, including rust and leaf spot, may strike with the warmth and humidity of August thunderstorms following hot weather. Remove all infected leaves and try to improve air circulation. Keep plants well watered.

Inspect plants for aphids, as always, and battle on with slugs and snails. Take precautions against the second generation of carrot fly and be on the look out for pear and apple scab. If you find it remove all affected fruits and prune back for a good circulation of air. Watch for tomato and potato blight and blossom end rot in tomatoes.

+ Sow a few seeds of winter spinach, spring cabbage and Japanese onions at intervals of two weeks. Timing is a bit of a gamble. If they are too small when the first frosts come they may not survive winter. If too large they may bolt. The best policy is to plant a few a week or so apart. Spring cabbage will be ready to eat as early greens, and will heart up in spring.
+ Sow Welsh onions for next spring.
+ Sow corn salad to grow under cover for eating in autumn. It will carry on through winter if given fleece or cloche protection.
+ Sow maincrop turnips under collars. Turnips resent transplanting so sow in situ in cool, damp soil in partial shade.

Thin when only 2.5 cm (1 in) high so they can get their roots down in time for winter. They can be harvested when they are the size of a tennis ball, up until the New Year. The tops can be used as greens.
+ Sow pak choi, Chinese cabbage, mizuna and mibuna greens, headed Chinese cabbage, komatusna and rocket.
+ Sow mustard greens in the south.
+ Sow winter radish (mooli or daikon) for autumn eating and winter storage.
+ Give texcel greens and rocket a rest.
+ Keep picking courgettes, but if you want marrows leave a few to mature.
+ Tomatoes and beans need picking almost daily when they are perfect.
+ When the 'silks' turn brown on sweet-corn, they will be ready to eat. They are so delicious when picked fresh.
+ Pick cucumbers before they go yellow, and aubergines and peppers while they are still shiny.
+ Continue to lift and dry onions.
+ Clear away the last of the mid-early potatoes and start to dig up the main-crop ones.
+ Sow winter spinach, winter radish (mooli), and turnips.
+ Collect seed – broad beans and peas are a safe bet.

FRUIT
+ Continue summer-pruning raspberries, gooseberries, cherries, redcurrants, damsons, cordons and espaliers.
+ Prune plums and damsons immediately after fruiting. Cut out any dead wood and broken branches.
+ Strawberry runners, pegged down last month, can be severed from the parent

plant. Prepare a new strawberry bed and plant them out or buy and plant new certified stock.

✦ Test apples and pears for ripeness. Cup the fruit in one hand and twist the stem. When ready they will come off easily with the stalk intact. Apples are picked when perfectly ripe but pears when still hard. They are taken home to finish ripening when needed.

✦ Continue tying-in and pruning the cane fruits. Leave the autumn raspberries.

✦ Keep harvesting stone fruit and all the berries and currants. Raspberries are picked while still firm, leaving the core or plug on the plant. Blackcurrants, redcurrants and whitecurrants are picked by the 'strig' or in little bunches. Blackberries are picked with the stalk still on. Blueberries ripen over the weeks, so if you don't have too many, freeze them until you have enough for a good serving.

HERBS

✦ Sow parsley and chervil for winter use under cloches. Net against carrot fly.

✦ Pot up chives for winter. Cut off old foliage and water.

✦ Take semi-ripe cuttings from shrubby herbs like rosemary, lavender and sage.

✦ Collect seed from dill, fennel, and coriander as they ripen. They can be re-sown at once outside, stored or used for flavouring.

✦ Keep an eye on the prolific self-seeders like fennel, and cut off the seedheads as they develop.

✦ Trim lavender after flowering, without cutting into the old wood.

GROWING FOR SHOWING

Digging for Victory proved to be an inspiration. The heyday of the flower show was after the last World War. Even now, particularly in August, you will not find many towns or villages that don't have a flower, produce and craft show. Among these are some 3000 societies affiliated to the Royal Horticultural Society where you can pick up a prestigious RHS medal. If you want to give it a whirl, get hold of the RHS 'Horticultural Show Handbook'. It sets out the rules that are closely followed across the country. They deserve studying as a single slip can get you disqualified as 'NAS' (not according to schedule). It gives invaluable tips on growing, point-scoring and presentation. If you get a taste for showing, move onto the National Societies. The prizes are substantial, you will get tips from the best growers in the country and will become a member of the elite.

September

Temperatures start to cool this month and there will be the first touches of frost in some areas. In a good year there can be an Indian summer, although temperatures usually cool down this month and the first touches of frost are likely. This is the month for harvesting potatoes and the last of the onions and for ripening tomatoes before the frosts come.

The autumn months are the best time for 'earthworks' – digging or making raised beds and improving the soil. Harvesting continues unabated. Tender crops need to be gathered before the frosts next month. Apples, pears and plums, late raspberries and blackberries should be at their peak and need to be harvested. Enjoy the last of the globe artichokes, fresh beans, autumn cauliflowers and Florence fennel and the first sweet potatoes. Ripen the last tomatoes and a pumpkin for Halloween. Maincrop potatoes are lifted for storing this month as are the last of the onions. As plants go over, there should be plenty of good material to build up a grand compost heap. It is the beginning of the autumn clearance and time to think about ordering new seed catalogues for next year.

GENERAL MAINTENANCE

✦ Clear autumn debris and falling leaves.
✦ Slow down on feeding. You don't want plants outside to put out soft growth now as they can be knocked back by frost.
✦ Start a new compost heap.
✦ Start collecting leaves for leafmould.
✦ Sow green manure crops on vacant ground if you haven't done so in August. Winter beans, Italian rye grass or grazing

Last Chance...

❈ Plant strawberries for next year.
❈ Ripen all the tender vegetables before the frosts.
❈ Get your onions in.

WEATHER

SUNSHINE: Edinburgh 118.4 hours, Durham 124.3 hours, Nottingham 121.3 hours, Lowestoft 147.1 hours, London 138.1 hours, Cardiff 141 hours, Exeter 133.3 hours.

RAIN: Edinburgh 11.5 days, Durham 8.3 days, Nottingham 8.8 days, Lowestoft 8.5 days, London 7.9 days, Cardiff 10.7 days, Exeter 8.9 days.

AIR FROST: Edinburgh 0.1 days, Durham none, Nottingham none, Lowestoft none, London none, Cardiff none, Exeter none.

MAXIMUM TEMPERATURE: Edinburgh 16.1°C, Durham 16.8°C, Nottingham 17.5°C, Lowestoft 18.2°C, London 19.1°C, Cardiff 18.3°C, Exeter 18.4°C.

MINIMUM TEMPERATURE: Edinburgh 9°C, Durham 8.7°C, Nottingham 9.3°C, Lowestoft 10.9°C, London 10.7°C, Cardiff 10.4°C, Exeter 9.9°C.

rye are good for autumn sowing and spring digging. September is a good time to dig heavy clay before the rains make it harder work.
✦ Incorporate some pea shingle and compost to help drainage.
✦ Cover light soils for winter so they don't leach, either by growing green manures or covering with polythene.
✦ Hoe and weed.
✦ Provide water and food for the birds.
✦ Collect seed as it ripens. Before the advent of the big seed companies and

the garden centres, everyone had to grow their own seed. There is no mystique about it. It saves money and can preserve wonderful old varieties that might die out otherwise. Many of the best have come down to us as family heirlooms. Start off with the simple ones like peas. They are anuuals so you don't need to over-winter them, they rarely cross-pollinate and are easy to collect and clean.

VEGETABLES

✦ Harvest maincrop potatoes on a warm sunny day and leave to dry out in the sun. Store in paper sacks and keep in the dark in a frost-free place. Burn the leaves or bin them.

✦ Lift root vegetables – beetroot, maincrop carrots and turnips – and store in boxes with sand or in clamps. Leave parsnips that you don't want to eat now in the ground as the frost improves the taste.

TROUBLE-SHOOTING

Pests should be less of a problem now, but clear out debris where they can overwinter. Trim back any shoots affected with mildew and burn them. Continue to watch for aphids, slugs and snails. Fix grease bands on the trunks of fruit trees; they will trap the female winter moths and other insects as they crawl up the trunks to lay their eggs or hibernate. Protect ripening apples and pears from birds and wasps. Prune mildew-infected shoots of apples and pears and burn them.

✦ Dig out any onions still in the ground and keep in a cool dry place. Bring under cover if necessary.

✦ Continue to earth-up (or blanch with sections of pipe or newspaper collars) trench celery for the last time this year. If frost is forecast, throw fleece over the tops of the plants. They should be ready next month.

✦ Take out the stakes and lay cordon tomatoes plants down on straw. Cover with cloches to speed ripening in the sunshine. You are now in a race to maximize the crop before the frosts get them. Try ripening green tomatoes in a draw with a ripe banana – it is said that the gases given off the banana will help speed the process.

✦ Cover Chinese and spring cabbages with cloches.

✦ When the leaves of Jerusalem artichokes go black after the first frost, mark where the plants are for harvesting later.

✦ Let marrows, pumpkins and squashes ripen and dry in the sun or under cover, and store in a cool dry place. Clear away old plants.

✦ Cut down asparagus foliage when it goes brown. Wear gloves as they have sharp spines on the stems. Pile plenty of garden compost or well-rotted manure onto the beds.

✦ Stake tall Brussels sprouts plants for overwintering in exposed areas.

✦ Start to harvest autumn brassicas – Brussels sprouts, Hamburg parsley, cauliflowers – also young leeks and parsnips.

✦ Plant garlic. It needs a period of cold weather to grow well. If starting fresh, buy bulbs especially cultivated for planting. If you have saved a bulb of your own, divide it into cloves, remove the papery skin and plant it with the tip pointing up. Over the years it will adapt to your particular conditions and become your own strain.

✦ Plant Japanese onion sets and autumn-sown onions.

✦ Transplant spring cabbages sown last month. Cover with netting or fleece against the birds. Pigeons are particularly partial to them.

✦ Sow hardy winter lettuce like 'Winter Density' outside covered with cloches or in the cold greenhouse. It will be ready to harvest in January.

✦ Make a final sowing of mizuna, mibuna and mustard greens.

✦ Sow summer cauliflowers.

✦ Sow spinach for spring eating. Make several small sowings a few weeks apart and choose the sturdiest to overwinter under cover.

✦ Sow forcing carrots in the cold frame for spring eating.

✦ Start to force chicory.

FRUIT

✦ Keep young strawberries well watered.

✦ Plant new blackberries or increase your stock by pegging down the tip of a new shoot into the soil. It will be ready to be severed from the parent in spring. Freeze the fruits as they ripen individually until you have enough. After fruiting, cut out the old canes and tie in the new.

✦ The autumn-fruiting raspberries should be ready now. Leave the canes unpruned until late winter or early spring.

✦ Have protection to hand in case of frost.

HERBS

✦ Sow lovage on good rich soil in full or part sun. Split established plants.

✦ Sow fennel or plant a piece of root.

✦ Make a last sowing of coriander in warm parts of the country.

✦ Protect parsley and chervil with cloches to carry on through autumn.

✦ Split large clumps of chives, making sure that each division has plenty of roots. They die back in winter but if you pot them up you can keep them going inside on a sunny windowsill.

✦ Dig up mint plants, pot them up and bring inside.

✦ Divide and replant established plants of sweet marjoram.

✦ Harvest all the basil or pot it up for growing on the kitchen windowsill as it won't survive a frost.

✦ Trim back lavender, sage, thyme and other shrubby herbs to tidy them up for winter.

October

October will see temperatures drop and clear, frosty nights are likely in most places. The days are drawing in so there is less time to work on the allotment. It is a good month to plant new fruit trees while the soil is still warm, and to get on with any digging.

As you finish the autumn harvest and clear the beds, decide how you will leave them over the winter. Heavy soils can be left roughly dug for the winter weather to break them down. Light soils should be covered with green manures or polythene to prevent them leaching. You might want to cover still-weedy areas with black polythene or make raised beds for next year. Put up insect hotels, bird boxes and other habitats for your wild friends.

GENERAL MAINTENANCE

✦ Clear the garden of debris. This is a good month to make a big compost heap quickly to rot down through the winter months. Burn anything affected by pests and disease.

✦ Keep weeding and hoeing but don't be too tidy. Leave seedheads for the birds to eat and some cover where useful insects can hibernate.

✦ Rake up falling leaves and pile them up for making leafmould or add to the compost heap.

✦ Try to get hold of a big heap of horse manure to rot down through winter.

✦ Dig borders while the soil is not too sticky. Break up heavy soils before the onset of winter when it becomes much harder work.

Last Chance...

❋ Harvest apples and pears.
❋ Ripen all the tender vegetables before the frosts.
❋ Get your onions in.

WEATHER

SUNSHINE: Edinburgh 94.1 hours, Durham 93.3 hours, Nottingham 86.6 hours, Lowestoft 106.1 hours, London 101.9 hours, Cardiff 93 hours, Exeter 90.2 hours.

RAIN: Edinburgh 11.5 days, Durham 9.5 days, Nottingham 10.6 days, Lowestoft 9 days, London 8.3 days, Cardiff 13.2 days, Exeter 11 days.

AIR FROST: Edinburgh 0.1 days, Durham 1.1 days, Nottingham 0.4 days, Lowestoft none, London 0.1 days, Cardiff 0.5 days, Exeter 0.7 days.

MAXIMUM TEMPERATURE: Edinburgh 13.1°C, Durham 13.2°C, Nottingham 13.7°C, Lowestoft 14.4°C, London 15.3°C, Cardiff 14.7°C, Exeter 15°C.

MINIMUM TEMPERATURE: Edinburgh 6.5°C, Durham 6.3°C, Nottingham 6.8°C, Lowestoft 8.5°C, London 8.1°C, Cardiff 7.9°C, Exeter 7.7°C.

✦ Cover ground with polythene on light soils to prevent nutrients leaching from winter rains.

✦ Sow green manures.

✦ Feed the birds. Strangely, wildlife is thriving in town allotments, parks, gardens and churchyards while the countryside is seeing a worrying decline. Even the once common sparrow and starling are on the danger list. In October there should be plenty of seeds, nuts and berries on the allotment but put out extra food and water. When the ground is frozen many birds will die of hunger. Oily seeds are nourishing. The seeds of sunflower, flax and rape will be enjoyed by the insect eaters as well as the seed eaters when there is ice on the ground. Make sure the feeders can be washed out and have a little roof to keep them dry. Once you start, don't stop as the birds will become dependent on you.

+ Check stores.

VEGETABLES

+ Clear tomato, aubergine, and pepper plants away.

+ Harvest any remaining French or runner beans still on the plants.

+ Decide how to store your winter root vegetables. With the exception of the iciest places you can leave carrots, parsnips, beetroot, swedes and turnips in the ground with extra protection later in the season. Alternatively, you can store them in stacking wooden trays or boxes in layers covered with just–moist sand and keep them in a cool frost-free place. Another method is to make a clamp (see page 66) and keep them outside on the allotment. Never store damaged produce as it can affect the rest.

+ Peas and beans can be frozen or dried.

+ Potatoes go in hessian or paper sacks and must be kept in the dark.

+ Onions must be kept dry and are stored in airy trays, in nets or plaited into onion ropes.

+ If you haven't already done so, cut down the foliage of Jerusalem artichokes, marking the spot so you know where to dig them up through winter. Harvest them as and when you want them.

+ Start to harvest trenching celery. If frost is forecast, cover the tops with straw kept in place with chicken or plastic netting, or fleece pegged into the ground.

+ In cold areas protect globe artichokes with straw or bracken, leaving the crowns of the plants exposed.

+ Force seakale from now until January. Cut the plants right down and clear any debris from the base. Cover with about 10 cm (4 in) of straw in cold areas and top with a bucket or a large flower pot with the hole blocked. It should be ready to harvest in about three months.

+ Plant garlic, spring cabbage, Japanese and autumn onion sets.

+ Sow a few winter lettuces (like 'All Year Round', 'Arctic King' or 'Winter

TROUBLE-SHOOTING

On the whole, pests are in the decline in the cooler weather. Sprays are not very effective at this time of year. Botrytis and mildew are common now the weather is damper – cut off and burn or bin affected parts of plants when you spot them. Courgettes and marrows are particularly prone.

Remove yellowing leaves from Brussels sprouts, cabbages, cauliflowers and broccoli. They also encourage botrytis and grey mould. Practice good hygiene as always.

Check for viral infections, particularly in your fruit, and discard any plants that seem unhealthy. Put greasebands on fruit trees to trap the female winter moths.

Density') in the cold greenhouse. Water sparingly at the base rather than from overhead as they are prone to botrytis and rotting off.

✦ Keep up the succession of radishes and winter salads. You can plant them in the growbags used for tomatoes. Give them a regular liquid feed and protect the plants with a cloche.

✦ Sow broad beans outside and cover with cloches. The seeds will germinate quickly and grow slowly through the winter for harvesting in early summer.

✦ Now there is room, tidy and clean out the greenhouse.

✦ Feed the birds and provide habitats.

✦ Watch out for ripening seeds.

FRUIT

✦ Finish picking maincrop apples and pears this month.

✦ Clean up strawberry beds, removing yellow foliage and any remaining runners. Keep young plants well watered so they can develop well before winter.

✦ Store apples and pears. Freeze or make jam with the last of the soft fruits.

✦ Prune blackberries and their hybrids when the fruit has been harvested.

✦ Take hardwood cuttings of black-, red-, and whitecurrants and gooseberries.

✦ You can prune blackcurrants now but the job is more easily done when the foliage has dropped off in December. Take cuttings if you want more bushes.

✦ Order trees, bushes or canes. Plant as soon as possible while the soil is warm. If the weather isn't right for planting when they arrive, heel them in or cover with wet sacking.

HERBS

✦ Lift parsley, chives and some mint, if you haven't already. Pot up and keep on the kitchen windowsill for winter use. Cover this season's chervil and more parsley outside with cloches. Clear away any from the year before as they are likely to bolt in their second season.

✦ Tidy up winter savory and apply a mulch to the soil.

✦ Dig up the annual herbs now, such as dill, coriander, summer savory and sweet marjoram.

November

In November, you will need to prepare your allotment for the onset of winter. It is generally damp, wet and frosty at night. In the west of Scotland and Ireland, there can be up to five days of gales. Sunshine is blocked by low cloud and snow is likely in the north. Make sure that your plants are protected against cold weather. On warmer days, carry on digging on heavy soils for the frosts to break them down further. Use up the last of the compost and build up a good heap to rot down through the winter.

Hurry to gather in the last of the summer crops and plant for winter. Put the plot to bed for the cold months. Carry on digging on fine days, planting green manures and enriching the soil with the last of the old compost and manure. If you have a bonfire, burn any diseased material. Winter vegetables will be coming in now – kale, cabbage, spinach, leeks, Oriental mustards, chards, beets and Jerusalem artichokes, scorzonera, salsify and trench celery. Parsnips and sprouts are sweeter after the first frosts.

GENERAL MAINTENANCE

+ Clear leaves and stack up for leafmould.
+ Dig heavy soils on good days when the conditions are right. This is a good time to convert to the deep bed, no–dig system. Leave light soils until spring.
+ Sow green manures on bare ground to replenish the soil before spring planting
+ Tidy beds. Clear away old foliage.
+ Keep going on the compost heap. If you and your neighbours have a lot of woody material, hire a shredder between you, or get your committee onto it.
+ If you are planning a bonfire, check for hibernating hedgehogs and frogs.
+ Protect vulnerable plants from frost and wind with netting or fleece.
+ Lag downpipes from the shed to the water butt.
+ Check stakes and ties as winter weather is imminent.

Last Chance...

❋ Get tender crops in.
❋ Protect vulnerable plants from frost.

WEATHER

SUNSHINE: Edinburgh 65.2 hours, Durham 66.2 hours, Nottingham 58.1 hours, Lowestoft 61.5 hours, London 57.4 hours, Cardiff 69 hours, Exeter 68.3 hours.

RAIN: Edinburgh 10.6 days, Durham 11 days, Nottingham 10.7 days, Lowestoft 12.2 days, London 9.3 days, Cardiff 13.5 days, Exeter 11.8 days.

AIR FROST: Edinburgh 7.4 days, Durham 6.3 days, Nottingham 5.4 days, Lowestoft 3.2 days, London 3.2 days, Cardiff 4.3 days, Exeter 5.7 days.

MAXIMUM TEMPERATURE: Edinburgh 8.8°C, Durham 8.7°C, Nottingham 8.9°C, Lowestoft 9.7°C, London 10.5°C, Cardiff 10.5°C, Exeter 11°C.

MINIMUM TEMPERATURE: Edinburgh 2.8°C, Durham 2.8°C, Nottingham 1.5°C, Lowestoft 4.4°C, London 4.5°C, Cardiff 4.3°C, Exeter 4.1°C.

+ In cold areas, insulate cold frames with polystyrene cut to size. With bubble wrap on top, this will keep out several degrees of frost. On bitter nights a piece of carpet on top will help. Take it off during the day to let light in.
+ Order horticultural fleece or mesh fabrics to protect your plants. Start to save newspapers, netting, old plastic bottles and blankets. They may all come in useful in the months ahead.
+ If you are on a windy site you might want to put up windbreaks.

✦ Cover compost bins.

✦ Check the shed for leaks before winter.

✦ Float a ball in the pond to prevent freezing.

✦ Clear out old bird boxes as they can harbour parasites. The birds will be looking for cosy winter roosts any time now. Put food and water out for them.

✦ Check your stores. Throw out or use up anything that looks less than perfect.

✦ Order seeds.

VEGETABLES

✦ Net all brassicas against hungry pigeons. Remove yellowing leaves from brassicas to discourage disease and burn them.

✦ Pick Brussels sprouts – starting from the bottom and removing old leaves.

✦ Prepare the onion bed for next spring. Onions like firm soil so prepare it now and let the bed settle over winter.

✦ Harvest parsnips after the first frosts in cold areas and store them in the same way as the other root vegetables.

✦ Lift a few leeks if there is frost about. They are impossible to dig out in icy conditions. Bury them horizontally with the tops sticking out in a sheltered spot.

✦ Protect the curds of cauliflowers by tying the leaves over them.

✦ Sow broad beans and winter peas outside under cloches in mild areas.

✦ Force chicory and seakale.

✦ Cut down globe artichokes and pack straw around them in cold areas.

✦ It is not too late to plant Japanese and autumn onion sets.

FRUIT

✦ Begin winter-pruning of apple and pear trees, gooseberries and currants when the leaves have died off.

✦ Weed carefully and top dress all soft fruit with a layer of organic matter.

✦ If you haven't already done so, put grease bands around the trunks of fruit trees.

✦ Propagate rhubarb by digging up and splitting into smaller pieces. Repeat every three years. Start to plant newly bought crowns now.

✦ Take hardwood cuttings of redcurrants, blackcurrants and gooseberries.

✦ Plant new fruit trees while there is still some warmth in the soil.

✦ Check stored fruit from time to time.

HERBS

✦ Put cloches over parsley, winter savory and chervil.

✦ Dig up mint and chives and grow them on in containers at home or in the cold greenhouse.

✦ Protect young plants of French tarragon, sage and rosemary with straw or leaf–mould around the roots.

TROUBLE-SHOOTING

There aren't too many pests around in November but watch for corners where they can lurk. The less places they have to hide, the less trouble you will have next year. Clean out old pots and trays and give tools, stakes and flowerpots a scrub and disinfect.

If rabbits are a nuisance, net your plants with chicken wire and protect tree trunks with rabbit guards.

Check apples and pears for canker and renew sticky bands on fruit trees if necessary.

December

Little is really urgent this month, though it is good practice to get any digging done on heavy soils by the end of the year. In the New Year it will be harder work and there will be fewer opportunities. Take advantage of any short, sunny days on offer to get ahead. However, as long as you have battened your hatches, harvested, stored and protected your plants from the cold, you can relax and do some armchair gardening. Browse the catalogues and make plans for next year. Work out your rotation, decide on any changes, and order your seeds.

Enjoy the produce from your groaning larder – nutty Brussels sprouts, spring carrots, petits pois, French beans, potatoes and parsnips, fresh salads, not forgetting your bountiful store of chutneys, jams and fruit pies. It is a just reward for all the work, and should be a matter of great pride.

GENERAL MAINTENANCE

✦ Test the soil pH. Apply lime if necessary. Don't use it at the same time as manure as it will react against it.

✦ Move plants that are in the wrong place when the soil is not frozen or water-logged, taking as much soil as possible with the rootball.

✦ Winter dig when conditions are right.

✦ Keep clearing debris but leave a few hidey holes for beneficial creatures – small piles of leaves, stones and logs.

✦ Carry on collecting leaves for leafmould. Use planks, hands or a 'gripper' to pick up leaves rather than a fork, to avoid harming dormant creatures.

✦ Give plants protection against severe cold and strong winds.

✦ Cover small vulnerable plants with little polytunnels and cloches.

✦ Insulate cold frames and the greenhouse with bubble wrap if you are planning to use them through winter.

✦ Rig up a polystyrene box to raise seed in the cold greenhouse. Glue sheets together and cover the top with a piece of glass or see-through plastic.

✦ Put sheets of polystyrene under lettuces and other plants in pots or trays in the cold greenhouse for insulation.

✦ Get in a good supply of horticultural fleece to protect plants from sharp frosts until the end of May in many places.

WEATHER

SUNSHINE: : Edinburgh 40.2 hours, Durham 45.6 hours, Nottingham 41.4 hours, Lowestoft 40.4 hours, London 34.6 hours, Cardiff 46.5 hours, Exeter 50.8 hours.

RAIN: Edinburgh 10.3 days, Durham 11.2 days, Nottingham 11.7 days, Lowestoft 11.5 days, London 9.4 days, Cardiff 13.8 days, Exeter 12.3 days.

AIR FROST: Edinburgh 10.4 days, Durham 10.1 days, Nottingham 9.7 days, Lowestoft 6.8 days, London 8 days, Cardiff 7.7 days, Exeter 8.5 days.

MAXIMUM TEMPERATURE: Edinburgh 7.1°C, Durham 6.6°C, Nottingham 6.7°C, Lowestoft 7.2°C, London 8.2°C, Cardiff 8.4°C, Exeter 9°C.

MINIMUM TEMPERATURE: Edinburgh 1.5°C, Durham 1.1°C, Nottingham 1.5°C, Lowestoft 2.4°C, Greenwich 2.6°C, Cardiff 2.8°C, Exeter 2.9°C.

✦ Check existing stakes and ties and put in new ones where necessary.

✦ Repair fences and sheds. Make a cold frame and tackle other DIY projects.

✦ Take hardwood cuttings.

✦ Make a small hotbed in the cold green-house if you can get some manure.

✦ On mild days open up the cold frame or cold greenhouse to let air circulate for an hour or two.

✦ If you haven't already, clean your tools. Remove rust with wire wool and oil them, sharpen blades. Scrub flower pots and seed trays to get rid of any lurking pests and diseases.

✦ Feed the birds. Don't trim down any ornamental plants that provide food for the birds in the depth of winter. The seedheads of asters, teasel, thistles (echinops) and the berries of cotoneaster and honeysuckle will be greatly appreciated. Make sure the birds have water. Provide bird feeders and nesting boxes.

✦ Check on stores.

VEGETABLES

✦ Earth-up spring cabbages and winter brassicas to avoid wind rock. Keep removing yellowing leaves which could harbour disease.

✦ Cut leaves from the crowns of kale to encourage side shoots to grow for harvesting in late winter.

✦ Put straw or bracken around perennials like globe artichokes to keep the worst of the frost off. Leave the crowns clear as they may rot off.

✦ If you still have maincrop carrots, parsnips, turnips, swedes and beetroot in the ground, cover them now with a thick layer of straw, bracken or leaves, earth them up or put cloches over for extra protection. In cold areas, lift them

TROUBLE-SHOOTING

There shouldn't be too much to worry about in December – one advantage of the cold weather. Still watch for slugs and snails as they may be lurking in the cold frame or greenhouse. Inspect apples and pears for canker.

and store in the shed or in a clamp.

✦ Harvest celery and leeks. If severe frost threatens, lift some and heel them in where you can get to them easily. Plants left in the ground can be protected from frosts by covering with straw. Harvest Jerusalem artichokes as required.

✦ Continue to force seakale and chicory.

✦ After the first frosts, start forcing rhubarb.

✦ Pick Brussels sprouts regularly from the bottom up and remove yellowing leaves.

✦ Sow early crops of lettuce, summer cabbage, radishes, round varieties of carrot, spinach, salad onions and turnips. They don't need a high temperature – 13°C (55°F) is enough. If started on a windowsill in good light, they can go outside under cloches or fleece in February. Cover with newspaper on icy nights but remove in the morning.

✦ Protect brassicas from birds.

FRUIT

✦ Check tree stakes, supports and ties.

✦ Winter-prune apples, pears, gooseberries and currants on days without hard frost.

✦ Force rhubarb for harvesting in January.

✦ Clear away straw under strawberries.

✦ Carry on inspecting your stores and remove any bad fruits.

✦ Spread a layer of compost or well-rotted manure around fruit bushes and trees.

HERBS

✦ It may not be too late to pot up mint and bring it indoors for early sprigs.

✦ Cut down on watering indoor herbs to a minimum.

✦ Protect young plants of French tarragon, sage and rosemary with a straw or leaf-mould around the base in cold areas.

chapter 5

DIRECTORY OF VEGETABLES

POTATOES
(Solanum tuberosum)

Potato growing has a great history on allotments. In the late 18th and early 19th centuries, it represented survival to the poor. Their staple diet was potatoes and bread.

Allotments sprung from the need to give the poor the means to provide for themselves and their families, particularly in times of food shortages. The first plots were often divided into two, one part for grain and the other for potatoes. Alongside the allotments were the 'potato grounds'. These were corners of fallow fields or areas of wasteland offered by landowners to agricultural workers on a temporary basis.

The tradition continues and it's rare to see a plot without them. Potatoes are gratifying to grow. One little tuber will produce a multitude, and harvesting is like digging for treasure. You need, however, to be very careful to avoid potato diseases, particularly on an allotment where they are probably already present in the soil.

Don't attempt to grow from your own stock or use potatoes from the green grocer. It was the exchanging of a few varieties that caused potato blight and the dreadful Irish famine of 1845–6. Always buy top-quality, certified virus-free seed potatoes from a reputable merchant. Keep up the rotation system. For extra security, choose modern cultivars which have disease resistance.

How to grow potatoes

Start off the seed potatoes in egg boxes with the end with the most 'eyes', or buds, facing upwards. Keep them in a light place out of direct sunlight, at a temperature of about 18°C (64°F). Move them to a cooler place when they start to shoot. Around six weeks from starting, the shoots will be 2.5 cm (1 in) long and the potatoes will be ready for planting.

Potatoes need a sunny, open site. They are not frost hardy and will not thrive in cold wet conditions, so delay planting if need be. The soil should have been well manured the autumn before. The ideal pH is 5–6. Add a good general fertilizer or line the trench with comfrey leaves. Plant them in individual holes or in a trench 7.5–15 cm (3–6 in) down and add an extra 2.5 cm (1 in) of soil on top. As they grow, earth them up by drawing soil over them with a hoe to prevent the tubers reaching the light and going green. An alternative is to grow them through thick black plastic on the no-dig system. This is a good way to combine weed clearance with growing crops. The only downside is that it encourages slugs. While excessive water can bring on too much leaf growth at the expense of the tubers, they need to be kept moist. A really good dousing every two weeks in dry weather is recommended, and again when the flowers are forming.

EARLIES OR MAINCROP?

Potatoes come as 'first earlies', 'second earlies' and 'maincrop'. The first and second earlies, eaten as new potatoes, are faster to mature and less likely to run into trouble. The main crop produces bigger potatoes which store well.

Traditionally, potatoes are planted on Good Friday (the first holiday since Christmas for the rural poor), but any time between March and May will do, depending on the weather.

On some allotments there is often friendly rivalry around who can harvest the first potatoes of the year. For the fun of the race, some take calculated risks. The aim, however, is to get the earlies planted a month before the end of the frosts. If they come up while frost is likely, they need to be protected with cloches or by earthing up.

Varieties

As there are over 200 varieties of potato, I sought advice from potato expert Alan Romans, author of the *Guide to Seed Potato Varieties* (Thompson and Morgan 2002). For the allotment, where people want a reliable crop to feed the family, and where there is likely to be eelworm and potato blight in the soil, he recommends choosing disease-resistant varieties bred after 1970. These varieties have built-in resistance to these diseases and high food value.

EARLY:

'*Orla*' – This variety is remarkably resistant to blight, and has some resistance to scab and blackleg. High early yields, and a good appearance.

'Premiere' – Good flavour. Makes fine chips. Some blight resistance.

'Cara' – Both early and late. A 'red-eyed tough guy for the allotment'. Vigorous, high yielding and resistant to disease.

Seed potatoes to harvest: 14–16 weeks

SECOND EARLY:

'Kestrel' – This has good disease-resistance and the slugs don't like it. Dominates show classes.

Seed potatoes to harvest: 16 weeks

MAINCROP:

'Saxon' – High-yielding, general-purpose potato with a pleasant creamy flavour. Disease-resistant.

Needs mild conditions.

'Remarka' – Flavoursome baking potatoes. Good all-round disease resistance though can be susceptible to blackleg. Needs plenty of moisture and careful weeding.

'Pomeroy' – Brand new potato. Winner at tastings. Good all-round disease-resistance.

Seed potatoes to harvest: at least 18 weeks

Potato problems

Potato and tomato blight, potato common scab, potato cyst eelworm, wireworm, potato blackleg, and slugs.

BRASSICAS – THE CABBAGE FAMILY

Primitive forms of cabbage grow wild on the chalky coastlines of southern England through most of Europe and as far as North Africa. Over the centuries these have evolved (with a little help from humans) into the very diverse and familiar group of vegetables – cabbage, cauliflower, Brussels sprouts and spinach, to mention but a few.

Brassicas are a large tribe of nutritious, cool-climate crops with much the same needs as each other. They like fertile, well-drained but moisture-retentive soil. Being leafy, they need plenty of water in dry spells. A good soak 10–20 days before harvest will make a big difference to the crop.

Some are sown outside where they are to grow as they are likely to bolt when transplanted. Others – particularly the slow-growing brassicas – are generally started in the seedbed or in modules. It gives them a more controlled, pest-free start and saves space. Move them outside when they have five or six leaves in as many weeks. They like firm ground. It is important for the brassicas that will overwinter outside to get a good roothold.

The soil should be prepared well in advance so it has time to settle down. Land that has been manured for the previous crop is ideal – neither too rich nor too poor. Many brassicas grow away again after the first cut to send out a second harvest of greens. Summer sowings are harvested when ready but the winter ones can stay in the ground until you need them.

Brassica problems

Clubroot is the worst enemy of brassicas. It is a soil-borne disease that can live in the soil for up to 20 years. Getting rid of it completely is nearly impossible. As it thrives best in acid soil, keep the soil neutral (pH7) by liming if necessary. Rotation is vital to prevent a build-up. Where plot holders have grown brassicas, year in year out on the same ground, it is likely to be rampant.

If there is eelworm on the allotment site, avoid treading over infected soil and accepting gifts of plants that might carry it. You don't have to worry so much about the fast-growing brassicas – radish, texcel greens, rocket and some of the Orientals – though it is still good practice to rotate them with the others.

Brassicas are popular with many different pests. Protect the plants from cabbage root fly with collars of rubber-backed underlay or the commercial equivalent, or by growing under fine netting or mesh.

Watch out for cabbage moths, cabbage white butterflies, mealy cabbage aphids, cabbage whitefly, cutworms, birds and (as always) slugs and snails. Flea beetle might appear in dry weather. Brassicas can also suffer from downy and powdery mildew as well as leaf spot.

SLOW STALWARTS
Brussels sprouts
Brassica oleracae

Brussels sprouts (which arrived from Belgium in the 18th century) are an allotment staple. If you plant early, mid and late varieties, they will supply you from September through to April. Given the right conditions, they are straightforward. The modern cultivars make life even easier and are bred to produce good quantities of tightly packed sprouts. For those who like the unusual, try the red varieties. Remember that Brussels sprouts are going to be in the ground for many months to come and are expected to withstand the worst of winter. Allocate them a sunny and sheltered place on the allotment with good fertile soil.

For autumn sprouts, sow an early variety in March under cloches for planting out in May and eating in autumn onwards. For crops for New Year to spring, sow a late variety in April for transplanting in June.

Sow in shallow drills and cover with netting to keep the birds off. When you transplant, protect them against cabbage problems with collars or fleece. Keep watered in dry weather until they are well established. After that they should be fairly self-sufficient.

As winter approaches, earth up stems and stake tall varieties to prevent wind rock. Remove any yellowing or diseased leaves on a regular basis.

Harvest from the bottom of the plant upwards, picking a few sprouts from each plant. Dig out entirely at the end of the season but wait until they have made one final departing gesture by throwing out a tasty top shoot.

As sprout plants are rather slow-growing and columnar in shape, they are good candidates for undercropping with salad leaves or fast-growing greens.

Varieties

EARLY:

'Peter Gynt' F1 – Tried and tested, dwarf variety. Fast growing, crops from September to January.

'Diablo' (AGM) – Good flavour. Early crops. Smooth sprouts are well-spaced and easy to pick. Resistant to powdery mildew.

'Igor' (AGM) – Vigorous plants producing good yields of tight buttons. Excellent frost tolerance.

'Noisette' – A nutty French variety which crops from October to February.

LATE:

'Cascade' (AGM) – Prolific.

'Wellington' F1 (AGM) – British bred. Smooth, dark buttons. Very hardy, crops from December to March.

'Braveheart' – Reliable tall variety, mildew resistant, crops Christmas to spring.

'Rubine' – An epicure dwarf red sprout with outstanding flavour.

Seed to harvest: 20 weeks

Cabbage
Brassica oleracea

By using different varieties you can have a supply of fresh cabbage every week of the year. The range is wide enough to be bewildering. There are eight main types and many new introductions. Some seed merchants offer collections of different types of cabbage seed in one packet – an economic way to experiment and see what suits you. Cabbages are not hard to grow as long as you provide them with good soil, continuous moisture and take action against pests and diseases. The main types are usually divided by their harvesting times.

SUMMER CABBAGE can be sown in February under cover in mild areas or in March to April in the seedbed. The seedlings are planted out and firmed when they have five or six leaves some six weeks later. Be extremely careful not to let the roots dry out through the summer months. All summer cabbages are hearting types. Earlies are pointed or round, while late summer ones are more compact and solid.

Varieties

EARLY:

'Derby Day' (AGM) – Popular old variety. Excellent light green ball-headed type. Bolt-resistant.

'Hispi' F1 (AGM) – Quick-growing, reliable, pointed type. Good flavour.

'Greyhound' – An old favourite. Fast growing and compact with good flavour. Can be sown successionally.

'First of June' (AGM) – Very popular, hardy, medium-sized, dark ball-headed type.

LATE:

'Stonehead' (AGM) – Large, solid, crisp round cabbage with a white heart. Crops from September and lasts well into autumn.

'Quickstep' (AGM) – Good quality and can take the heat.

Seed to harvest: 20–35 weeks

WINTER CABBAGE is sown in the seedbed in April or May and transplanted when the seedlings have about six leaves in July. Plant slightly deeper than in the nursery bed and tread down the soil. Start harvesting when the heads are firm in November and carry on through to March. Dutch white types or 'winter whites' store well. The Savoy cabbages with their crinkled, blue-tinged leaves are particularly hardy. 'January King', which has many modern cultivars, is noted for flavour as well as for lasting well into spring.

Varieties

'Tarvoy' (AGM) – Extremely hardy, Savoy type.

'Celtic' F1 (AGM) – A cross between a white and a Savoy with a crisp white heart.

'January King 3' and 'Flagship' (AGM) – Crosses between 'January King' and the Savoy cabbage. Very hardy and last well in the ground until spring.

Seed to harvest: 20–35 weeks

SPRING CABBAGE is sown in the seedbed in July or August and planted out in autumn when it has five or six leaves. Timing is critical. It could bolt if sown too soon but won't survive the winter if sown too late. The safe course is to make sowings a couple of weeks apart. As they stay small through winter and put on a spurt when the weather warms up, they are usually planted close together and thinned in spring. The thinnings can be eaten as greens while every third plant is left to heart up. They will be encouraged by a liquid feed in early spring.

Varieties

'Duncan' F1 (AGM) – Early greens which you can keep going all year. Dark green pointed cabbage. Bolt-resistant.

'Myatt's Offenham Compacta' Offenham 1 group (AGM) – Makes good spring greens and

hearting cabbage later. Tasty.
'Pixie' (AGM) – Early and small with a good heart.
Seed to harvest: 20–35 weeks

THE BROCCOLIS

Broccoli came from the Mediterranean in the 17th century. There are three main types. Sprouting broccoli over-winters and is eaten in late winter or early spring. It is an easy and productive plant which produces delectable sprigs for some six weeks on the cut-and-come-again principle. Calabrese (also commonly known as broccoli) has one big head per plant and is a summer crop. Its pretty cousin romanesco is harvested in late summer or early autumn. Perennial broccoli (or 'nine star') comes up every year for harvesting in spring. They are all called broccoli in supermarkets and sometimes in catalogues. To add to the confusion, winter cauliflowers were also known as broccoli until recently.

Sprouting broccoli
Brassica oleracea Italica Group

This is an overwintering hardy plant and the easiest of the group. As it takes up space for the best part of a year, it is not widely grown in gardens but is an excel-lent choice for the allotment. It produces many small florets on succulent stems. It is sown in April or May in the seedbed and trans-planted in June or July for harvesting in late winter or spring. Pick sprigs when the buds are formed but before they flower. Cut the central stem first to encourage side shoots to grow.

Keep picking these a few at a time over the next six weeks. The shoots dwindle in size towards the end of the season.

The aim is to grow sturdy plants which will survive the winter. The soil should be well drained and not too rich in nitrogen as you don't want much soft leaf growth. Don't let the plants dry out. Earth up as winter approaches and cover with netting to protect against pigeons.

Varieties
'Red Arrow', *'Red Head'* and *'Red Spear'* (AGM) – All are noted for hardiness, high yields and flavour.
'Early Purple Sprouting Improved' (AGM) – This will be ready to harvest in February to March. It is a well-tried, popular and tradi-tional choice with a long cropping season.
'Late Purple Sprouting' (AGM) – This is for April picking. It is a good for overwintering and extends the season.
'Early White Sprouting' and *'Late White Sprouting'* – These are white varieties.
'White Eye' and *'White Star'* (AGM) – White varieties noted for their hardiness.
Seed to harvest: 8–12 months

Perennial broccoli

Perennial broccoli or 'nine star' is grown in the same way, though it will need support as it grows up to 90 cm (3 ft) high. At the end of the season in spring, all the white flower heads should be cut off and the plants given a top dressing to build up strength for the following year. Plants are usually replaced every three years. Personally, I wouldn't recom-

mend growing it as it won't be rotated very often and you could be risking an attack of clubroot.

Calabrese

Calabrese is the familiar vegetable with a single head like a small, dark green cauliflower, and is a fast-growing summer treat. The soil should be friable, well-drained and fertile. Station sow two or three seeds where you want the plants to grow in a sunny and sheltered spot. For a succession through summer, sow a few every couple of weeks. Thin to the strongest, leaving 30 cm (12 in) between plants. Don't let them dry out. Romanesco is a pretty form of calabrese. The curd is cone-shaped and lime green. It is harvested in late summer or early autumn.

Varieties
'Shogun' (AGM) – An undoubted star with blue-tinged heads and a fair tolerance of wet weather and a range of soils.
'Cruiser' – A mid-season type which has some resistance to bolting in hot weather.
'Emperor' and *'Citation'* F1 – These are high yielding and have resistance to downy mildew.
'Minaret' – A romanesco calabrese.
Seed to harvest: 11–14 weeks

Cauliflower
Brassica oleracea Botrytis Group

Cauliflowers, which came over from the Mediterranean in the late 18th century, are notoriously temperamental – a challenge even to the most experienced gardener. The seeds often come up 'blind', without a central bud. They are more sensitive to acidity than the other brassicas and generally don't thrive in acid soil even when it has been limed. They dislike being transplanted and hate loose soil. They need a sunny place out of the wind and with top-quality, moisture-retentive soil.

The cauliflower bed should be dug over and limed (if necessary) the autumn before planting, and trodden down hard. A constant level of moisture is essential. For this reason, the early summer varieties, which are ready before the full heat of summer, are the easier choice.

MINI CAULIFLOWERS

These are another good bet. They are sown in April and ready to eat in July. An additional bonus is that, being small and quick growing, they can be sown in situ.

To minimize transplanting shock with the others, grow in modules and transplant early, about six weeks after sowing. Water the evening before you move them. Remember to firm them in thoroughly. Mulch and keep well watered. Cover the curd with the leaves in summer to shade it from the sun, as it will turn it yellow; in winter to protect it from harsh weather.

SUMMER CAULIFLOWERS

These are sown under cloches in September or outside (the easier choice) in April. The minimum germination temperature is 7°C (46°F). The cauliflowers should be ready in June, July or August depending on variety.

Varieties

'*Alpha 5 – Polaris*' (AGM) – Early. Resistant to bolting or 'premature curding'.
'*All the Year Round*' – An old and reliable favourite that can be grown for summer or autumn.
'*Aubade*' (AGM) – This has a good flavour.
'*Doc Elgon*' (AGM) – Late summer. Large cauliflower – a favourite for exhibition.
'*Predominant*' (AGM), 'Garant' and '*Idol*' – These are mini cauliflower varieties.
Seed to harvest: 16 weeks, minis 15 weeks

AUTUMN CAULIFLOWERS

Sow outside mid-April to May and transplanted six weeks later. Remember to keep well watered right through the summer to harvest in autumn.

Varieties

'*Limelight*' (AGM) – An interesting variety being lime green and (comparatively) easy to grow.
'*Plana*' F1 (AGM) – Big and showy.
Seed to harvest: 16 weeks

LATE WINTER or EARLY SPRING CAULIFLOWERS

These need a cold spell. They are the most difficult of the group. While the plants are hardy, the curds are not. Unless your allotment is in a very mild, frost-free part of the country they are not worth trying. Other disadvantages are that they take up a good deal of space for most of the year and come out more like broccoli than cauliflower. They are sown in the cold frame or under cloches in May, and should be transplanted in July for cutting the following late winter or early spring. Protect the curds from frost, rain and direct sunlight by covering them with the leaves. Don't give them too much nitrogen as it will produce soft lush growth that will collapse in the cold.

Varieties

'*Inca*' – Suitable for mild areas. '*Walcherin Winter Armado May*' (AGM) and '*Walcherin Winter 3 – Thanet*' (AGM) – These are hardy as winter cauliflowers go. *Seed to harvest: 40 weeks*

Kale (borecole)

Brassica oleracea Acephala Group

Unlike the sensitive cauliflower, kale comes into its own in the worst of the British winter. It is a useful standby for the hungry gap. Some are gorgeous looking and would brighten up the dreariest of allotments in the cold winter months.

They have real character. 'Chou Palmier', the palm tree cabbage, is like a small palm tree in shape. Curly kale is as bright and frilly as parsley. 'Chou Cavalier', the giant Jersey kale, has a topknot of leaves on a stem so sturdy that it can be made into a walking stick for you to lean on later. There are also the varieties with pink and white markings that were enjoyed for bedding schemes in the 19th century.

Kale is not prone to pests and disease and is the least fussy brassica when it comes to the soil. Make sure it has good drainage and remember to plant firmly. Don't overdo nitrogen fertilizer as

you want to encourage sturdy growth for winter. Sow in May and transplant in July or August. Stake tall varieties, earth up in autumn and tread down once more to prevent wind rock. Pick off yellowing leaves as they appear.

Kale can be harvested from late summer onwards but is at its best after the frosts. If you cut a few young leaves from the crown in early winter you will encourage side shoots to form for picking in the New Year.

Kale sometimes looks bedraggled in early winter but soon perks up, sending out fresh new leaves – only harvest the youngest. Compost the rest as they grow tough and bitter with age. An alternative is to grow a seedling crop under glass in January for cutting a few weeks later as young greens. Once regarded as little more than cattle fodder and peasant food, kales are now all the rage among the chattering classes.

Varieties

'*Darkibor*' F1 – Productive with curly leaves that can be harvested from autumn onwards. Very hardy. '*Nero di Toscana*' – Vigorous plants with crinkled leaves that taste like spring greens. '*Red Russian*' (AGM) – Frilly with reddish leaves and veins. Good flavour. '*Thousand Head*' – An exceptionally hardy old variety. It produces succulent shoots in early spring. Keep picking every few days while young and tender. '*Ragged Jack*' (Heritage cultivar) – The leaves and midribs are tinged pink. *Seed to harvest: from 7 weeks*

Seakale

Crambe maritima

Seakale grows wild on the coasts of the Atlantic, Baltic and Black Sea, so it can cope with the windiest allotment site. Though popular with Victorian gardeners who grew it as a winter substitute for asparagus, it is rarely grown nowadays. It is a hardy perennial that dies back in winter. If the plants are covered over with forcing pots (or an old bucket or bin) to blanch them in November, the young leaves and flowering shoots can be cooked and eaten in late winter and early spring. After two or three cuts, they are uncovered, given a boost of fertilizer (seaweed meal is good) and allowed to build up strength for the following year.

They make handsome plants about 90 cm (3 ft) tall with grey leaves and sweetly scented flowers. If you are serious about harvesting the shoots, the flowers should be removed. Being a coastal plant, seakale is happiest in deep, free-draining sandy soil in an open airy position in sun. Though slow to germinate, it can be grown from seed sown outside in spring. The easier choice is to propagate it from root cuttings or 'thongs' (*see page 44*).

If you have a neighbour with a plant over three years old, they may be happy to give you a few. The thongs are the side shoots of the roots which can be cut off to make new plants. The buds will grow at the plant end of the root. Stand them upright in a pot of sand and leave in a shady place. Rub off all the growing tips bar one and plant out in March with the bud 2–3 cm (about 1 in) below ground. Don't harvest until the following year. The one disadvantage of seakale is that it could encourage pests and diseases as it stays in the same spot for a few years.

Varieties
'*Lily White*' and '*Ivory White*'.

TURNIP, SWEDE AND KOHLRABI

To get the best out of these three vegetables, grow sweet young turnips for spring, early summer and autumn; kohlrabi in summer as it can take the heat, and swedes – the hardiest of the three and the best for storing – for winter use.

Swede

Brassica napus Napobrassica Group

Swedes have nourished man and beast since time immemorial. 'Swedish turnips' are also the classic ingredient for the bashed neeps that go with haggis on Burn's Night. They are sweeter and milder than turnips and the introduction of disease-resistant cultivars has made growing swedes easy.

Prepare the bed in a sunny place in the autumn, liming if necessary. Sow seed under fleece in March or in April to May and thin out when still small – about 2.5 cm (1 in) high. Water regularly but not too much. If kept short of water the roots will go woody. If they are drenched after drying out they may split. Lift swedes as you want them from autumn through to spring or store in a cool dry place in December.

Varieties
'*Marian*' – Purple-top variety, resistant to club root and mildew, good flavour.
'*Best of All*' – An old favourite, hardy and reliable.
'*Ruby*' – Sweet tasting and resistant to mildew.
'*Joan*' and the new variety '*Brora*' – Good for early sowings.
Seed to harvest: 20–26 weeks

Turnip

Brassica rapa Rapifera Group

Turnips, which originated in southern Europe, are faster growing but less hardy than swedes. Providing you deter cabbage root fly with collars, and don't let them dry out or starve, they are easy to grow. They don't mind a little shade and are good for intercropping and successional planting.

The early or 'bunching' turnips, which come flat, cylindrical or round, can be harvested when they are a golf ball size. A cold snap in March can cause bolting so warm the soil with cloches for a couple of weeks before sowing, or wait until the weather is set fair in April or May.

The maincrop turnips are sown in July or August for eating in October onwards. A further sowing of turnips in autumn will give you spring greens in March. Prepare the bed the autumn before planting and lime if your soil is acid. Sprinkle on a general fertilizer. They don't like being transplanted so sow them where you want them to grow. The crop can be lifted in November for storing but they don't keep as well as swedes.

Varieties

EARLY:

'Ivory' and *'Tokyo Cross'* (AGM) – Early and sweet tasting.

'Snowball' – An old variety.

'Purple Top Milan' – Flat, early, with white flesh.

'Golden Ball' – A fast-growing maincrop turnip with yellow skin and flesh.

'Veitch's Red Globe' – An old maincrop variety.

'Market Express' – Late, hardy maincrop with a good flavour.

Seed to harvest: 6–12 weeks

Kohlrabi

Brassica oleracea Gongiloides Group

Kohlrabi comes from northern Europe where it is widely grown as a summer substitute for turnips. It is a strange but decorative vegetable. Unlike swedes and turnips, it is not the root but the swollen stem that is eaten. It comes with pale green, white or purple skin. The purple types are slower but hardier and are usually planted later for autumn eating. As it has a spreading root system, it copes well with dry spells and rarely falls prey to the common cabbage diseases.

Kohlrabi is grown from February onwards in mild areas under cloches, though it is safer to wait as a cold snap can make it bolt. The temperature needs to be over 10°C (50°F). Sow a few seeds every few weeks where they are to grow, from spring through to September. Harvest them when quite small, no bigger than a tennis ball.

Kohlrabi isn't too fussy about soil though it shouldn't be acid, to avoid club root. While not needing copious watering, if

given too little it will become tough and unappetizing. It doesn't store well, so eat shortly after harvesting.

Varieties

'Kongo' and *'Quickstar'* (AGM) – Fast-growing, green varieties.

'Azur Star' – Striking, blue-purple variety.

'Purple Danube' (AGM) – Sweet tasting and purple.

'White Danube' – Juicy white variety.

'White Vienna' and *'Purple Vienna'* – Traditional kohlrabis.

'Purple Delicacy' – An heirloom variety.

Seed to harvest: 8–12 weeks

ORIENTAL BRASSICAS

The Oriental brassicas are fast-growing, naturally healthy plants, excellent for cut-and-come-again in salads and stir-fries. They can be harvested at any time through their growing period. In general, the older the leaves the hotter they get. Some seed companies produce Oriental saladini, stir-fry and spicy mixtures which are ideal for trying out the different types. Some are pretty plants – mizuna greens and pak choi are particularly elegant. Seeds can be sown in succession, outside in the summer and under cover in spring, autumn and winter.

When it comes to growing to maturity, there are one or two points to watch. Most are likely to bolt in the UK, both in hot dry summers and cold springs. The safest bet is to sow in late summer and overwinter under cover for spring eating. Spring sowings,

even under floating mulches, are risky except for mizuna and mibuna greens.

Oriental brassicas need constant moisture, fertile soil and warm temperatures until established. Most have shallow roots which must not be allowed to dry out. New bolt-resistant varieties and F1 hybrids are being introduced from Japan all the time, so watch the catalogues for developments. They are prone to the same pests and diseases as the other brassicas.

Chinese broccoli

Brassica rapa var. *alboglabra*

Chinese broccoli, also known as Chinese kale, tastes like calabrese with a mustardy kick. The young flowering stems in bud are a true delicacy. Probably the easiest of the Oriental brassicas, Chinese broccoli can take some heat and even frost. For a maincrop, sow at any time through summer but the best crops come from seed sown in midsummer for autumn eating. An early autumn sowing under cover should bring a spring crop unless the winter is severe. Harvest the top shoot first to encourage side shoots. Any tough stems can be peeled and cooked.

Varieties

'Green Lance' (F1) – vigorous

'Kailaan White Flowered'

'Tenderstem' – A cross with calabrese.

Seed to harvest: 6–10 weeks

Chinese cabbage

Brassica rapa var. *pekinensis*

Chinese cabbage is the familiar crisp vegetable that looks like a tightly packed pale green cos lettuce. Less familiar are loose-leaved and round types. They make good cut-and-come-again crops. You will get 3 or 4 harvests of tender leaves, followed by the young flowering shoots.

Unlike the others, though, they are quite difficult to grow well to maturity in garden conditions in Britain. They seem to attract cabbage pests and diseases – particularly clubroot. They bolt easily if too cold or too hot. If you are determined, try the F1 hybrids which have some built-in resistance. You need to be vigilant, the soil must be rich and watering copious.

They are best sown in situ in July or August for autumn eating. They can also be sown in May or June under the cover of floating mulches. This is chancy, as is an overwinter crop sown in autumn.

Varieties

'*Spring A1*' and '*Jade Pagoda*' F1 – These are resistant to bolting.
'*Eskimo*' F1 – White leaves at the heart.
Seed to harvest: 8–10 weeks

Komatsuna

Brassica rapa var. *perviridis*
Komatsuna is a group of plants like spinach with a milder kick than the mustard greens. They are hardy and undemanding and can be grown outside without worries. They can be sown from spring, right through summer. For a winter or spring crop, sow in late summer and grow under cover. You can treat them as cut-and-come-again, or allow the plants to mature.
Seed to harvest: 4–12 weeks

Mizuna greens

Brassica rapa var. *nipposinica*
Mizuna greens are a Japanese relation of the turnip. Pretty plants with feathery leaves, they are the hardiest and most heat-tolerant of the Oriental vegetables. It is reasonably safe to sow them in spring in situ under cover once the soil has warmed up. Carry on successional sowing through summer and make the last one in autumn outside for a seedling crop. For mature plants in spring, sow under cover.

Varieties

'*Tokyo Beau*' – Good cold resistance.
'*Mizuna Greens*'
'*Purple Mizuna*'
Seed to harvest: 2–10 weeks

Mibuna greens

Brassica rapa var. *nipposinica*
Mibuna greens are a fairly new arrival. Though less resilient, they are much like mizuna but have long elegant leaves. Make the main sowings in midsummer for an autumn crop or stick to cut-and-come-again.
Seed to harvest: 2–10 weeks

Mustard greens

Brassica juncea
Mustard greens are a diverse group of peppery, leafy plants. They come in many shapes and colours – green, red or purple, with jagged or smooth edges. They are highly nutritious and get hotter as they run to seed. They are grown in the same way as Chinese cabbage but are less temperamental. Start them off in warm, fertile, moist soil outside in July in cold areas (August or

September in warmer ones) to grow on through winter. Early crops are risky. Excellent for cut-and-come-again, or they can be left to mature.

Varieties

'*Green in the Snow*' – With jagged leaves.
'*Red Giant*' – Crinkly red leaves.
'*Sheurifong Improved*' – Resistant to bolting.
Seed to harvest: 2–8 weeks

Pak choi
Brassica rapa var. *chinensis*
Pak choi, or celery mustard, is a delicious fresh green and a practical proposition to grow in the UK. It is great for cut-and-come-again. For mature plants it is best sown in situ in late summer for autumn eating. It can be grown early or late but this is taking a chance. It will bolt if exposed to either cold or long days. It needs the same conditions as Chinese cabbage. Either pick off leaves for baby leaf salads or wait for the mature plant.

Varieties

'*Cantong White*' – With white midribs.
'*Choko*' – With green midribs
'*Joi choi*'
'*Nikaine Taing*' – Bolt resistant.
Seed to harvest: 2–10 weeks

Texcel greens
Brassica carinata
Texcel greens are an exciting new vegetable developed from Ethiopian mustard. They taste like spinach and cabbage combined, with a mustardy, garlic tang. They grow at great speed and are first-class for intercropping or as cut-and-come-again for salads and stir fries. Take great care to eliminate every single weed to avoid eating them by mistake. Keep picking when young, as the leaves coarsen quickly. In the heat of summer they are happiest in light shade. They are ideal for intercropping and undercropping They can be grown outdoors from spring to autumn, though you may want to leave a gap in midsummer as they may bolt in hot weather. The best soil for them is fertile, non-acidic and well drained. However, as they grow so fast you can get away with almost any – some even say in clubroot-infested soil. Broadcast the seed every three weeks for a succession and keep moist.
Seed to harvest: 3–8 weeks

SALAD BRASSICAS
Rocket
Eruca sativa
Peppery rocket leaves are highly fashionable in salads and expensive to buy. They are very easy to grow, though they run to seed quickly. To keep up the supply, wait until one crop is showing a couple of leaves and sow a few more. Make sowings from February to June and from August to October. In the winter months carry on under cloches.

Alternatively grow them as a cut-and-come-again crop. They like moisture-retentive soil and some shade, otherwise they are not particular. Water in dry spells. No particular problems, though they may be susceptible to flea beetle. Being brassicas they should be planted with them and follow their rotation.
Seed to harvest: 4–12 weeks

Summer radish
Raphanus sativa
The summer radish is fast growing. It needs to be harvested as soon as it is ready as it coarsens quickly. Sowing a few seeds every couple of weeks in summer is the best plan. You can start as early as March or April outside if you give it cloche cover.

Radishes like a sunny spot (except in midsummer when they appreciate dappled shade) and fertile, moisture-retentive soil. Keep watered in dry spells but don't overwater as this will encourage leaf growth at the expense of the roots.

Varieties

'*Cherry Belle*' (AGM) – Cherry shaped and coloured. Not too hot, crunchy and delicious.
'*Scarlet Globe*' (AGM) – Good for early cropping under cloches. Round, bright red roots.
'*Summer Crunch*' (AGM) – Long roots, deep pink. Crisp with a good flavour.
'*Easter Egg*' – A white variety.
'*Rainbow Mix*' – Red, white and purple.
Seed to harvest: 4 weeks

Winter radish
Raphanus sativus
Winter radish, including the hot Oriental mooli (or daikon) radish, can grow longer than a parsnip. The smaller ones are eaten in salads while the bigger ones are cooked. The leaves can be used as 'greens'. The autumn varieties have white flesh but the skins can be black, purple, yellow or green as well as red. They are sown in summer for autumn eating and winter storage.

Dig over the ground before planting and remove any stones. They like soil manured for a previous crop, light, free draining but moisture retentive. Rake in some fertilizer before sowing and keep (but not overly) watered. They need to grow fast for best results. They can stay in the ground, protected with straw, until you want them or you can dig them up, twist off the leaves and store them in boxes of sand.

Varieties

'Round Black' – Fast-growing winter radish which keeps well.
'Minawasa Summer' – A Japanese variety with tapering roots, not too hot.

'Green Goddess' – Green skinned with mild flavour. Good for salads and stir-fries. Stands well through Christmas.
Seed to harvest: 20 weeks

THE MOOLI OR DAIKON RADISH is sown in late summer as it needs cool temperatures and short days. Allow one plant to flower so you can collect seed from the pods for the following year.

Varieties

'Sakurajima' – A sweet variety from Japan. Slow growing but lasts well through winter.
'April Cross' F1 – Long white roots, good for salads or cooking.
Seed to harvest: 7–8 weeks

THE BEETROOT FAMILY

Most of the beetroot family, spinach, chards and leaf beets, are grown for their leaves. True spinach has the most delicate taste but is quite temperamental. New Zealand spinach is undemanding and crops over a long period. The chards are just as easy and some are really eye-catching. All need fertile, neutral to alkaline soil with a high nitrogen content and plenty of water in dry weather. Problems are generally few as they grow too fast for anything to get a hold. Downy mildew, leaf spot, shot hole, magnesium deficiency, cutworms, slugs, snails and birds could affect the plants. Spinach beet and chard might get leaf miner or beet leaf spot.

Spinach
Spinacia oleracea

True spinach comes from China and likes cool damp conditions. It will run to seed in hot weather, so consider the new bolt-resistant cultivars. It needs very fertile soil with a high nitrogen content and plenty of organic matter for moisture retention. In poor soil it becomes bitter. It must never be allowed to dry out. It won't tolerate high acidity (aim for pH 6.5–7.5). Treat as cut-and-come-again, or allow to mature.

Traditionally, the summer varieties are smooth-seeded and those that stand through winter have prickly seeds. However, modern breeding has produced seeds that can be planted both for winter and summer use.

Sow summer spinach thinly in situ from March (late February in mild areas) on pre-warmed soil under cloches, or through a plastic sheet mulch. This has the added bonus of keeping the leaves clean. Thin as soon as the plants touch each other by harvesting alternate ones.

Winter varieties are sown in August or September for the following spring. Sow a few batches as timing is something of a guessing game. You want them to be large enough to survive the winter but not to have bolted before the cold weather arrives. They will need winter protection.

Varieties

'Atlanta' (AGM) – Frost resistant with thick, dark green leaves.
'Sigmaleaf' (AGM) – Hardy throughout the British Isles.
'Monnopa' (AGM) – Autumn or summer, vigorous yet slow to bolt, thick leaves.
'Palco' (AGM) – Mildew resistant, slow to bolt.
'Spokane' (AGM) – Mildew resistant, slow to bolt.
Seed to harvest: 2–10 weeks

New Zealand spinach
Tetragonia tetragonioides
This is the spinach that Captain Cook ordered for his crew to prevent scurvy. Unlike true spinach, it has no tendency to bolt in hot summers and is generally easy-going. It is a low and sprawling plant, making good weed cover. Allow plenty of space between plants, about 60 cm (24 in). The seeds have hard coats so soak them overnight before sowing.

Sow outside after all danger of frost has passed as it is not hardy. New Zealand spinach likes a deep, sandy soil. Water in dry periods. Harvest from late June to September, regularly picking the outer leaves. The more you pick, the more will come.
Seed to harvest: 6–7 weeks

Spinach beet and chard
Beta vulgaris Cicla Group
Spinach beet, also known as leaf beet or perpetual spinach, is a more straightforward proposition than true spinach. It doesn't bolt and is resilient enough to withstand seaside conditions – handy if you are on a windy allotment. Excellent for cut-and-come-again crops, it also makes good winter greens outside under cover.

Sow in March or April outside for summer and autumn croppings, and in August for winter leaves. The soil should be fertile. Pick leaves from the outside when young and succulent. If the plants look tired, cut them down to the ground and they will put out fresh growth.

The chards (also known as Swiss chard, and rhubarb or ruby chard) can be treated in the same way. They are the glamorous side of the beet family. Swiss chard, which has marked white veins and leaf stalks and large crumpled green leaves is the tastier type. Rhubarb or ruby chard is a star potager plant and comes in a rainbow of colours. It would certainly cheer up the allotment on dreary winter days. The fleshy midribs can be cooked separately, like asparagus.

Varieties

'Perpetual Spinach' (AGM) – Tough, hardy and succulent.
'Rhubarb Chard' (AGM) – Near-fluorescent scarlet midribs and stems with dark green leaves with a purple tinge.
'Bright Lights' (AGM) – An astonishing plant with a combination of pink, red, orange, purple, gold and green midribs.
Seed to harvest: 12 weeks

Beetroot
Beta vulgaris
Beetroot is an easy crop to grow and rarely suffers from pests or disease. If you use 'bolt-hardy' cultivars you can start them off indoors in spring or sow a few outside every two weeks from April to June for a succession. The choice lies in round, long or oval shaped roots, which are red, yellow or purple in colour or striped. The seed usually comes as 'multi-germ' so several seedlings will appear from each and will need to be thinned out.

Beetroot likes light, sandy, alkaline soil and plenty of sun. Keep them well watered so they don't go woody, giving extra water when the roots begin to swell. When harvesting, twist the leaves off, taking care not to break the skin as beetroots 'bleed'. The globe and long cultivars are best for storage.

Varieties

'Bolthardy' (AGM) – A good bolt-resistant variety excellent for early sowings. Round red type.
'Bonel' (AGM) – Bolt-resistant early cropper. High yielder, round, red and tasty.
'Cheltenham Green Top' (AGM) – An old variety with a tapered root.
'Burpees Golden' – A yellow

variety with orange skin. Doesn't bleed when cut.

'Moneta' – A monogerm type which saves thinning.

'Bulls Blood' – An old variety

with dramatic red foliage.

'Chioggia' – Comes with red and white striped flesh.

Seed to harvest: 8–13 weeks

LEGUMES

The pea and bean tribe have nitrogen-fixing nodules on their roots so they need less fertilizer than other vegetables. Providing you leave the roots in the ground to rot down, they will enrich the soil and their foliage will make a good addition to the compost heap. Runner beans, French beans and broad beans are among the most popular crops, being easy and prolific. The more you pick, the more will come.

French and runner beans are tender and will twine around a support by themselves. Peas and broad beans are hardy, cool weather crops. Supports should go in before planting. Peas cling on by their tendrils and will happily scramble up a row of peasticks or hazel twigs, or netting supported by stakes. There are also leafless varieties that need no support. All need sun to do well.

To give them the best start and avoid the mouse problem, sow the seeds (having soaked them overnight) under cover in a piece of guttering *(see page 41)*. This is a neat way to start them off as you can just slide them off the guttering when transplanting, without disturbing the roots. They can also be station-sown outside with cloche protection. Sow three or four per station outside as others will have their eye on them. As the old saying goes: 'One for the mouse, one for the crow, one to rot and one to grow'.

Once transplanted, keep the plants moist and protect from

weeds with mulch. Keep them on the dry side as this will encourage growth in the leaves rather than the flowers and seeds. Water generously, however, when the plants start to flower to maximize the crops.

Apart from broad beans which like clay, legumes prefer a light but rich soil on the alkaline side (pH 7–7.5). Organic matter should be well mixed into the soil before planting.

Legume problems

Rotation is important. Broad beans are particularly prone to black bean aphid and chocolate spot. Pea and bean weevil, root aphid and red spider mite can occur. French beans can get anthracnose and halo blight. Birds (particularly pigeons), rodents, slugs and snails, can also be a nuisance.

Broad beans
Vicia faba
The broad bean is the only bean that is hardy. It is delicious when eaten younger than you can find

135

in the shops (complete with pods, if young enough). It is a five-star allotment plant. Types vary from dwarf to tall, and variations include green, near-white or red pods – opinions vary as to which are the tastier. The flowers are sweetly scented.

The Longpod types have eight seeds and are very hardy and high yielding. They are the usual choice for early crops. The shorter Windsors, with four seeds, are considered the more epicurean and are generally grown later in the season. Breeders have combined the two for new varieties with the merits of both.

The hardiest varieties can be grown from February onwards under cloches once the soil temperature has reached a minimum 5°C (41°F). They can be sown a row at a time every month for a succession. Switch to maincrop sowings from March to May for beans throughout summer. In mild areas, you can sow in November to overwinter, though this is not without risk. The dwarf types are usually sown for late summer.

The easiest way to support broad beans is to run stakes along the row about 1 m (3–4 ft) apart and tie round with string. While preferring a rich and free-draining soil, broad beans won't fuss unless the soil is waterlogged or very acid. However, it is important to dig it over well as they have a hefty tap root which needs to grow down through it. They like an open, sunny site.

Varieties

'Witkiem Manita' (AGM) – One of the earliest of broad beans for spring sowing, with high yields and a good flavour.

'Express' (AGM) – A strong, hardy plant with mild-tasting beans, good for freezing. The quickest grower for spring planting.

'Aquadulce Claudia' (AGM) – A very hardy Longpod suitable for autumn planting. A top favourite since 1844.

'The Sutton' (AGM) – Dwarf variety, excellent flavour. Prolific and doesn't need staking.

'Red Epicure' – Has attractive red seeds and flowers.

Seed to harvest: spring sown 12–16 weeks, autumn sown 28–35 weeks

French beans (flageolet and haricot)
Phaseolus vulgaris

French beans are well worth growing. An easy and prolific crop, they are a true delicacy when fresh and young. If for some reason you forget to pick them, all is not lost. They will mature into flageolet beans (to be shelled and eaten like peas) and finally into haricot beans for drying and storing. To add to the fun, consider unusual colours – red, purple, yellow and flecked as well as the usual green. They have pretty purple, lilac or white flowers. The beans come flat or pencil shaped. Modern cultivars are usually stringless.

They are fast-growing annual plants from central Mexico and need warm conditions. For good results, don't attempt to grow them before the soil has reached 13°C (55°F). The climbing varieties will cling and can be grown up supports in the same way as runner beans. The dwarf types make low bushes which have the advantage of fitting neatly under cloches in cooler areas.

French beans are self pollinating and like a light, fertile soil of about pH 7. Sow in late spring, having warmed the soil if necessary. If you would like a continuous supply, sow a few seeds every two weeks until midsummer. Mulch well and keep the plants moist. Water copiously when in flower. The more you pick, the more you will get.

For dried haricot beans, pull out the entire plant at the end of the season and hang it out to dry in an airy place.

Varieties
CLIMBERS:

'Algarve' (AGM) – Stringless slicing beans up to 25 cm (10 in) long. Good, consistent cropper with excellent flavour.

'Hunter' (AGM) – Strong-growing, heavy cropper with straight stringless pods, 23 cm (9 in) in length. White seeds. Popular for exhibition.

'Eva' (AGM) and *'Diamont'* (AGM) – Early varieties with long round pods and black seeds. Resistant to bean mosaic virus.

'Barlotta Lingua di Fuocco' – The Italian 'fire tongue' bean has bright green, flat pods with red markings (which disappear when cooked). A delicious bean mostly grown for drying.

DWARF:

'The Prince' (AGM) – Produces masses of delicious, slender, flat pods. Good for exhibition.

'Sprite' (AGM) – Stringless continental variety with dark green, round pods.

'Cantare' (AGM) – Early variety

which is high yielding and resistant to viruses.

'Cropper Tepee' (AGM) – Pencil-podded cultivar with a good high yield. 'Purple Tepee' is the purple version.

Lima or butter beans
Phaseolus lunatus

The butter bean is a decorative tropical plant with white flowers. The climbers can grow to 3 m (10 ft) and take three months to mature, while the fastest-growing bush varieties will be ready in about two months. It is rather unpredictable in the British climate but can be grown in warmer parts if germinated at 18°C (64°F) and planted out in a warm protected spot under fleece. Let the bees get in when it is in flower on sunny days so the plants can be pollinated. It needs well-drained, reasonably fertile soil. Pick when young. The beans can be eaten green or dried, and the sprouted seeds are beansprouts.

Varieties

'Fordhook 242' – A reliable bush variety.
'Christmas Lima' – A productive climber. The beans are white with brown flecks.

Runner beans
Phaseolus coccineus

Runner beans are easy to grow and delicious. Originally brought to Europe from Mexico as ornamentals, they are elegant plants with broad, bright green leaves and red flowers – though there are variations with white and two-tone flowers. They are frost-tender, vigorous climbers, growing to 2.5 m (8 ft) or more. There are also dwarf varieties which are good for early crops under glass.

Runner beans need to be pollinated and like warm, sheltered conditions – the optimum conditions for bees to do their work. The soil should be deep and fertile and at a minimum temperature of 12°C (52°F) before sowing. Warm with plastic or cloches for a few weeks if necessary.

They are self-twining but will need strong supports put in place before planting. The traditional and most practical method is a row of criss-cross poles tied at the crossover point with wire or string, and anchored at each end by a short stake (*see page 56*). Attractive alternatives are to grow them up wigwams or over trellises like any other climber. They combine well with sweet peas.

The seeds can be sown under cover in May (use biodegradable tube pots or root trainers as the roots grow long) and transplanted after the last possibility of frost. Alternatively, sow outside in June or July. Mulch well and keep moist at all times. Pinch out the tips when they reach the tops of their supports. As the flowers appear, give them a really good dousing of water to improve the crop. Keep picking the beans to encourage more to come.

Sometimes runner beans suffer from 'poor setting' when – despite the fact that the plant appears to be in perfect health – the beans are distorted or have dry patches. This can be caused by frost, bad weather resulting in poor pollination, or dry soil.

Varieties

'Enorma' (AGM) – Big cropper, long slim tender beans; good for showing.

'White Emergo' (AGM) – Known for its vigour which helps it to cope with bad weather. Prolific cropper with traditional taste and texture. White flowers and seeds.

'White Lady' (AGM) – A new variety with white flowers, which is very prolific. Said to be less prone to birds and good at coping with high temperatures.

'Desiree' and *'Lady Di'* (AGM) – Almost stringless and prolific croppers.

'Painted Lady' – Introduced in 1855, it is the oldest and most aristocratic variety of runner bean. Exceptionally pretty with scarlet and white flowers, it is sometimes known as 'York and Lancaster'. A very good cropper with plenty of flavour, it can be harvested over many weeks.

'Red Rum' (AGM) – Early variety with little foliage but masses of beans. Halo blight tolerant.

'Scarlet Emperor' – Introduced at the turn of the last century, a great favourite said by many to be unbeatable in flavour.

'Pickwick' – A modern, early, dwarf variety growing no higher than 60 cm (24 in). If picked young, the beans are stringless.

'Hestia' – A new variety which stands clear of the ground (making it easy to pick) and needs no support. Disease resistant. Heavy cropper with red and white flowers. Grows to 45 cm (18 in).
Seed to harvest: 8–12 weeks

Peas, mangetout and snowpeas
Pisum sativum

Young peas, cooked within half-an-hour of picking, before the sugar turns to starch, are ambrosial. While not the simplest of crops to grow, nor the most economic for the space they take, many believe that they are worth every bit of effort.

Probably first cultivated in Turkey centuries ago, peas thrive in alkaline, fertile, light and free-draining soil. Don't attempt to grow them in cold wet clay. They can take a little shade, particularly in the heat of summer. There are different types suited to the changing seasons. The round-seeded varieties are used for the cooler conditions of spring and autumn.

✦ For the earliest peas in May or June, sow early types under cloches in warmed soil in late February or March.

✦ For peas to harvest in June and July, plant wrinkled and round second-earlies in mid-March to mid-April outside.

✦ For peas in August, sow the maincrop wrinkled types. These are taller and slower but are of the best quality and crop more heavily.

✦ For autumn peas in mild areas, make a last sowing in July with fast-growing early round types with mildew resistance.

Some cultivars can be sown at any time which saves a lot of bother. New developments include the leafless and semi-leafless pea which don't need support and are less prone to being eaten by birds. There are also dwarf types with heavy yields. Varieties also include petits pois, sugar snap and mangetout.

Prepare the bed in the autumn, putting at least two bucketfuls of well-rotted compost or manure into each square metre (square yard) of soil. Warm the beds for a few weeks before sowing in February or March. If in doubt, it is safer to wait or to grow the earliest peas in guttering under cover for trans-planting later (*see page 41*). If planting outside, sow individually where they are to grow.

Traditionally they would be planted in a V-shaped trench about 5 cm (2 in) apart. Mulch to keep in moisture. Protect them against mice and birds from the moment they go in. Wire mesh is the most effective method. When the peas have grown to about 7.5 cm (3 in) and put out the first tendrils, put twiggy sticks around them or netting for them to clamber up. Keep moist and give them plenty of water when in flower to improve the crop. When they are ready to harvest, you need to pick them nearly every day to catch them at their best.

Varieties
EARLY:

'Early Onward' (AGM) – A faster-growing relative of the second early *'Onward'*, possibly the most popular pea ever. Disease resistant and a heavy cropper, it is very reliable with plump, dark green pods.

'Kelvenden Wonder' (AGM) – Another classic choice. An early dwarf, it can be grown for any season. Good mildew and pea

wilt resistance.

'*Little Marvel*' (AGM) – Good flavour. Makes a tidy bush to go under cloches and easy to pick.
Seed to harvest: 11–12 weeks
SECOND EARLY:
'*Hurst Greenshaft*' (AGM) – Widely praised variety. Pods grow on the top of the plant which makes for easy picking. Resistant to mildew and fusarium wilt. Good choice for the show bench.
'*Onward*' – Excellent choice. See '*Early Onward*' (above).
Seed to harvest: 12–13 weeks
MAINCROP:
'*Rondo*' (AGM) – Some say this is better than '*Onward*' for quantity and quality of peas – an average of ten peas per pod.
Seed to harvest: 12–13 weeks
PETITS POIS:
'*Waverex*' – The most popular variety.
SUGAR SNAP PEAS:
'*Sugar Snap*'
'*Sugar Anne*'
MANGETOUT:
'*Oregon Sugar Pod*' (AGM) and '*Sugar Dwarf Green*'(AGM) – Both extremely popular heavy croppers, resistant to powdery mildew and virus.
'*Carouby de Maussane*' – Purple flowering. Large flat pods.

Asparagus pea
Lotus tetragonolobus
The asparagus pea is something of a rarity. It is not a pea at all but a small creeping vetch, no higher than 15 cm (6 in) and 60 cm (24 in) wide. It is not a great cropper but is so pretty that perhaps it is worth growing for looks alone. It has enchanting red flowers and the winged pods are a delicacy as long as they are picked when they are young.

As it is a Mediterranean plant, it likes warm dry conditions. It will enjoy a sunny spot in light but fertile soil. Sow seeds under cover in April or May, barely covering the seed. Once hardened off, they will be ready to plant out six weeks later for eating eight or ten weeks after that. A good watering when in flower will help the crop.
Seed to harvest: 14–15 weeks

ROOTS

Carrot, Hamburg parsley, parsnip, Jerusalem artichoke, salsify, scorzonera and sweet potato come from diverse families but they all produce their crops at or below ground level.

These plants do best on soils with plenty of organic matter, though not recently manured. Obviously all need stone-free and well-cultivated soil so the roots can push through effortlessly. If you have heavy clay soil, you can get round it by making a V-shaped trench (or individual holes) filled with proprietary compost – used growbag compost would be fine. The alternative is raised beds or growing them in barrels. Crop rotation (*see page 29*) is important to help to keep down pests and diseases, particularly eelworm and parsnip canker. Root crops are generally sown from seed where they are to grow. They don't transplant well or respond well to 'checking' – so grow them fast and in the best conditions. The aim is to encourage the roots to grow down strongly. Only water if they start to flag, so that they will seek out moisture down in the soil. Protect early crops against cold with fleece.

Carrot
Daucus carota

Carrots are among the most widely grown crops. They come in myriad shapes and forms – long, round or short, yellow, white, purple or orange. There are those for autumn and summer planting and for forcing. When buying, check the packet for the recommended season as new breeding has made the picture even more complicated. In general, use quick-growing Amsterdam and Nantes types for spring. Big maincrop Chantenays are for summer, while Berlicum and Autumn King varieties are for autumn and winter use and for storing.

Carrots are straightforward as long as you get the soil right and take precautions against carrot fly. All need light soil which is easy for the roots to push through. If you haven't got the right soil, grow them in a barrel or raised bed. Go easy on the manure as too much will make them fork.

The earliest crops are sown under a cold frame in February or March in mild areas. Don't sow seed outside until the soil temperature has reached a minimum of 7.5°C (45°F). As the old saying goes: 'Wait to plant carrots until you can work

outside in your shirt sleeves all day'. Sow a few seeds outdoors of different types through the seasons every two weeks from April onwards and you'll have a succession of carrots until early winter. For winter storage, sow carrots in May or June to harvest in October.

Keep carrots on the dry side for sweetness of flavour but not too dry or they will fork. Try to maintain a low but constant level of moisture. Sow the seed, which is as fine as fairy dust, as sparsely as possible by mixing it with silver sand. Thin plants to 10 cm (4 in) apart. Possible carrot problems include carrot fly, root aphids, downy and powdery mildew and violet root rot.

Varieties

'Amsterdam Forcing' – the traditional tried-and-tested first Carrot of the Year.
'Flyaway' (AGM) and *'Sytan'* (AGM) – Breakthrough carrots with good flavour and some built-in resistance to carrot fly. Early.
'Parabel' (AGM) – Sweet round roots. Early.
'Early Nantes' – An old favourite for successional planting.
'Nantes 2' – Follows on for an early main crop. Virtually coreless.
'Panther' (AGM) – Stumpy quick-growing maincrop. Vigorous.
'Autumn King 2' (AGM) – Fine quality, cylindrical, deep orange roots. Stores well and can be left in the ground for some time without losing flavour.
'Kingston' (AGM) – Autumn King type. Handsome carrot, long and pointed. Good for showing and autumn storage

'New Red Intermediate' – A heritage variety. Good show carrot.
'Giganta' – Large Autumn King type, good for showing.
Seed to harvest: earlies 9 weeks, maincrops 20 weeks

Hamburg Parsley
Petroselinum crispum var. *tubersosum*

Hamburg parsley has a root that tastes like parsnip and a leaf that tastes like parsley. Two vegetables in one, it is widely grown in Eastern Europe for soup. Having warmed the soil with plastic, sow in March or April, and cover with cloches. Mulch around them well as it can be slow to germinate and it is important to keep the area moist and free of weeds. The roots should be ready by autumn and can be left in the ground over the winter to harvest when you want them. Though very hardy, cover with straw for safety's sake.

They are generally trouble free, though they may suffer from parsnip canker, carrot fly, downy and or powdery mildew and violet root rot.
Seed to harvest: 30 weeks

Parsnip
Pastinaca sativa

Parsnips, enjoyed since ancient times for their sweet nuttiness in winter, have one drawback – germination can be slow and erratic. To improve your chances, buy seed fresh each year. Parsnips can be given a head start with pre-germination, growing in biodegradable modules or by using the fluid sowing technique (*see page 43*). If you are sowing directly outside (which is preferable if conditions are right) sow three seeds at each station for thinning later. As they are miserable in cold, wet soil, delay until late spring if necessary.

Site them in sun or partial shade. Prepare the ground carefully and warm it for a week or so with polythene. Keep weed free. When the leaves start to droop in autumn, they are ready to harvest. They can be left in the ground right through winter but will begin to go woody towards the end.

It is worth leaving one or two in the ground to produce a tall graceful flower the following summer, not only for your own pleasure but because it will attract beneficial insects.

As parsnips are slow to germinate, try using the old method of marking the row with radishes. Sprinkle the radish seed thinly along the drill and then put in the parsnip seeds, two or three per station. Punch them down if they are in a windy spot. Rake them over and mark the ends of the rows. The radishes will be up in 14 days and by the time you have pulled up the last, the parsnips will be showing.

Generally trouble free, though they may suffer parsnip canker, carrot fly, downy and powdery mildews or violet root rot.

Varieties

'Tender and True' (AGM) – An old variety. Nearly coreless, sweet tasting and canker resistant. Tapering roots for deep soil and exhibition.

'Cobham Improved Marrow' (AGM) – Canker resistant, a popular stubby, wedge-shaped

parsnip with good flavour.
'Gladiator' F1 – High resistance to canker. Vigorous.
'White Gem' – With broad 'shoulders' and white skin. Resistant to canker. Heavy cropper. Sweet flavour and not too fussy about soil.

Jerusalem artichoke
Helianthus tuberosus

The Jerusalem artichoke is not related to the globe artichoke but has a similar flavour. It makes a leafy screen up to 3 m (10 ft) high – excellent for some privacy in summer or as a wind break. It is an easy crop to grow.

You can order them from seed merchants or just buy some tubers from the greengrocer to plant in early spring. Choose tubers about the size of an egg. Plant these in spring 10–15 cm (4–6 in) apart.

They will thrive in most soils, though moisture-retentive, sandy soil will produce the best tubers. Stake and earth them up as they grow if you are on a windy site. Let the plants grow on through summer.

Water in dry spells and remove flowers to improve the crop. Cut them right down a month after flowering or after frost has killed off the tops. Leave the tops over the patch for winter protection. Jerusalem artichokes don't store for long, so dig them up as you want them through winter. Clear the ground in spring and replant a few for the next year's crop. If you don't get them all out, they can become rampant.

They are generally trouble free, though wireworms and slugs may be a problem.

Varieties

'Dwarf Sunray' – This variety doesn't need peeling.
'Fuseau' – An old French variety with long, smooth tubers.
Planting to harvest: 20 weeks

Salsify
Tragopogon porrifolius

Salsify, the vegetable oyster, is a biennial root vegetable from Southern Europe. The white roots, young shoots and flower buds can be cooked like asparagus.

It is slow to grow and you don't get a great deal to eat from it. However, it is a pretty plant and if left unharvested until the following spring, it will produce purple daisy flowers which attract useful predators.

Prepare the ground so that the tap root can push through with ease. Salsify likes fine sandy soil not recently enriched as this can make the roots fork. If you don't have the right conditions, dig a long trench and fill it with sandy soil or compost. Plant seeds in spring about 30 cm (12 in) apart in a sunny spot.

The roots should be ready from October onwards and can be left over the winter to lift when you want them. The roots are quite brittle, so take care when you lift them. If you find that the roots have forked, leave the plant to make new shoots and buds to harvest the following spring. These are generally trouble-free plants.

Varieties

'Mammouth Sandwich Island'
'Mammouth White'
'White Skinned' – Very hardy.

Scorzonera
Scorzonera hispanica

Apart from having a black skin and yellow flowers in summer, scorzonera is very similar to salsify. It should be treated in the same way. The big difference is that it is a perennial so if you discover the roots are not worth harvesting, leave the plant to grow on for another year. Generally no problems.

Varieties

'Russian Giant' – Long rooted, black skinned, very hardy.
'Habil' – Possibly the best for flavour.
'Long Black Maxima'
'Black Giant Russian' – Very hardy.

Sweet potato
Ipomoea batatas

The sweet potato is widely grown in tropical countries. It needs a sunny and sheltered spot – aim to create a little patch of Peru. It likes a rich, sandy soil (pH 5.5–6.5), dug over well with plenty of compost and a general fertilizer.

Sweet potatoes are usually grown from 'slips' in the UK to give a head start in our short summers. As they need four months to mature, you really need to plant in May to get a long enough stretch for the tubers to grow to maturity. However don't plant before the soil has reached at least 12°C (52°F). To maximize your chances, warm the soil with black polythene or cloches before the tubers arrive. If the conditions aren't right, they can be stored for a few days in a bucket with the roots in water.

Plant them 15 cm (6 in) deep and 30 cm (12 in) apart with at least two leaf nodes buried under the soil. To keep them warm, grow them through fleece, black polythene or under cloches. Keep well watered throughout their growth and avoid damaging the tubers when hoeing off the weeds. With luck they can be harvested in the same way as potatoes in September. The ones with orange or yellow flesh are the sweetest. They may suffer from leaf spot.
Planting to harvest: 16 weeks

ONIONS

Bulb onions, leeks, garlic, Japanese bunching onion, pickling onion, shallot, spring onion and the Welsh onion are closely related. All need an open site with plenty of air circulation to avoid downy mildew. They dislike acid soil so liming may be necessary to bring the pH to 7 or more. The aim is to grow them dry and hard. Once they have established, only water if they show the earliest signs of wilting. The soil needs to have organic matter mixed in ahead of time as onions grown in freshly manured ground will grow soft and be more susceptible to disease. Buying sets of certified bulb onions is recommended for ease of cultivation and speed. The heat-treated ones are resistant to bolting. Growing from seed has the advantage of offering a wider choice of types and less chance of bolting as well. It is cheaper but takes longer. If you want small onions, plant them close together. If you prefer larger ones, space them wider.

ONION PROBLEMS

The onion family is prone to fungal diseases, particularly onion neck rot and onion white rot. Others are eelworm, onion fly, virus and bolting. Sparrows like to pull the newly planted onions right out of the soil. Dig out (carefully), replant and protect with fleece or netting. Put up bird scarers.

Bulb onions
Allium cepa

The bulb onion comes with brown, yellow, white or red skin and can be bulb shaped, flattened or elongated.

GROWING FROM SETS: plant out when recommended in spring, so that the tips just show. You can hold off planting them out by potting them up if the soil is too cold and wet. Water them until established. The ones which have been heat-treated against bolting – a process that takes several months – go in a little later.

Autumn-planted onions are a fairly recent development. They will only store for about three months but mature in midsummer when you might have a gap. Treat in exactly the same way as the common onion but plant sets in autumn.

SOWING FROM SEED: Sow seed in late winter indoors at 10–16°C (50–61°F). Keep them on the cool side when germinated, about 13°C (55°F). Prick out when they are 1 cm (½ in) high. Harden off and plant out when they have two true leaves in spring.

Alternatively, having warmed the ground, sow outside under cloches in early spring when the ground is workable. Use the thinnings as spring onions. The onions can be harvested 'green' or when ripened in late summer (*see page 67*).

Varieties
FROM SETS:
'Centurion' (AGM) – Heavy cropper, early maturing, good for storing.
'Struron' (AGM) – Big globe-shaped, straw-coloured onions.

Resistant to bolting, excellent flavour, will store until the following spring.

'Turbo' (AGM) – Globe type with golden skin. Slow to bolt with a good yield.

'Rijnsburger 5 Balstora' – A pale yellow globe. Good keeper.

'Radar' – For autumn planting. Good tolerance to bad weather. Early maturing, mild and crunchy.

'Silvermoon' – An early variety for autumn or spring planting. Round with white flesh.

Sets to harvest: spring planted 18–20 weeks, autumn planted 40 weeks

FROM SEED:

'Red Baron' – Flashy red-skinned onion with concentric red and white rings inside.

'Rayolle de Cevennes' – Big onion with yellow skin, mild and sweet from Cevennes in France.

'Ailsa Craig' – Old-fashioned heavy cropper. Winner of many shows.

Seed to harvest: 20–24 weeks

Shallots
Allium cepa Aggregatum Group

Shallots are just the same as onions except they grow in a bunch, are smaller and less prone to disease. They take longer to grow but are ready earlier, to fill the gap until the onions appear. They can be used for cooking or pickling, even for salads.

Shallots are usually planted as sets as early as January in mild areas. If grown from seed, you will just get one bulb so you might as well grow onions instead. Shallots will be ready to harvest by July or August. You can save some of the bulbs to plant and grow on the following year.

Varieties

'Sante' – A big round shallot with brown skin and pinkish flesh. Stores well and yields prolifically. Mild taste.

'Golden Gourmet' – Yellow skinned, pear shaped, stores well.

'Piquant' – Bolt resistant with brown skin.

'Topper' – Round golden bulbs which store exceptionally well.

'Hative de Niort' – Pear-shaped bulbs, dark skin – a favourite for exhibition.

Sets to harvest: 20–24 weeks

Japanese onions
Allium fistulosum

Japanese onions, also known as 'short day' onions, are planted in late summer for early crops the following year. Before the invention of the autumn-planted onions, they were the only way to get fresh bulb onions in June.

The planting time for Japanese onions is tricky and critical – plant them too early they may bolt in spring and too late and they won't survive the winter. You want them to be at least 15–20 cm (6–8 in) tall by the time the first frosts arrive.

If you are growing Japanese onions from seed, sow a few outside at two week intervals through August, earlier in the north and later in the south. Sets are sturdier and can be planted in September to November.

Varieties

'Express Yellow' F1 – Matures two months ahead of the main crop.

'Keepwell' F1– Good for storing, with flattened round bulbs.

Seed to harvest: 40 weeks

Sets to harvest: 28–36 weeks

Pickling onions
Allium cepa Cepa Group

These are sown from seed outside in spring. Plant close together and don't bother to thin. If you want to keep them white, sow them deep at 5 cm (2½ in) down. Just as with ordinary bulb onions, you can tell that they are ready when the leaves die down. They can be stored in just the same way or pickled.

Varieties

'Paris Silverskin' – Pearly white cocktail onions for stews or for pickling.

'Jetset' – Mini brown-skinned onion. Matures quickly and is resistant to bolting.

'Purplette' – The first purple-skinned variety. Can be harvested early for salads. The flesh turns pink when pickled or cooked.

'Shakespeare' – Reliable, brown-skinned variety.

Seed to harvest: 20–24 weeks

Welsh onions
Allium fistulosum

Welsh onions are like coarse chives with hollow stems, 30–45 cm (12–18 in) tall. They are a common ingredient in Chinese and Japanese cooking and useful for winter salads. Coming from Siberia (not Wales) they are perfectly happy standing out through winter and need little attention. Though most are perennials, they are usually treated as annuals. Modern cultivars are self-blanching. Spring-sown seeds should be ready by autumn, and those sown in late summer are ready the following spring. Treat exactly like bulb onions and keep the area free of weeds.

Varieties

'*Welsh Red*' – Hardy plants from Siberia with a strong flavour.
Seed to harvest: 24 weeks

Japanese bunching onions
Allium fistulosum

The Japanese bunching onion is a refined version of the Welsh onion, rather like a cross between a spring onion and a leek. Seed can be sown at any time from spring and they can be cropped in six weeks. They can be pulled out or snipped at any time for a bit of onion flavour or left in the ground where they will continue to grow for many months, finally reaching leek proportions. They carry on through mild winters.

Varieties

'*Ishikura*' – Long white stems. Fast grower.
'*Kyoto Market*' – Good for early sowings.
'*Redmate*' – Interesting red-tinged base to the stems.
Seed to harvest: 6 weeks onwards

Spring onions
Allium cepa

Sow seed every two or three weeks for non-stop production from early spring to midsummer. The hardier types can go on well into autumn.

Varieties

'*Ramrod*' (AGM) – Long straight white stems. Good for frequent sowing, and hardy.
'*White Lisbon*' – Quick grower for successional crops.
'*Deep Purple*' – New cultivar with violet, torpedo-shaped bulbs.
Seed to harvest: 12 weeks

Garlic
Allium sativum

Garlic bulbs come in pink, purple and white, with various strengths of flavour. As long as they have sunshine, they are really easy to grow. They can be eaten green or dried. You need to start off with bulbs from a nursery or seed merchant, as they will be certified free of disease. After that you can grow from your own stock. Garlic seems to adapt to any given conditions over time so you can develop your own allotment strain.

Garlic is grown from cloves as it doesn't set fertile seed. Some types produce a flower stem. If you cut it back by half a couple of weeks before flowering, the bulbs will be substantially larger. Elephant garlic needs no further description. The flavour varies from mild to strong. It should be harvested just before the flower opens in mid summer.

In the UK, garlic is planted in autumn or winter as it needs a month or two of cold weather at 0–10°C (32–50°F). Split up the cloves, discarding any weaklings, and plant the right way up, 7.5–10 cm (3–4 in) deep in light sandy soil. They need little attention apart from weeding and watering in dry spells. When the leaves go yellow the following late spring or summer, dig them up, taking care not to bruise them. Dry outside or in an airy shed for a week or so.

Varieties

'*Early Wight*' – Adapted to the British climate on the Isle of Wight. Purple variety, early.
'*Thermidrome*' – Selected for our

climate. Plant in November.

'Elephant' – Just that. Mild, sweet flavour.

Clove to harvest: 16–36 weeks

Leeks
Allium porrum

If sprouts and spuds are the commoners, the leek is king on the allotment. It is the subject of much friendly contest in Durham and thereabouts. A hardy crop for winter picking, leeks come as earlies (from late summer) and maincrop (lasting right through to spring), and slim or stout types. They are easy to grow and will rarely sicken.

Early varieties are slim, tall and less hardy than the others. Sow seed in spring in the cold greenhouse, cold frame or nursery bed when the temperature is at least 7°C (46°F) between March and May. Warm the soil if necessary with polythene. When the young leeks are about 20 cm (8 in) tall, they will be ready to be hardened off for transplanting any time between June and August.

If you are moving them to the potato patch, a dressing of nitrogen will be helpful. Make holes with a dibber and drop the leeks in.

Don't backfill as they are delicate little wands at this stage. Contrary to general practice, don't trim the roots. Just water them in. As they grow, earth them up a little to keep the stems white. Try not to get soil between the leaves.

Alternatively, place collars (small sections of plastic pipe or cardboard tubes will do) around the necks. Keep watered until they are established. The maincrop leeks are spaced more widely and can be dug up through winter.

Varieties
EARLY:

'King Richard' – An abundant cropper with long white 'shanks' and a mild taste.

'Jolant' (AGM) – Long season of cropping for an early type.

'Mammouth Blanch' – Starts late summer.

MAINCROP:

'Autumn Giant Cobra' (AGM) – Medium length, bolt resistant.

'Toledo' (AGM) – Early winter to late spring.

'Upton' (AGM) F1 – Good rust resistance.

'Bleu de Solaise' – A fine blue-leafed leek from France. Carries on until spring.

Seed to harvest: 16–20 weeks

FRUITING VEGETABLES

Tomatoes, aubergines, peppers and sweetcorn come from hot countries and need long summers to ripen. Some cold resistance in contemporary F1 seed has made it much easier to grow them outside in Britain.

If you grow these plants from seed you will need to give them your attention for many weeks, keeping them at a minimum temperature of 16°C (61°F) for germination and a few more degrees warmth for the seedlings. This can be done in a heated propagator, followed by a sunny windowsill. Make sure the temperature doesn't drop below this at night. You can save yourself a lot of bother by buying young plants from a reputable nursery or garden centre, though you won't have the same choice of interesting varieties.

Choose the sunniest, most sheltered spot for them and warm the soil with plastic sheeting for a week before planting out. Either grow through slits in the sheets or mulch well to prevent evaporation and to keep down the weeds.

Fruiting vegetables are rather insatiable and need fertile soil with plenty of organic material incorporated, a general fertilizer applied before planting and top-ups of liquid feed. They also need good drainage. When they are in flower and fruit, watering should be copious.

Tomato
Lycopersicum esculentum

The tomato is native to South America. It is well worth growing as, freshly picked from the vine, it is delicious. There is huge diversity in size from the giant beef tomatoes down to tiny cherry ones. There are wonderful heritage varieties and a fun range coming in green, yellow, purple, even striped, and in an assortment of different shapes.

The two main divisions, however, lie between vine (indeterminate) and bush (determinate) varieties. The vine tomatoes are usually grown in the greenhouse. They produce a main stem which needs to be tied onto a sturdy central support as the plant can become top heavy. As they grow, the side shoots are pinched out and, towards the end of summer, the leader is 'stopped' (or nipped out) to make the plant concentrate less on growing ever taller and more on producing fruits. The bush varieties are more practical for outside as they don't need training. Growing in the open air makes them less prone to disease and produces tastier crops.

Raise the seeds in a greenhouse, or at home on a windowsill, in early April or six to eight weeks before the last frost. Pot on when there are three true leaves. Harden off in May when the flowers are just forming and plant out in June, weather permitting.

Some of the problems include aphids, red spider mite, blossom end rot, mosaic virus, potato blight and virus.

Varieties

CHERRY TOMATOES:
'Gardener's Delight' (AGM) – One of the most popular tomatoes ever. It never stops producing trusses of sweet cherry tomatoes.
'Sweet Million' (AGM) – Non-stop tiny sweet fruits.
'Sun Baby' (AGM) – Yellow fruited. Prolific.
Seed to harvest: 7–12 weeks
BUSH TOMATOES:
'Tornado' (AGM) F1 – Generous cropper. Large fruit with good flavour.
'Tigerella' (AGM) – Medium-sized tomatoes with decorative stripes.

'Shirley' (AGM) F1 – Quick to mature and disease resistant.
Seed to harvest: 7–12 weeks
VINE TOMATOES:
'Alicante' (AGM) – Another great favourite. Prolific and reliable.
'Yellow Perfection' (AGM) F1 – Popular old variety. Productive and juicy.
'Beefsteak' – Strong and tall growing with hefty fruits.
Seed to harvest: 7–12 weeks

Aubergine
Solanum melongena

Aubergines are grown in the same way as tomatoes, though they are even more sensitive to cold and take longer to grow. Their ideal temperature when ripening is 25–30°C (77–86°F). They can be grown outside in hot summers if started off in the greenhouse. Soak the seed overnight before sowing in spring at 20°C (68°F). Pot on when there are three true leaves. Hold off planting them out under a cloche until the minimum temperature at night is above 15°C (59°F). Taller varieties will need a stake.

For sizeable fruits, restrict each plant to five by nipping off any additional buds. Give a liquid feed weekly. Harvest while the fruits are still shiny. When they go dull they are bitter. Aubergines are usually purple but there are violet and pink varieties, even white ones the size of an egg.

Possible problems include aphids, whitefly, red spider mite and botrytis.

Varieties
'Black Beauty' F1 – Good old stager with big purple fruits.

'*Moneymaker*' F1 – An early variety bred to cope with slightly cooler conditions. Good flavour.
'*Easter Egg*' – A modern variety. It is a quick grower with small white fruits.
'*Violetta di Firenze*' – A pretty violet version, which is occasionally striped.
Seed to harvest: 16–24 weeks

Peppers and chillies
Capiscum annuum
Sweet peppers, bell peppers and chillies are native to Mexico and Central America. They grow fast. The hotter the weather, the more fiery they become. Sow seed under cover in March or April, potting on or transplanting into growing bags when there are three true leaves. Keep the plants warm until they can go outside under cloches when night temperatures are over 16°C (61°F). Ideally, this should be when the first flowers are forming. They will need staking. Feed weekly and keep well watered. Pick the fruits while still shiny and green, to encourage more to come.

They may suffer attacks from slugs, whitefly, red spider mite and aphids.

Varieties
SWEET PEPPERS:
'*Gypsy*' (AGM) F1 – Large pale yellow pepper, red when ripe. Prolific and popular.
'*Canape*' (AGM) F1 – Bred for cool climates. Good yields of red fruits. Ready in 60 days.
'*Lipstick*' – Productive and easy. Green turning to red.
'*Ace*' (AGM) F1 – Fast maturing, large green pepper.

CHILLIES:
'*Ring of Fire*' – Cayenne type. As it turns from green to red it lives up to its name.
'*Jalapeno*' – A fiery ingredient in Mexican cooking. Dark green changing to red.
'*Tabasco Habanero*' – This will blow your head off. Used in West Indian sauces.
Seed to harvest: 20–28 weeks

Okra
Abelmoschus esculentus
Okra does need a constant temperature between 20–30°C (68–80°F). Unless you can grow it in hothouse conditions, it is best bought as a young plant and kept under a cloche in rich soil in the sunniest and most sheltered spot. It will need staking. Cut the pods as soon as they form before they become stringy. Possible attacks from aphids, red spider mite and whitefly.

Variety
'*Clemson's Stringless*'

Sweetcorn
Zea mas
Sweetcorn, freshly picked and barbecued before the sugar turns to starch is a treat not to be missed. Modern American cultivars include the 'supersweet' types which are very sweet indeed and take longer to grow. There are also quick-maturing varieties more suited for the British climate. Sow seed under cover in April at 10°C (50°F) in modules (root trainers or tubes) as sweetcorn resents disturbance.

Warm the soil at the end of May or beginning of June with polythene. It needs to be at least 16°C (61°F). It is a good idea to plant through the polythene for extra warmth and to keep down weeds. Cover with cloches. Corn has shallow roots so don't hoe around them. Plant in a block about 30 cm (12 in) apart to encourage wind pollination. Earth up the plants as they grow for extra root anchorage. A good watering when in flower and when the kernels are swelling will improve the crop. When the tassels, or 'silks', turn brown, the corn is ripe. Test it further by pushing a fingernail into a kernel. If the juice is milky, it is ready to eat. Sweetcorn suffers few problems, apart from mice and birds.

Varieties
'*Sundance*' (AGM) F1 – Good vigorous variety for the UK.
'*Kelveden Sweetheart*' – A fast maturing variety with long, well-filled cobs.
'*Start-up*' (AGM) – A supersweet variety.
'*Conquest*' – Supersweet, early and better than most on cold soil.
'*Honey and Cream*' and '*Peaches and Cream*' – With white and yellow seeds.
Seed to harvest: 16 weeks

CUCURBITS

Courgette, marrow, summer squash, pumpkin, winter squash, cucumber and gherkin all belong to the same family of half-hardy plants. They are bushy, trailing annuals, so fast growing that they can be sown outside to fruit in a short British summer. They need sunshine and shelter, pre-warmed soil, cloche cover (with ventilation in summer to avoid scorching) and a good supply of water and nutrients. They prefer soil on the acid side, about pH 6–6.5.

Cucurbits have male and female flowers on the same plant and you will need to remove any covers when they are in flower for the insects to pollinate them. Thirsty plants, they benefit from having a piece of open-ended pipe, or a sawn-off plastic bottle inserted into the ground to get water down to the roots. It is almost impossible to give them too rich a diet and many people grow them in the manure or compost heap.

Courgette, marrow and summer squash
Cucurbita pepo

Courgette, marrow and summer squash are variations on a theme. The courgette is just a young marrow, so you can get two different crops from the same plant if you let a few grow on to maturity. Summer squashes come in amusing shapes.

All are easy, vigorous and give a prolific harvest. Sow indoors in early May at 18°C (64°F) or outside in late May on pre-warmed soil under cloches. You can time it to two weeks before the end of frosts or be safe and wait until they are over. You can grow them up sturdy posts, pinching out the top when it reaches the desired height. Feed at least once a fortnight with liquid feed and keep well watered. Harvest them by cutting them off when young and succulent to encourage more to come. They should be eaten fresh as they don't store. They may suffer from powdery mildew, cucumber mosaic virus, slugs and snails. In the cold frame, red spider mite and whitefly may attack.

Varieties

COURGETTES:
'Bambino' (AGM) – Small, tender fruits. Early and prolific.
'Early Gem' (AGM) – Dark green, lots of fruits.
'Jemmer' (AGM) F1 – Prolific yellow variety.
'Defender' (AGM) – Dark green, good resistance to cucumber mosaic virus.
'Rondo di Nizza' – A round Italian courgette.
Seed to harvest: 6 weeks
OTHER MARROWS:
'Tiger Cross' (AGM) F1 and *'Badger Cross'* (AGM) F1 – Both are resistant to cucumber mosaic virus.
'Long Green Trailing' – Prolific traditional striped marrow.
Seed to harvest: 7–8 weeks
SUMMER SQUASH:
'Sunburst' F1 – Yellow flying-saucer-shaped fruit.

'Vegetable Spaghetti' – Pale yellow. When cooked the flesh inside looks just like spaghetti.
'White Patty Pan' – With a pretty scalloped edge.
Seed to harvest: 6 weeks

Pumpkin and winter squash
Cucurbita maxima

Pumpkins and winter squash develop a hard skin and are usually grown for winter storage, though they can be eaten when immature like courgettes. Winter squashes have real character. Types include the turban, the warted hubbard, buttercup and banana. They are mostly large, sprawling plants though there are bush varieties. As they take between three and five months to mature, sow around the end of April indoors in modules.

Plant out in the same way as courgettes and marrows. In mild areas, they can be sown in situ after the frosts. Mark the centre with a stick so you can see where to water. They make a good, strong root system so they are not as thirsty as courgettes and marrows once established. Put a layer of straw or a board under the fruits to keep them clean. Let them ripen in the ground until they sound hollow when tapped. Dry them further in the sun, underside up, before storing.

Varieties
WINTER SQUASH:
'Turk's Turban' – The name describes the shape. Possibly the most exotic, it has orange, cream and green splotches and stripes. Good for soup.
'Crown Prince' – A more modest

character with grey skin but delicious, nutty orange flesh.
'Crown of Thorns' – Spherical with spikes.
'Butterball' – Bred to mature in three months, so a good choice for the UK climate. Sweet tasting orange flesh.
Seed to harvest: 12–20 weeks
PUMPKINS:
'Atlantic Giant' – Truly gigantic. The world-wide, record-breaking, exhibition pumpkin.
'Triple Treat' – Perfect for Halloween. Not too big, it is round and orange with tasty flesh. The seeds are great for toasting.
Seed to harvest: 12–20 weeks

Cucumber and gherkin
Cucumis sativus

Modern breeding of Japanese and 'Burpless' cucumbers have made it possible to grow swish hothouse types out in the open. Cucumbers were traditionally divided into indoor and outdoor types. The greenhouse types are longer, more elegant and have smoother skins than their country cousins – the rugged, ridged, outdoor varieties. They are also trickier to grow and more susceptible to pests and disease. Gherkins are just small cucumbers grown for pickling, though they can be eaten fresh.

Sow outdoor cucumbers under cover at 20°C (68°F) in late spring, timing it a month before the last frosts. Sow in biodegradable modules as cucumbers resent disturbance. Sow two seeds in each module and thin to the strongest. Keep the seedlings warm (no lower than 16°C or 61°F at night).

Don't be too free with watering at this stage as they are prone to damping off.

The traditional way to plant out is to make ridges, hence the name 'ridge' cucumber. A couple of weeks before the plants are ready to go out, dig a trench, half-fill it with well-rotted manure or compost and pile back the soil on top to make a ridge. Plant out at the three-leaf stage under cloches, a little less deeply than before to avoid neck rot. Another option is to sow straight outside in June, or when the soil temperature is 20°C (68°F).

Cucumbers can be grown on the ground or trained up a wigwam, trellis, wires or netting. This is practical as it has the double effect of keeping the fruits clean and protecting them from slugs. Stop the plant by nipping out the growing tip when it reaches the top of the support.

Keep well watered, and mulched. When the plants are in flower, remove any covers so the insects can pollinate them. Give liquid feeds, particularly when the fruits form. Harvest before they go yellow.

Problems include cucumber mosaic virus, slugs, aphids, red spider mite in hot weather, powdery mildew and neck rot.

Varieties
OUTDOOR CUCUMBERS:
'Marketmore' (AGM) – Ridge type, high yielding. Resistant to cucumber mosaic virus. Good for cooler climates.
'Bush Champion' (AGM) F1 – Compact. Resistant to cucumber mosaic virus.
'Burpless Tasty Green' F1 –

Mildew resistant, crisp and well flavoured. Good cropper. Possibly the best of the new outdoor varieties producing glasshouse quality.

'Tokyo Slicer' – Japanese variety with slender fruits. Perfect for cucumber sandwiches.

'Crystal Lemon' – An interesting cucumber that looks not unlike a lemon with a tangy taste. It can be used for pickling as well as eating.

Seed to harvest: 12 weeks
GHERKINS:
'Fortos' (AGM)
'Gherkin' – Fast growing with masses of small prickly fruits.
'Vert Petit de Paris' – Prolific, tasty French variety.
Seed to harvest: 12 weeks

SALAD LEAVES

The price of gourmet salad leaves is perfectly ridiculous when it is so easy and cheap to grow them on the allotment. With a little thought, you can have a constant supply.

Chicory, corn salad, endive, frilly lettuce, mustard and cress, rocket, summer and winter purslane and the Oriental brassicas are fast growing plants and can provide you with gourmet salads all the year round.

There are just a few points to watch. Leaf salads are sensitive to temperature. The ideal is within the range of 10–20°C (50–68°F). Any lower and germination will be erratic and established plants may bolt, any higher will make them coarse and unappetizing. For this reason, it is best to start them in modules either in the propagator or covered with a plastic bag at home where the temperature can be controlled.

If growing outside, cover early sowings with a cloches or fleece. When the weather is warm, sow in dappled shade. Salad leaves, being fast and low growing, are ideal for intercropping, under-cropping and catch cropping. If you choose suitable cultivars you can keep endive, chicory, corn salad and rocket going through winter with protection or through forcing along with cut-and-come again salad crops.

Lettuce
Luctuca sativa

The easiest to grow are the loose-leaved types like 'Lollo Rossa' and 'Salad Bowl'. You can buy mixtures of these which should set you up for summer. They are good for cut-and-come-again, and are slow to bolt. Among the cos types, the mini lettuces like 'Little Gem' are pretty reliable, hardy and quick growing. The big cos lettuces are also hardy but slow to mature and best in spring. The hearting types – crisphead lettuces like 'Iceberg' and the cabbage-like butterheads – are more demanding, needing large quantities of water and fertilizer.

The earliest lettuces can be sown indoors from winter to early spring and transplanted out in early spring under cloches. Lettuces for summer can be sown where they are to grow. If you sow a few seeds every couple of weeks from spring until midsummer you will have a continuous supply until autumn. Many are pick-and-come-again which saves trouble. Hardy lettuces planted in autumn will stand out through winter (under cloches or in the cold frame) in mild areas. In colder places they can be sown in late winter for spring eating.

Lettuces like a cool germination temperature 10–20°C (50–68°F) and an open sunny situation in sandy, fertile, moisture-retentive soil with free drainage. If your soil is heavy and wet, it is best to raise the beds. If the temperature is over 25°C (77°F) in the day, lettuce seed can become dormant several hours after sowing, so wait until evening. Soil which has been fertilized for a previous crop is ideal. They shouldn't need any fertilizer unless the soil is poor. Thin when about 5 cm (2 in) high.

If sowing indoors, use biodegradable modules as lettuces suffer badly from transplanting shock. Move them when they have six leaves, taking care to plant them so the leaves are just clear of the ground.

Lettuces may suffer from aphids, cutworms, slugs, snails, and tip burn.

Varieties

LOOSE LEAF LETTUCES:
'Salad Bowl' – A pretty frilly green lettuce.
'Red Salad Bowl' – The same as above with bronzy red tints.
'Oak Leaf' – An old variety aptly named. Green with brown tints.
'Lollo Blonda' – The pale green

version of 'Lollo Rossa'.
Seed to harvest: 4–14 weeks, depending on season and variety
COS LETTUCES:
'Little Gem' – A winner since the 19th century. A small but delicious, it is a good candidate for early sowings. Everyone's favourite.
'Lobjoit's Green Cos' (AGM) – Delicious old variety. Spring and summer.
'Winter Density' – A first-class candidate for winter growing under a cloche or coldframe. Dark green with a good heart. Medium sized.
'Pinnokkio' (AGM) – Disease tolerant. Crisp and sweet tasting. Medium sized.
Seed to harvest: 4–14 weeks, depending on season and variety
CRISPHEADS AND BUTTERHEADS:
'All Year Round' – A winner for spring, summer or winter.
'Webb's Wonderful' – A popular and reliable variety.
'Minigreen' (AGM) – A neat little crisphead, just right for one.
Seed to harvest: 4–14 weeks, depending on season and variety

Endive
Cichorium endiva

Endives are generally trouble-free, bitter, lettuce-like plants. They make a good addition to the salad bowl, especially off-season. The new cultivars are not as bitter as the old, unless left to coarsen. Related to chicory (and dandelion, hence the bitterness), the two are often confused. The frisee endives have frilly leaves, are decorative and are grown mostly in summer. The Batavians (or escaroles) are broad-leaved, upright plants that will survive

light frosts. Under cloche cover they can go well into winter. Both can be grown to maturity or be used for cut-and-come-again.

Neither are particular about soil. If you are keeping them in cold weather, site them in a sheltered spot with good drainage. Sow and treat in the same way as lettuce. If you dislike the bitterness, blanch them by covering them with a bucket. If you just want to blanch the centre, use an old plate. Make sure they are completely dry first.

Endive may suffer from problems with slugs and snails, aphids (lettuce root aphid), caterpillars and tip burn.

Varieties
'Jeti' (AGM) – Attractive, bright green, curly leaf.
'Pancalieri a Costa Biancha' (AGM) – Bolt resistant with a curly leaf.
'Grosse Pancalieri' – Self-blanching. Curly with rosy midribs. March to September.
'En Cornet de Bordeaux' – Batavian type. Hardy old French variety for cut-and-come-again through winter.
'Escariol' – A crisp Batavian chicory, slow to grow but withstands frost.
Seed to harvest: 12 weeks

Chicory
Cichorium intybus
The chicories provide good bitter leaves to perk up cool-weather salads. They enjoy the same conditions as lettuce but need less cosseting. They fall into three groups. The witloof (white leaf), or Belgian chicory, is grown for forcing in autumn for winter

eating. Radiccio is a decorative, hearting chicory that flushes red for autumn eating. The sugarloaf (or non-forcing) is like a big, hearty cos lettuce. Discard the outer leaves and eat the heart which is naturally blanched and mild tasting – hence the name.

WITLOOF: Sow sparingly outside in summer. Water until the seeds come up. After that leave them fairly dry to encourage root growth. In autumn they can be forced for winter eating.

RADICCIO AND SUGARLOAF
Radiccio (or red chicory) and sugarloaf chicories are sown mid-spring indoors, or outside at any time through summer when the temperature is above 10°C (50°F). They can be grown as cut-and-come-again crops. If you grow them to maturity, leave the stump in the ground when you harvest to resprout.

If covered with cloches or fleece in autumn, they will continue to grow for some time. You can extend the season further by lifting them, and growing them on in pots indoors. They don't go over quickly like lettuce but will keep in the ground for several weeks.

These are generally trouble-free plants, but they may be attacked by slugs and snails.

Varieties

WITLOOF:
'Witloof de Brussels' – A great traditional variety.
'Witloof Zoom' F1 – A new self-blanching variety which doesn't need earthing up.
Seed to harvest: variable

RADICCIO:
'Palla Rossa' (AGM) – Old favourite. Dark red with bright white veins.
'Rossa di Treviso' (AGM)
Seed to harvest: variable
SUGARLOAF:
'Sugarloaf' – Resistant to cold, a good choice for winter under cloches. A big hearted chicory. Mild tasting.
Seed to harvest: variable

Corn salad
Valerianella locusta

Corn salad, lamb's lettuce, or mâche, is another gourmet green leaf for winter salads. It grows almost as easily as a weed and will self-sow if allowed. Provided it is kept covered in cold weather, it will carry on through winter – a real winner. The French type is compact with small leaves. The English or Dutch types are more sprawling. If sown before midsummer, they may bolt.

It is best sown in late summer and thinned to 15 cm (6 in) in well-drained soil for harvesting in autumn and through winter. Pick single leaves for a cut-and-come-again crop. The French type looks decorative in salads picked whole. Generally free from problems, though tempting to slugs and snails.

Varieties

'Vit' – A modern variety with dark green leaves. Vigorous, good for winter production.
'Cavallo' (AGM) – Small-leaved, neat French type.
'Verte de Cambrai' – Traditional French variety. Small leaves, looks good harvested whole in salads.
Seed to harvest: 4–12 weeks

Good King Henry
Chenopodium bonus-henericus

Good King Henry is an old-fashioned perennial, rarely grown nowadays. It tastes rather like asparagus. It is an undemanding plant, happy in semi-shade. It survives in almost any soil but performs best if it is moist and fertile. It grows to 90 cm (3 ft). Don't crop until the second year. It is advisable to split the plants every third year. Problems are unlikely.

Seed to harvest: 2 years, then harvest every year

Red orach
Atriplex hortensis var. *rubra*

Red orach makes a pretty addition to salads if the purple-red leaves are picked young. The older ones can be cooked like spinach. Sow outside in spring when the soil is warm, in dappled shade. Rich soil and constant moisture will produce the best

crops. It grows fast to 1.2 m (4 ft). Pinch out the flowering tips as they appear.

Generally no problems, but it can become rampant if allowed to self-seed.

Amaranthus
Amaranthus gangeticus

Amaranthus is known as Chinese spinach, *bayam* in Indonesia, and *calaloo* in the West Indies where it is the classic accompaniment to salt fish. It is the 'leafy' type, not unlike spinach, that is usually grown in allotments in the UK for cooking. The very young leaves can be used in salads. The lowest soil temperature for germination is 10°C (50°F). Either raise it under cover in early spring or wait until the soil is warm in late May and sow outside – a better choice if the weather allows, as it may bolt when transplanted.

The seed is very fine so mix it with a little sand or fine soil. It

can be used as a cut-and-come-again crop or thinned and allowed to grow on. Amaranthus is usually harvested by pulling out the entire plant with its roots when about 20–25 cm (8–10 in) high. It needs a reasonably fertile, fairly loose soil and sunshine. It's a very fast grower. The occasional liquid feed with high nitrogen will help, especially for cut-and-come-again.

Fenugreek
Trigonella foenum-graecum

Fenugreek or methi, is widely used in southern Asian cuisine. Both the leaves (fresh or dried) and the toasted, ground seeds are a traditional ingredient for curries. It can also be sprouted as a bitter salad green. Fenugreek, an easy and hardy plant, is sown in late spring in fertile, well-drained soil in sun. The leaves are picked in summer and the seeds when ripe. It is generally trouble free.

STEM VEGETABLES

Celery, celeriac and Florence fennel are grown for their edible stems. Celery and Florence fennel are tricky plants to raise as, given the slightest hitch, they will bolt. All need fertile, well-drained but moisture-retentive soil with plenty of organic matter and an open site.

Celery needs high nitrogen feeds and a constant supply of water. If it doesn't get them, it will become stringy and tough. Celery, celeriac and Florence fennel are grown for their edible stems. Celery and Florence fennel are tricky plants to raise as, given the slightest hitch, they will bolt. All need fertile, well-drained but moisture-retentive soil with plenty of organic matter and an open site.

Celery
Apium graveolens var. *dulce*

The classic French celery is unbeatable for flavour but is demanding and takes up a good deal of space. The newer self-blanching celery is much easier and quicker to grow, though less hardy. Both need deep, well-drained soil (pH 6.5–7). If you soil is acid, add liime.

The seeds can take a long time

to germinate if the temperature is too high – 10–15°C (50–59°F) is about right. They are best sown under glass in late March or April. Celery is one of the few plants that germinates in the light, so scatter seed on top of the compost. When the seedlings have five or six true leaves in early summer, they can be hardened off and transplanted.

If temperatures drop below

10°C (50°F) for any length of time at this stage they will bolt. If the weather isn't right for them to go out, you can hold them back by cutting them down to about 7.5 cm (3 in). When you transplant them, cover with fleece or cloches for a few weeks. Water in well. If celery receives any set backs it will become stringy. Keep an eye on it. If you see signs of flagging or any yellowing in the leaves, give it a boost with liquid feed. The traditional way to grow trench celery is to plant it in a trench (hence the name) and earth it up to keep the stems whole. Nowadays it is usually sown on the flat and each plant is blanched with an individual collar made from cardboard covered with black polythene, tied round with string. The self-blanching types are planted in a block to shade each other and only the outer ones are given collars. Leaf miner, celery leaf spot, slugs and calcium deficiency can be a problem with celery.

Varieties

SELF BLANCHING:
'Celebrity' (AGM) – Early, nutty and crisp with bolting resistance.
'Latham Self-blanching' (AGM) – Hearty and well-flavoured early variety.
'Ivory Tower' (AGM) – Nearly stringless.
Seed to harvest: 12–16 weeks
TRENCH CELERY:
'Giant Pink – Mammoth Pink' (AGM) – The name describes it. Hardy.
'Hopkins Fenlander' – Green celery, stringless and good flavour.
Seed to harvest: 9 months

Florence fennel
Foeniculum vulgare var. *azoricum*

Florence fennel, or finnochio, with its aniseed taste and elegant feathery foliage, thrives in temperate to sub-tropical climates. It is not the easiest to grow, being inclined to bolt at the slightest difficulty – if it is too cold or too hot, doesn't have enough water or if it is disturbed for transplanting. For this reason it is worth buying fast-growing, bolt-resistant seed. To improve your chances further, sow outside to avoid transplanting shock, from the end of April to late summer, using fleece at each end of the season.

Find fennel a sheltered sunny site, with well-drained, moisture-retentive soil that has been enriched with organic matter the previous year. Spread mulch around the plants and keep them well watered.

When the bulbs start to form, either earth them up to halfway up the bulb or tie cardboard collars around them to blanch the stems. Cover with fleece as the nights start to draw in. Sometimes bulbs don't swell at all but you can still eat the rest of the plant. Slugs may be a problem. The leaves are a classic accompaniment to fish.

Varieties

'Zefo Fino' (AGM) – Good bolt resistance. Medium-sized, well-filled white bulbs.
'Zefo Tardo' – Bolt resistant variety. A fast grower.
Seed to harvest: 10–15 weeks

Celeriac

Apium graveolens var. rapaceum

Though a close relative of celery, celeriac is hardier and less temperamental. The swollen stem can be grated raw or cooked, and the leaves can be used for celery flavouring. It can stay in the ground with cloches, or a covering of straw, right through winter. It does, however, take six weeks longer to mature than celery, so you may not achieve the size you find in the shops.

Sow in March at 16°C (61°F) indoors, or outside in the cold frame in April or May. Harden off before planting outside after the last frosts. If the temperature drops, delay by clipping off the tops. Plant so the crown is just above soil level.

Like celery, it needs rich soil with plenty of humus. It can take a little shade and likes a damp spot. Mulch around it and keep up the watering. Give it some liquid feed every week or so. In midsummer, remove side shoots and any extra growing buds (if there is more than one). Snip off the outer leaves of celeriac to help ripen the crowns.

Apart from slugs, celeriac is generally trouble free but can suffer from the same pests and diseases as celery.

Varieties

'*Monarch*' (AGM) – Succulent firm white flesh. Harvest in autumn or early winter.
'*Prinz*' (AGM) – Early variety with big bulbs. Slow to bolt.
Seed to harvest: 26 weeks

DISTINGUISHED PERENNIALS

Asparagus and globe artichokes will stay in the ground for years, dying down in winter and re-emerging in spring. Site them carefully where they will not cast shade on other plants and prepare their beds for a long stay. Once established, perennial vegetables need little attention other than routine care.

Globe artichoke

Cynara scolymus

The artichoke makes an architectural spire up to 1.5 m (5 ft) in height. If you don't harvest it you will get a beautiful bright blue thistle flower, irresistible to bees. It is no trouble to grow. Buy or beg some offsets.

Globe artichokes like a sunny, sheltered site and will do best in fertile, free-draining soil (pH 6.5–7). Plant in spring with the crown just above the surface. Mulch to keep in moisture and water well in the first season. Cover with straw in winter.

Dig and divide globe artichokes (*see page 44*) every three years for top-quality artichokes. You may get a few in the first season but more will come in the following years. Harvest before the flower buds begin to open, starting at the top. They have very few problems, but may suffer an attack of aphids.

Varieties

'*Violetta di Chioggia*' – Decorative variety with purple heads. Not very hardy.
'*Vert de Laon*' – Hardy and a good flavour. Productive.
'*Green Globe*' – Popular variety with big succulent heads.
Offset to harvest: 16 weeks, and every year after

Asparagus

Asparagus officinalis

Asparagus will produce gourmet spears for twenty years. Site it in an open, but sunny and sheltered place. The traditional bed is 1.2 m (4 ft) wide with the crowns planted in two staggered rows 45 cm (18 in) apart. The autumn before, dig a trench about a spit deep and remove every last trace of perennial weeds.

Asparagus will rot if it is too wet, so if you have heavy soil, add grit, manure and leafmould or raise the bed. If it is acid, add lime the following spring. The ideal pH is 6.5–7.5.

Plants grown from seed take three years to mature, so it saves time to buy one- to three-year-old 'crowns'. Male plants produce fatter spears. In spring, build ridges in the prepared trenches and place the crowns straddled across them with the roots going downwards. When you fill the trench, the asparagus crowns should be about 15 cm (6 in) below the soil surface.

Don't cut the asparagus in the first year, and ration yourself in the second. Your patience will be rewarded. In the third year, the asparagus can be harvested for six weeks from May to June. After that, allow the stalks to grow into fern-like leaves. Cut these down every year when they turn yellow in autumn. Top-dress with a good quantity of well-rotted manure. Sprinkle on some fertilizer the following spring.

Slugs, asparagus beetle and violet root rot can cause problems. Late frosts can spoil an early crop without protection.

Varieties

'Connover's Colossal' (AGM) – A favourite since the 19th century. Early, large spears with a fine flavour.

'Giant Mammouth' – Tolerates heavy soil.

'Gijnlim' (AGM) – All-male hybrid. Prolific and early.

Crown to harvest: 2–3 years

DISTINGUISHED PERENNIALS

DIRECTORY

OF FRUIT

SOFT FRUIT

The prospect of home-grown fruit gives you an extra incentive for a trip down to the allotment in summer. Fruit is easy to grow and perennial. Unless things go badly wrong, it needs little attention other than routine care and pruning. Fruit is long-lived: trees produce for decades, while gooseberries and blackcurrants are great old stagers, performing well for twenty years, raspberries for fourteen.

Autumn raspberries will bear fruit the year after planting. Summer raspberries, blackberries and gooseberries fruit in the second year and redcurrants and whitecurrants in the third. Blueberries can take more than three years to build a good crop but then grow well. The slower fruits are usually bought as two- or three-year-olds to speed things up. Strawberries are renewed from runners every three years and replaced every ten.

All soft fruits like soil on the acid side. It is important to site the plants in a sheltered spot well away from frost pockets. Soft fruits flower early and if they get caught by frost there will be no crop. Choose late varieties for extra insurance. Birds love fruit, so netting is essential.

Avoid planting where soft fruit has been before as it can lead to replant disease which shows as stunted growth. Raspberries, blackberries and strawberries share diseases caused by fungi in the soil. To avoid the fatal viral diseases – the single greatest danger – buy stock that has been certified free of pests and disease. The only soft fruits for which there is no certificate are red- and whitecurrants. If you buy plants 'bare-rooted', soak the roots overnight and plant as soon as you can. If you need to delay, heel them in or cover with wet sacking.

Strawberries
Fragaria x ananassa

To get top crops, prepare the ground carefully. Strawberries grow best in well-drained, moisture-retentive, humus-rich soil. Add lots of well-rotted compost or manure and a sprinkling of phosphate (bone meal will serve). Give them a sunny site.

Buy certified disease-free plants. Plant them in late summer as they need a period of cold to flower and fruit the following year. Space them about 60 cm (24 in) apart, making sure that they are at the same depth as before. The crown – the point where the leaves join the roots – should be at soil level. Too low and the plant might rot, too high and it won't establish well.

They can be grown through weed-suppressing horticultural plastic. Keep moist in dry spells but avoid watering from overhead and wetting the leaves in summer. Net against birds.

The mid-season strawberries will produce a good crop in the first year. Early and late varieties need to be held back. Pick off all the flowers in the first year for a rewarding harvest the next.

Strawberries send out a lot of runners. These should be removed to conserve the plant's energy, unless you want to propagate. If so, leave about four on each plant and snip off the rest. As strawberry plants need to be moved every three years, the general practice is to propagate about a third every year (*see page 45*).

Put straw under the plants as the fruits form to keep them clean. After harvesting, tidy the plants by cutting plant back to 10 cm (4 in) and removing any tatty leaves. Clear the straw in winter. Buy new stock every nine or ten years.

Problems include grey mould (particularly if the plants are over-crowded), powdery mildew in dry weather, aphids, vine weevil, red spider mite, viruses, slugs, snails and birds.

Varieties

EARLY:
'Honeoye' (AGM) – Firm and glossy with great flavour. Fair resistance to botrytis. Ready with cloche protection in May and carries on until early July.

MID-SEASON:
'Pegasus' (AGM) –Vigorous with big juicy fruits. Resistant to virus and to grey mould and mildew to some degree.

'Cambridge Favourite' (AGM) – A mid-season bright red, medium-sized, luscious strawberry that copes with a wide range of soils. Resistant to powdery mildew, grey mould and virus. Very reliable.

'Hapil' (AGM) – A Belgian variety. A high-yielding and delicious variety. Vigorous and heavy cropping.

LATE:
'Aromel' (AGM) – Large fruits which keep coming from July to October – even November under cloche protection.

'Symphony' – Produces a heavy crop of firm berries. Vigorous.

CANE FRUIT

Raspberries

Rubus idaeus

Summer raspberries crop in the second year, while autumn raspberries will produce a harvest in the first.

They like an airy spot with sunshine for at least half the day. They don't need rich soil but it should be fertile, free draining and on the acid side, the ideal being pH 6.5. Raspberries don't prosper in alkaline, chalky soils or soggy ones. At the same time they do need adequate water as their roots are close to the surface.

Raspberries are usually bought as bare-rooted plants in the dormant season, or can be container-grown. Make sure you buy certified virus-free stock. Aphid-resistance is also a good idea as it is aphids that carry deadly viruses from plant to plant. Autumn raspberries are generally

grown as free-standing plants and don't need staking, except in windy places. A post-and-wire support for summer raspberries is ideal as it allows for plenty of air circulation.

To plant, dig a trench, get rid of any weeds and mix in some well-rotted compost or manure. A sprinkling of bone meal will help rooting. Plant a little below the nursery mark. Once planted, cut the canes back to 15 cm (6 in). As the summer ones grow, tie them in to the support and cut them off when they reach the top.

A good mulch of manure in winter will help to keep the pH low, conserve moisture and keep back weeds. If you do need to weed, be careful not to damage the roots that lie just below the surface. Raspberries are picked when still firm, leaving the core and 'plug' on the plant.

You may experience problems with aphids, grey mould, viruses, raspberry beetle, raspberry cane spot and raspberry spur blight.

Varieties

SUMMER:
'Glen Moy' (AGM) – Early cropper with berries from late June. Spine-free canes. Aphid resistant.

'Glen Ample' (AGM) – A new variety, getting an accolade. Very heavy cropper from July onwards with good flavour. Spine-free canes. Resistant to aphids.

'Malling Jewel' (AGM), *'Malling Delight'* (AGM) and *'Malling Admiral'* (AGM) – All have outstanding flavour.

AUTUMN:
'Autumn Bliss' (AGM) – Crops heavily from August to the first frosts. Succulent fruits. Resistant to root rot and aphids.

Considered to be the best autumn raspberry.
'Golden Everest' – A yellow variety with sweet-tasting, mellow fruits.

Blackberries and hybrids
Rubus fruticosus

Blackberries are not the most popular fruits to grow. Free to passers-by in hedgerows, many say the wild ones taste the best. Much work, however, has gone into taming their vigour and their sharp spines by crossing them with raspberries and with each other. The resulting hybrids – loganberry, tayberry, boysenberry, tummelberry, veitchberry, youngberry, sunberry, dewberry and Japanese wineberry – are usually earlier, sweeter and less rampant. Some are thornless. They make excellent jam.

The hybrids need the same conditions as raspberries – with well-cultivated, fertile, slightly acid soil. Blackberries will grow almost anywhere but will revel in these conditions. The hybrids need sun, while blackberries are content in partial shade. They need little feeding other than an annual dressing of well-rotted compost. Keep them mulched and well watered, particularly as the fruits form.

Buy virus-free stock. The bare-rooted 'stools' are usually sent off by the nurseries in November. You can also buy them potted up which, though more expensive, gives you leeway on planting times. Give them plenty of space, planting up to 3 m (10 ft) apart depending on the variety, against a sturdy post-and-wire support.

Cut down to about 25 cm (10 in) above the ground. Tie in as they grow to stop them tangling (*see page 62*).

The stems that grow in the current year will bear fruit in the next. You need to net them against birds once the fruits appear. Unless you want to propagate from them, don't let the stems touch the ground as they will root themselves (*see page 45*). Harvest the berries, taking care not to handle them, with the stalk on. Choose a dry day as they deteriorate quickly when wet.

Problems are unlikely, though keep an eye out for raspberry beetle, aphids, grey mould, viruses and birds.

Varieties

BLACKBERRIES:
'Fantasia' (AGM) – Large, shiny, black berries. Full of flavour. Vigorous, heavy cropper. Sharp spines. Mid-season to late.
'Loch Ness' (AGM) – A thornless variety. Long, shiny, black berries. Grows short upright canes, making it easy to manage.
Hybrids are usually sold under their own name, for example *'Boysenberry'*.

Blackcurrants
Ribes nigrum

Blackcurrants make large free-standing bushes about 1.5–1.8 m (5–6 ft) tall, though there are compact forms. Unlike redcurrants and whitecurrants they don't lend themselves to training. They perform best in an open but sheltered position in sun or partial shade. Avoid planting them in frost pockets as they flower early and choose late varieties for this reason.

Blackcurrants need a good depth of soil for their roots to spread. As they are cut back hard, it needs to be fertile. They prefer soil on the acid side (pH 6.5). To plant, dig the soil well, remove all weeds and put in plenty of well-rotted compost or manure.

Buy a two-year-old certified virus-free, bare-rooted 'stool' in autumn. If you buy container-grown plants, they can be planted at any time, though the best time is between October and March. Plant 5 cm (2 in) deeper than previously. Cut down to one bud above ground level. Pile on a mulch of organic matter around the plant to keep in moisture and keep down weeds. Water well in dry spells. The current year's shoots will bear the best fruits in the next year. When harvesting, pick whole bunches, or 'strigs', as these keep better than individual berries.

Problems include blackcurrant gall midge, aphids, capsid bugs, big bud mite, American gooseberry mildew, reversion and leaf spot. For training and pruning information, *see page 63.*

Varieties

The 'Ben' series have resistance to cold and they flower late.

'*Ben Sarek*' (AGM) – Makes a smaller bush than most. Big crops of large berries. Good resistance to gooseberry mildew and some to leaf midge. Tolerant of frost at flowering time. Mid to late.

'*Ben Lomand*' (AGM) – Flowers late with some resistance to frost and mildew. Upright rather than spreading.

'*Ben Connan*' (AGM) – Exceptionally sweet berries. Resistance to leaf midge, mildew and leaf spot.

'*Boscoop Giant*' – Vigorous with luscious berries but early in flower, so vulnerable to frost.

Redcurrants and whitecurrrants
Ribes sativum

Redcurrants and whitecurrants are easy to grow. They are happy in semi-shade and don't need as luxuriant conditions as the others. Whitecurrants are a nearly colourless variety of the same plant but some say they have a sweeter taste. They fruit in the third year.

If you are going to grow them as bushes, buy a two- or three-year-old with a single short stem, or 'leg', and well-balanced side branches. There is no virus certificate so rely on a good nursery. They need a sheltered spot to avoid frosts as they flower early.

Prepare the ground as for blackcurrants but leave out the manure as it can make them grow too fast. Plant to the same depth as before.

Cut the branches back by half to an outward-facing bud and trim off the side shoots to three buds. If you want to train them as a cordon or espalier, buy a one-year-old plant.

Mulch with straw and water well in dry spells. Give them a dressing of well-rotted compost every three years. They are harvested by the string, or bunch. For training and pruning information, *see page 64.*

They are generally trouble free, but net against birds. Look out for aphids, gooseberry sawfly, American gooseberry mildew, coral spot and grey mould.

Varieties

REDCURRANTS:

'*Jonkheer van Tets*' (AGM) – Heavy cropper, early fruiter and good flavour.

'*Red Lake*' (AGM) – Mid-season variety, with plentiful tasty fruits.

'*Stanza*' (AGM) – Late season (good for chilly places), with lots of tasty fruit.

WHITECURRANTS:

'*White Grape*' (AGM) – Mid-season variety with plenty of sweet flavour.

'*White Versailles*' – A very popular variety, reliable with big juicy fruits.

Gooseberries
Ribes grossularia

Gooseberries are European natives. They aren't fussy about soil and are not prone to viral diseases. While preferring sun to ripen the berries, they don't mind a little shade – a spot with sun for half the day is perfect. They can be grown as bushes, trained as cordons or mop-headed standards, or be grown in a barrel. They produce fruit in their second year and are always the first soft fruits of the season. The disadvantage of their forwardness is that they flower so early that frost can destroy the crops.

Buy a two- or three-year-old plant with a clear stem of 10–15 cm (4–6 in). Choose a sheltered site away from frost pockets but with air circulation. Treat the soil in the same way as for their near-relative, the redcurrant. Plant during the dormant season to the same depth as they were in their pots.

As you want to keep the fruit away from the ground where

slugs, snails and fungal infections may lurk, inset four canes around the plant at an outward angle and tie string around to lift the branches. If you are growing them as bushes, prune in winter, aiming for a balanced and open goblet shape. Keep the stem clear by cutting off any new side shoots on it. Prune the leader to half of its new growth every year so that the plant makes strong side branches to support the fruit. As plants establish, reduce these by one-third after harvest. Cover with fleece when frost threatens. Gooseberries are susceptible to the same problems as redcurrants.

Varieties

'Careless' (AGM) – An old mid-season variety grown for its outstanding flavour. Crops well, is quite vigorous and is not too fussy about the soil.

'Jubilee' (AGM) – Developed from 'Careless' with additional virus resistance.

'Invicta' (AGM) – Mid-season, thorny but with a very good flavour. Mildew resistant.

'Whinham's Industry' (AGM) – A red dessert variety, producing prolific, big, succulent berries. Many declare it to be the sweetest gooseberry. A vigorous plant that can cope with poor soils, though rather prone to mildew.

'Leveller' (AGM) – Abundant, large yellow berries with good flavour. Not too vigorous. Needs good soil and drainage.

Blueberries

Vaccinium corymbosum

The 'high bush' blueberry, an American favourite, is gaining in popularity over here. It is both hardy and attractive. It has white bell flowers, blue fruits and dramatic autumn colour. It needs special conditions though – lots of moisture and extremely acid soil (pH 4–5.5). Unless you have this, grow them in large pots in ericaceous (lime-hating) compost, and water them copiously with rain water. They like sun but can take partial shade. Modern cultivars have reduced the blueberry from being a huge shrub to a size suitable for container planting. Though a single plant will produce fruit, more will come if it has a companion of a different variety flowering at the same time for cross-pollination.

Plants are usually sold container-grown as two- or three-year-old bushes. Plant in the dormant season. They take three to six years to produce a good quantity of fruit, but after that there is no stopping them. Prune in winter, cutting out about one-third of the old or damaged wood down to the base. Trim off the tops in spring to keep a neat shape. Harvest the berries over a few weeks when they are ripe and blue. A generally healthy plant, though protect from birds and keep a look out for blue mould.

Varieties

'Bluecrop' – The most popular choice, mid-season and good flavour. Fairly compact.

'Berkeley' – Big lush fruits and the bonus of yellow stems in winter. A big spreading plant.

'Herbert' – Late variety with extra-large fruits.

FRUIT TREES

When it comes to fruit trees on the allotment, think small – if at all. Large trees are generally banned with good reason, but small trees grown in barrels or trees trained flat as espaliers, cordons or fans are often allowed. Apples, pears and plums lend themselves to training in this way. So do peaches and nectarines but these are really for the enthusiast living in a warm part of the country. They need too much cosseting for most plot holders – a sunny wall, hand-pollination, protection against frost and a rain cover to stop them getting silver leaf disease.

CONSIDERATIONS WHEN BUYING

Most cultivated fruit trees are not grown from seed as the results can be unreliable. Instead they are budded and grafted onto rootstocks, usually from a different variety or close relative of the same type of fruit tree. This is done by the age-old practice of joining a shoot from one tree onto the root system of another. It is the root, rather than the shoot, that determines the eventual size of the tree, so be sure to choose a plant with the right rootstock for you. When planting, take care to plant to the same depth as before. If you plant near or above the graft, the shoot may put out its own roots and make the tree too vigorous.

Where possible, buy certified stock. It will have been grown in accordance to the Ministry of Agriculture Certification Scheme and will be guaranteed to be substantially free of pests and disease and true to name. Certificates aren't available for all fruit trees but cover commonly grown apples, pears and plums.

Look for the Award of Garden Merit awarded by the Royal Horticultural Society following extensive rigorous trials.

Always go to a reputable nursery. Fruit trees are generally lifted for sale in November. They come as one-year-old maidens, otherwise known as whips. Feathered maidens will have formative branches or side shoots. You can also buy a two- or three-year-old partially trained and shaped by the nursery. Though more expensive, these will give you a head start.

The cheapest option is to buy them bare rooted. If you buy them pot grown, make sure they are not pot-bound with roots so congested that they can't spread out comfortably in the soil. Sometimes the roots have twisted themselves round like a spring and, when planted, they can lift the tree right out of the ground. You can get some idea by checking the bottom of the pot. If a tangled mass of roots is poking out, you can be sure that it is pot-bound and is likely to be dehydrated.

Pollination

Some trees, like the Victoria plum, are self-pollinators, so you will get fruit with a single tree – but more if they are cross-pollinated. Most however, need to be fertilized by the pollen of a different tree of the same type. If you are buying several fruit trees that need cross-pollination, look for different varieties of the same fruit tree, making sure that they flower at the same time. Take advice from the nursery as some trees are ineffectual pollinators.

Most fruit trees are pollinated by insects, particularly bees, so avoid windy areas where they will be blown off course. If your trees flower early before the bees are about, you can hand-pollinate them with a soft paintbrush, moving from flower to flower (*see page 70*).

Flowering times

Frost will kill your crops stone dead if it gets to the flowers. Look for late-flowering types in cold parts of the country. Plant your trees in a sheltered spot and be ready to cover them with fleece when frost threatens.

Cultivation

Fruit trees are a long-term investment so it is worth getting the conditions as perfect as possible. Don't plant where there were fruit trees before as they can get replant disease. They need sun for the fruit to ripen. The topsoil should be deep, ideally around 60 cm (24 in), well-drained and slightly acid (pH 6.5).

Trees develop big roots, so dig a generous planting hole, mix in plenty of well-rotted compost or manure and sprinkle on bone meal for good rooting.

Put a stake in first and plant to the same depth as before. Firm the soil by stamping around the tree. Give it a tug to see if there is any movement and stamp some more if not. Water well to get rid of any air pockets.

An organic mulch around the tree to cover the root run will keep in moisture and keep back weeds. Don't let it touch the trunk of the tree, however, as it could set off rot. Keep well watered in the first summer until the roots get a good hold.

If you are buying bare-rooted trees, don't let the roots dry out any further – plant as soon as possible. If the ground is frozen or waterlogged when they arrive, cover them with wet sacking or heel them in. To do this, dig a trench deep enough to cover the roots and lay the young trees at an angle of 45 degrees. Cover loosely with damp soil.

A monthly spray of seaweed solution will keep the trees well.

Thinning fruit

For quality over quantity, it may be necessary to thin the fruit. To get less but larger and more luscious fruits, pick a few off as they form to get even spacing.

Protection against animals

Rabbits can cause great damage by nibbling the bark off young trees. If they chew the bark off all the way round the tree, it will die. If you have rabbits around, encircle the trunk with rabbit netting buried about 30 cm (12 in) deep.

Birds will be after your fruit. Bullfinches don't even wait for them to form. They will strip apples, pears and plums of the fruit buds. With dwarf stock it is easy to net them before the fruits form.

Apples

Malus domestica

Apples are hardy and late flowering by fruit tree standards. They flower in mid to late spring, so are a good choice for colder areas. The vast majority need to be cross-pollinated, some by two different types. There are so many varieties that it is generally recommended that you choose by tasting lots of different ones. Keep in mind the ones that are traditional in your neighbourhood.

If you are going to train them as a fruit fence, remember to get a 'spur bearer'. It will produce fruit along the length of the branches. The rootstock used to create small apple trees is M9 (which grows to 1.8–3 m or 6–10 ft) or M26 (which will reach 2.4–3.6 m or 8–12 ft) if left to grow to its full height. M26 is more robust and is the most widely used rootstock for trained fruit trees.

Look also for resistance to frost and diseases, and for late flowering. Take advice from the nursery on which varieties will cross-pollinate successfully and grow well in your area. Some of the most outstanding apple varieties can be quite difficult to grow. The superb Cox's Orange Pippin, for example, is prone to disease and doesn't do well in the cold.

Apple trees can suffer from canker, codling moth, apple sawfly, aphids, capsid bug, caterpillars, mildews, brown rot, blossom wilt and birds eating the fruit.

Varieties

'Sunset' (AGM) – Delicious, like a Cox's Orange Pippin. Small tree, very reliable. Fruits in early autumn.

'Falstaff' (AGM) – Late crisp sweet fruits. Reliable with some frost resistance.

'Ashmead's Kernel' (AGM) – Has an exceptionally good, nutty, russet flavour which makes up for less than abundant crops of small fruits. Prone to frost damage.

'James Grieve' (AGM) – Juicy green apple on the sharp side. Quite early flowering. It is rather prone to canker.

'Laxton's Epicure' (or 'Epicure') (AGM) – Crops late summer. Interesting aromatic taste.

Pears
Pyrus communis

Pears need more sun and flower several weeks earlier than apples. In gardens they are usually planted against a warm wall. If you are growing them on an open allotment in the North you may not get good fruit unless you can find them a very sheltered, south-, south-west or west-facing spot.

Prepare the soil as for apples. They need 45–60 cm (18–24 in) depth of well-drained but moisture-retentive soil. Ideally, it should be on the acid side (pH 6.5). Like most of the other fruits, pears don't do well on chalk. They respond well to hard pruning and can be trained flat in any form, even grown in a tub.

Pears are usually grafted on quince rootstocks. The smallest, 'Quince C', which makes the tree grow to 2.4–3 m (8–10 ft), is recommended for cordons and espaliers. Plant to the same level as

before. All pears need to be cross-pollinated. Take advice on which varieties are compatible. Look for late flowerers if you are in a frosty area and be prepared to give them protection. Pick the fruits when hard and ripen indoors.

Pears are less prone to pests and diseases than apples. However, look out for pear leaf blister, pear midge, aphids, codling moth, canker, pear scab, brown rot, blossom wilt, replant disease and birds eating the fruit.

Varieties

'Doyenne de Comice' (AGM) – A late, heavy pear and absolutely delicious.

'Conference' (AGM) – Early, very reliable and scab resistant.

'Williams' Bon Chretien' – Late with a musky flavour, slightly prone to scab.

'Concorde' (AGM) – Mid-season. Compact form, juicy fruits.

'Beth' (AGM) – A mid-season, reliable cropper with small but tasty fruits.

Plums, damsons and greengages
Prunus domestica and *Prunus italica*

Plums are grown in much the same way as pears. They need warmth and shelter but flower even earlier, so they are not recommended for places with late spring frosts. They are not too fussy about soil, but they need good drainage. The rootstock for training is 'Pixie' which will allow the tree to grow to 2–2.5 m (6–8 ft). If you are planning to train them as fans and cordons, look for the more compact types. There are many self-fertile culti-

vars. If you are growing a few cross-pollinators, get guidance from the tree nursery on flowering times and compatibility.

Never prune plums during the dormant season as it can expose them to silver leaf disease and canker. Plums are ready in August onwards and taste sweeter if left on the tree until they are fully ripe. Unless caught by the frost, fruiting is usually prolific.

Greengages make smaller trees than plums and are even more sensitive to frost. Otherwise they are grown in the same way.

Damsons, which are hardier than true plums and fruit later, are not usually trained but left to grow into bushy trees which rather rules them out on an allotment.

Plums, greengages and damsons can suffer from plum leaf curling aphid, brown rot, plum moth, silver leaf and blossom wilt.

Varieties

PLUMS:

'Blue Tit' (AGM) – A compact, mid-season culticar. Juicy blue fruits. Reliable.

'Early Laxton' (AGM) – Sweet-tasting yellow fruits with red tints. A compact cultivar.

'Opal' (AGM) – Late-fruiting, compact cultivar. Reliable with sweet-tasting, orange fruits.

'Victoria' (AGM) – The famous and classic golden plum. Fully self-fertile and reliable.

'Czar' (AGM) – Late-cropping, compact, very reliable, blue cooking plum. Frost resistant and self-pollinating.

GREENGAGES:

'Cambridge Gage' (AGM) – Reliable with sweet green fruits.

Peaches and nectarines

Prunus persica

Peaches and nectarines need cosseting. They can be grown in warm areas with the protection of a 2 m (6 ft) south-facing wall or a fence. The flowers, which are not hardy, come early and the fruits need plenty of sunshine to ripen.

The trees need deep, well-drained but moisture-retentive soil on the acid side. Prepare the ground by adding in generous quantities of organic matter. Plant them in autumn, as they start growth early. Spread a good mulch around them to keep them weed-free and to prevent them drying out. This needs to be repeated on an annual basis.

Peaches and nectarines respond well to fan training *(see page 61)* on 'St Julien A' rootstock. Keep them well watered and feed regularly with seaweed spray. They are mostly self-pollinating but, as they blossom before there are many insects about, hand-pollinate the plants as extra insurance. Make a shelter over them in late winter to keep the rain off as it will spread peach leaf curl on the new leaves as they open. Thin the developing fruits for a good crop.

RHUBARB

Rhubarb

Rheum x *hybridum (*syn. *R. cultorum)*

Rhubarb is easy to cultivate and a single plant is sufficient to yield enough satisfy a family of four. The seed does not come true to type, so it is better and quicker to start from root cuttings, or 'sets'. You can probably get these from a neighbour to start you off.

If not, buy the sets (with a virus-free certificate) from a reputable nursery. Rhubarb will grow almost anywhere, but the most succulent stalks will come from plants grown in free-draining soil enriched with organic matter.

Plant them away from frost pockets and in a sunny position during late autumn or early spring while the plant is dormant. Keep moist with a good mulch, taking care not to cover the crown as it could rot.

Don't harvest in the first year. In autumn, cut away the dead leaves and let the frost get to the crown to break the dormancy. The following spring start to pull (not cut) the stems, leaving about half the shoots on the plant. Stop around mid-summer to give it time to regenerate. Remove any flowers as they form. It can be forced *(see page 64)* after the first few frosts and should be divided every three years *(see page 44)*.

Don't forget that the leaves are poisonous. Rhubarb is generally trouble free, but watch out for crown rot and viruses.

Varieties

'Victoria' – Tried and trusted old variety.

'Timperley Early' – Vigorous and good for forcing.

'Early Champagne' – Quite delicious and sweet. Early.

chapter 7

DIRECTORY

OF HERBS

Allotment people are usually doubly talented. They are both good growers and fine cooks. The two skills go hand in hand. Having a good stock of herbs among the vegetables will inspire the chef, and you don't need many. The classic French mixtures are composed of a handful of commonly grown herbs.

In bouquet garni there is thyme, parsley, bay and sweet marjoram. The same mixture (without bay) makes the classic Herbes de Provence, with the addition of rosemary, tarragon and savory. For culinary use, it is best to stick to the common forms of the herbs — they have more flavour than the varieties bred for their looks.

Basil
Ocimum basilicum
Sweet basil is an Italian classic for tomato-based dishes and pasta sauces. It originates from tropical Asia and is a tender summer plant in the UK. Sow seed in warmth in spring or sow directly outside after the frosts in a really sheltered warm patch. Alternatively, small plants from the supermarket will grow on well as long as you harden them off carefully before planting them out. Keep pinching out the growing tips through summer to keep a neat shape. Either bring them indoors or harvest completely before the frosts. Basil doesn't dry or freeze well, but if you have a glut you can make wonderful fresh pesto and freeze that.

Chervil
Anthriscus cerefolium
Chervil has a mild aniseed cum parsley taste. It is popular in French cuisine to flavour eggs or fish and can be sprinkled on salads. Unlike basil it is very hardy and a boon in winter. The seed doesn't store for longer than a year, so make sure you have a fresh supply. For summer use, sow in late spring in light moist soil in dappled shade – in between tall leafy vegetables would be a good spot. It should be ready to pick in about seven weeks. As long as it is not allowed to flower, it will carry on through summer. For winter use under cloches, make a second sowing in mid-summer.

Chives
Allium schoenoprasum
Chives make an attractive garnish and the mauve drumhead flowers make an ornamental edging to your beds. They are very easy to grow. They spring readily from seed when the soil temperature is 19°C (66°F) in late spring. An even simpler method is to dig up a good-sized clump, pull the mass of little bulbs apart and replant them. They need to be divided every three years anyway. Chives like moist, rich soil and sunshine, though they can take a little shade. If they look tired, give them a haircut back to 2.5 cm (1 in) to encourage fresh new growth. They die back in winter but can be kept going, potted up, on the windowsill in the warm. Store them chopped up and frozen in ice cubes.

Coriander
Coriandrum sativum
The coriander leaf is a delicious addition to salad dishes and essential in Thai cooking, while the aromatic seeds are used in garam masala and curry dishes. You need to grow a good quantity to get a reasonable amount. Coriander likes sunshine and to be kept quite dry. As it is likely to bolt if it is transplanted, sow seed straight out after all danger of frost. Cover thinly with fine soil; the seedlings should emerge after a week or so. Thin them when large enough to handle. Make successional sowings through summer, allowing them to grow on if you want seed. They are lax plants so you may need to stake them at this stage. Prevent them from seeding themselves by pulling up the plants when the seeds are almost ripe. Hang the plants upside-down in the shed with the seedheads tied into paper bags.

Keep coriander plants well away from dill and fennel as they will cross-pollinate.

Dill
Anethum graveolens
The dill leaf is a marriage partner for smoked fish and the more strongly flavoured seeds are used in cooking. Sow in mid-spring outside in sun. As it grows wild in the Mediterranean, dill is happiest in well-drained soil in sunshine. It can grow to up to 1.5 m (5 ft) so it may need staking. Water in hot weather to prevent it bolting. Cut it back regularly to encourage the production of fresh leaves. Don't let it seed itself or you will have dill plants everywhere. Harvest the seeds in the same way as coriander. Keep it away from fennel and coriander as they will mix and marry.

Fennel
Foeniculum vulgare
Fennel, with its aniseed taste, is traditional in fish dishes and with fatty meats. It has been used as a digestive for thousands of years. It is a very elegant plant with bright green feathery leaves growing to a magnificent 2 m (6½ ft). Sow a few seeds in a sunny spot in well-drained loam after the frosts, or in spring under cover in biodegradable modules. Remove flowers in summer to prevent it seeding prolifically. Water in dry spells. It will die back in winter. Tidy it up at the end of the season and replace every three years. The leaves can be frozen in ice cubes and the seed saved for cooking. (see also Florence fennel, page 155).

Lovage
Levisticum officinale

Lovage tastes like celery and both the leaves and the seeds add flavour to soups and stews. It can also be cooked like spinach. It needs a period of cold so sow outside in autumn. It is another monster with a potential growth to 2 m (6½ ft) and half that width over five years. Prepare the ground well, incorporating plenty of well-rotted manure or compost. It is happy in either sun or partial shade. If you need more than one plant, thin to 60 cm (24 in) apart. Keep clipping the plants in summer to encourage fresh young leaves. Once it has established after a year or two you can divide it in spring or autumn. Cut off the flowering stems when the seeds are nearly ripe and harvest in the same way as described for coriander.

Sweet marjoram
Origanum majorana

There are many members of the marjoram family but the undoubted culinary star is sweet marjoram. It is half-hardy, originating in North Africa. A popular ingredient in Italian and Greek cooking, it is sprinkled on tomatoes and other salads or added at the last minute to soups and sauces. Either buy plants or sow seed outside after the danger of frost has passed. Alternatively, sow indoors at 16°C (61°F). Choose a sunny, well-drained site. It grows to a modest 60 cm (24 in) and is well suited to container growing. Trim after flowering in summer. In the UK it is treated as an annual, so discard it at the end of the season.

Mint
Mentha x piperita

The common garden mint is widely used for mint sauce, to flavour new potatoes, for tabbouleh and other Middle Eastern dishes. It is popular for mint tea and iced drinks such as Pimms. There are dozens of types (including ginger, lemon and spearmint), so finding a pure seed strain is difficult. The best policy is to buy a plant (having rubbed a leaf and sniffed it to make sure it's the one you want), or to get a root cutting from a neighbour. Any time during the growing season you can dig up an established plant and pull the roots apart, making sure that each division has some roots and shoots. Replant in sun or shade. Mint is a great colonizer, so sink a container (a bucket with the bottom sawn off would be suitable) into the ground and plant in that or grow it in a pot. Trim the plants right back in summer to encourage renewed growth of fresh young leaves. In autumn dig some up and plant in pots to go inside.

Parsley
Petroselinum crispum

Parsley must be the most widely grown culinary herb in Britain. Curly-leafed parsley is used mostly as a garnish and the flat-leafed variety (also known as Italian or French parsley) has a stronger flavour and is considered better for cooking. As parsley has a hungry taproot, it is best to sow it in situ in rich deep soil. Sow thinly from spring to summer with a further sowing in early autumn. Keep well watered. Be patient as parsley can take six weeks to germinate. For summer picking, sow in semi-shade, and for winter sow (under cloches) in a sunny, sheltered spot. Cut off flowers as they appear. It is best to start afresh each year as parsley runs to seed quickly in its second season. Take precautions against slugs. Curly parsley makes a pretty edging to a bed.

Rosemary
Rosmarinus officinalis

The smell of rosemary as it cooks really sharpens the appetite. Classic with roast lamb, it is also wonderful with any barbecued food and useful for flavoured oils and vinegars. As it is tricky to grow from seed, buy a small plant in spring or grow it from softwood cuttings. Give it a sheltered and sunny spot where you will brush past it to release its calming, aromatic scent. It needs soil with good drainage. Mulch young plants well in autumn to protect them against cold. Trim immediately after flowering. Try to keep the bush neat and avoid cutting into old wood as it doesn't put out new growth easily.

Sage
Salvia officinalis

Sage is widely used for stuffings and flavouring meat. It has the two-fold effect of aromatic flavouring and aiding digestion. You can grow it from seed outside, take softwood cuttings in late spring to early summer, or splash out and start off with a bought plant. Site it in a warm spot with free-draining soil, neutral to alkaline. Trim back after flowering in summer to

ORGANIC PEST AND DISEASE CONTROL

A pleasing development in the allotment scene has been the steep rise in demand for plots by the parents of young families. This seems to be largely due to the various food scares. Distrustful of the food industry and their tricks, the idea of growing fresh and affordable organic produce has never seemed so attractive.

Controlling pests and diseases organically is not as simple as changing from man-made sprays to organic ones. It is far more interesting as it is about creating a partnership with nature. It comes down to good husbandry, knowledge, observation and using your wits. With netting, traps, camouflage, timing and an increasing choice of disease-resistant varieties, you have a powerful armoury at your disposal to control them – without resorting to chemicals.

Keep plants healthy

Plants that are grown to be strong and vigorous will shrug off mild diseases and pest attacks. Give them first-class soil at the right pH for them. Find them the situation they prefer, in sun or shade. Raise them fast by sowing them at the right time, in their season.

Supply them with sufficient water and nutrients but don't overfeed as this will make them soft, sappy and attractive to pests. After a few years, the annual addition of well-rotted bulky organic matter will make the soil so fertile that most plants shouldn't need extra fertilizer. Don't overcrowd

> ## CASE STUDY
>
> A well-run garden will achieve a balance. There has to be an element of live and let live. Birds and wasps are useful in keeping down pests but they will have an eagle eye on your fruit.
>
> "Quite a few people see gardening as a challenge. They want to be top dog. I don't think we should deny the creatures that help us some reward by letting them take a small share of our crops." – *June Brandon, Site Manager, Barrowell Allotments, London.*

them or let them get choked by weeds. Nanny them carefully when they are young and vulnerable. Always avoid stress.

Crop rotation

Rotation is vital on allotments where the ground may have been used to grow the same vegetables for decades (*see page 29*). Moving crops around to a fresh site each year really helps to prevent colonies of soil-borne pests building up.

Beneficial predators

Many pests have their own natural predators, so by attracting these to your allotment, they will deal with many pest attacks for you.

✦ Ladybirds, hoverflies and lacewings demolish aphids, mites, scale insects, mealy bugs and small caterpillars at an astonishing rate.

✦ Ground beetles eat slugs, underground larvae and root aphids.

✦ Parastic wasps will eat caterpillars.

✦ Centipedes will eat slugs and snails.

✦ Earwigs eat caterpillars, aphids and the eggs of codling moths.

✦ Frogs, toads, hedgehogs, newts, shrews and slow worms demolish slugs and many other pests.

✦ Birds and bats eat a wide range of pests. Robins love caterpillars, cutworms and other soil-borne grubs. Starlings will go for wireworms and thrushes are skilled at dealing with snails.

Providing the right habitats

Providing water in the shape of a small pond will bring in frogs and toads to breed (*see page 71*). It will also provide bathing and drinking water for birds and many other useful creatures.

Frogs and toads like to retire for the winter into a secluded spot in the undergrowth. Keep the areas around your plants weed-free but allow a few chosen weeds to grow in odd corners as hideaways through winter. Leave some piles of logs and stones in corners for winter refuge. Some allotment sites are fortunate in

PRINCIPLES OF ORGANIC PEST AND DISEASE CONTROL

✦ Raise plants to be in top health
✦ Rotate crops
✦ Bring in the beneficial predators
✦ Camouflage your crops
✦ Keep hygiene levels high
✦ Nip problems in the bud

✦ Get to recognise the pests
✦ Buy resistant varieties
✦ Outwit pests with barriers and traps
✦ Get your timing right to avoid certain pests
✦ Practise companion planting

having hedges, trees and dense evergreen climbers to provide nesting places around the periphery of the site. Others plant a disused allotment plot with indigenous trees and shrubs as a small nature reserve.

Insect hotels

Parasitic wasps and solitary bees like to hole up in small hollow sticks in winter. It is easy to construct a habitat yourself by drilling out some short lengths of straight sticks and binding them together. Make the bundle water-tight and attach it to a post, tree or shed in a sunny, sheltered spot. Organic gardening catalogues offer many other insect hotels which are easy to copy.

Flowers to attract insects

To lure valuable pollinators and predators into the plot you need to grow flowers. They provide nectar, pollen and the right habitat for wasps, bees, lacewings and ladybirds. Simple daisy-type flowers in yellow or orange are particularly favoured. The hoverfly needs an open flower to get to the pollen as it only has a short feeding tube. It lays its eggs on the plant near a colony of

CASE STUDY

With a life-long passion for ornithology, Bernard Coote, the allotment representative at Ashley Vale Allotments, Bristol, has built up the bird population to an astonishing number. He has made and set up scores of different types of bird boxes including the upside-down teapots that robins love.

He provides the birds with food all year. In spring and summer, he says, they can have a lean patch if things go out of balance – for example if the green caterpillars don't coincide with hatching of the tits. He has also developed a colony of some 600 slow worms (which demolish slugs) by giving them the dry conditions they enjoy. He made a nest with open plastic breadbins on their sides, half-filled with hay or straw. Over these he has put a cage of wire netting held down by logs and covered with soil.

aphids and the resulting larvae demolish them. Some allotments are turning spare plots into nature reserves which is good for the environment, while helping the organic gardener. Plant with wild flowers, grasses and cereals to attract butterflies, bees and other useful insects.

Easy annuals that will bring in beneficial predators are nasturtiums, marigolds and the poached egg plant, *Limnanthes douglassii*. If you shake the seed out as they go over, they will carry on for years. To extend the season, plant a few

wallflowers for spring and Michelmas daisies for autumn. If you grow buckwheat, clover, lupins or phacelia as green manures, let a few flower as beneficial insects adore them. The flowers of parsnips are equally appreciated if you can wait for them until the following year.

Camouflaging your crops

Don't let your plants become a sitting target – they can't run away. Disguise them by mixing in flowers and edging your beds with pungent herbs. Many pest insects fly in a random and inaccurate way looking for specific crops. They need a big landing area. If you have small beds with different crops in them they may well miss the target altogether.

Hygiene – keeping up standards

Diseases are caused by fungi, viruses, and bacteria. Symptoms include spotting where parts of leaves die, cankers or scabs, changing colour (yellowing or silvering), wilting, wet rots and powdery or fluffy moulds or mildew.

Viruses are bad news as there is no cure. The symptoms are malformations and unnatural patterns on leaves (mottling or mosaic). They are likely to start on a single plant and be spread by aphids or anything that moves from plant to plant – and that includes you.

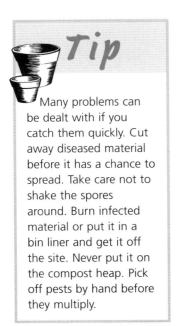

Tip

Many problems can be dealt with if you catch them quickly. Cut away diseased material before it has a chance to spread. Take care not to shake the spores around. Burn infected material or put it in a bin liner and get it off the site. Never put it on the compost heap. Pick off pests by hand before they multiply.

Be careful when accepting gifts of plants. On an allotment it is truly unwise to exchange potatoes, brassicas or onions. They may carry any of the worst of the soil-borne diseases such as eelworm, potato blight, clubroot or onion white rot.

Be wary of cross-infection. Dip your tools into disinfectant or alcohol between plants when pruning fruit as the plants are prone to viruses. Keep pots and containers well scrubbed. Mind where you tread if you have visited another plot where there may be diseases in the soil. Wash your hands between moving from plant to plant.

Get to know your pests

Some pests are large enough to be seen and identified, many are not or they dine at night. Detection skills come in here, either by night vigils with a torch and magnifying glass or finding clues from the type of damage.

✦ If there are holes in the leaves of a plant, the chances are that they are being eaten by slugs, snails or caterpillars.

✦ If it's the roots, underground larvae might be to blame.

✦ If the leaves are curling, most likely there will be colonies of aphids feeding on plant sap on the undersides.

✦ If you come in one morning and find your vegetables decapitated it could be the work of cutworms.

✦ If some newly planted seedlings have disappeared without trace, suspect mice.

Generally creatures that move fast are chasing prey and the slow ones are after your vegetables. But

not always – a ladybird larva, for example, could easily be mistaken for an enemy.

Disease-resistance

If certain diseases are a problem in your area, seek out disease-resistant cultivars. They really make a difference. For soft fruit, tree fruit, potatoes and other plants prone to viruses, always use certified virus-free stock.

Preventing pests reaching your plants

BARRIERS in the form of netting and horticultural fleece are highly effective at keeping out flying insects. Keep in mind that they need to go up before the pests arrive and the gauge of mesh needs to be in proportion to the pest (see page 55).

COLLARS of carpet underlay placed around plants will deter soil-borne creatures creeping up the stems. Many lay their eggs in the soil under a plant, which the larvae will then feed on when they hatch.

CLOCHES will keep out slugs as well as flying insects.

TRAPS Car grease spread on a board will trap flea beetles when the plant is shaken. Commercially bought sticky grease bands are effective against the wingless winter moths that crawl up the trunks of apples, pears and plums to lay their eggs.

Jars of beer sunk into the ground will send slugs off into drunken oblivion. Pheromone traps lure codling moths looking for a mate. They indicate their presence so you can take further action if necessary.

Get the timing right

Sometimes you can avoid pests and diseases by timing. Early potatoes are less prone to disease because they grow fast and are out of the ground before blight has got going. Overwintered broad beans are too tough for the black bean aphid to enjoy much and the first carrots are usually out before the breeding season of the carrot fly.

Companion planting

One area that is waiting for scientific research to prove its worth is companion planting. However, it has already been shown that French marigolds or nasturtiums will mask the smell of brassicas to the cabbage white butterfly, and if four rows of onions are planted around one row of carrots, they keep carrot fly at bay until the onion leaves go over.

Dwarf broad or French beans planted between brassicas of the same size in alternate rows show a lessened risk of aphid attack. While netting is more foolproof than this, these trials show that combined plantings can have an effect on pests and diseasea and will help, at the very least, to tip the balance.

Herbs, ancient plants useful to mankind for centuries, know how to defend themselves.

✦ Tansy contains an insecticide (thujone).
✦ Pennyroyal was used in the olden days to repel mice and insects in the house.
✦ *Tagetes minuta*, a herbal relation of the marigold (also known as 'stinking Roger'), excretes sulphur compounds from its roots to inhibit

eelworms and slugs, as does the mustard green manure, *Sinapis alba*.
✦ Lavender and rosemary produce clouds of essential oils that few pests would choose to cross.
✦ Chamomile, known as the plant's physician, is believed to bring good health to every plant around it.
✦ Members of the onion family and nettles are said to protect their neighbours from diseases caused by fungi and bacteria. Some good gardeners make infusions of these by steeping them in water overnight, dousing affected plants and laying the soaked stems around them.

Biological pest control

The use of nematodes and parasites to target specific pests is expensive and temporary. Although the idea is effective for the enclosed greenhouse, it is generally impractical for an area as big as an allotment. However, if you have a bad infestation, a biological control might be worth considering.

They are usually obtained by post. With one exception (the bacteria *Bacillus thuringiensis* which is sprayed onto caterpillars), they are microscopic forms of life which need to be released by watering onto the soil as soon as possible after delivery.

Highly susceptible to insecticides, these pest controls cannot be used in any joint programme. They need moist, well-drained soil to do their work and specific temperature bands. They should be introduced as early as possible

so they have time to breed and build up a big enough population to be effective.

Organic pesticides and fungicides

Organic chemicals should be used with as much care as their man-made chemical counterparts and only as a last resort. The organic organization, the Henry Doubleday Research Association, only gives the short list of chemicals below 'qualified acceptance'. Make sure that you have identified the problem accurately before you use them and target precisely. The main advantage of organic over inorganic chemicals is that they are non-persistent – in most cases being active for no longer than a day. Don't attempt to make your own – it is illegal in the UK.

COPPER FUNGICIDE acts against the spread of mildews and blights. It coats the leaves for several weeks. It comes in various cocktails, including Bordeaux mixture (copper sulphate and quicklime) and Burgundy mixture (copper sulphate with washing soda).
Warning: toxic to fish and can harm plants, particularly if they are under stress.

DERRIS (rotenone) comes as a powder or liquid and is made from the derris plant. It is an effective insecticide for dealing with aphids, spider mite and other small insects.
Warning: it is also poisonous to ladybirds, worms and fish, among others.

INSECTICIDAL SOAP is potassium salt soap and is used to control aphids, whitefly, red spider mites and mealy bugs. It only works on

GOLDEN RULES FOR SPRAYING

- ✦ Follow the manufacturer's instructions to the letter.
- ✦ Store chemicals away from children in the original labelled container.
- ✦ Use good equipment and wash thoroughly afterwards, having disposed of any leftover.
- ✦ Never spray open flowers for fear of harming bees.
- ✦ Only spray on windless evenings when the good insects have turned in for the night.

a direct hit and is only active for one day.

Warning: it will kill friendly insects on contact.

PYRETHRUM is extracted from *Chrysanthemum coccineum* and is used as an insecticide against aphids, small caterpillars and flea beetles, among others.

Warning: poisonous to fish and some friendly insects.

SOFT SOAP is a mild pesticide but is usually used as a medium, or wetter, to help other sprays to adhere to leaves.

SULPHUR is a fungicide. It comes as a spray or dust and can be used to control mildew.

Warning: harmful to beneficial insects.

COMMON PESTS AND DISEASES
American gooseberry mildew

This is a fungal disease usually caused by humidity or too much nitrogen feed. It shows as a white powdery fungal growth on the stems and leaves. Vulnerable young leaves may drop off and the fruit may become discoloured. Cut off affected parts of the plant as soon as you see the first signs. Prune to allow plenty of air circulation. Look for

disease-resistance in any future plantings.

Anthracnose

A fungus that can badly affect dwarf and runner beans. The first symptoms are sunken brown spots on the stems. The leaf veins may go red and the leaves drop off. The pods may get infected. Remove and burn or bin all sick plants and start again using resistant cultivars.

Aphids

There are hundreds of different types of this very common pest. They include greenfly and blackfly, mealy cabbage aphid, black bean aphid and lettuce root aphid. They breed rapidly, suck the sap and secrete honeydew which brings on sooty moulds (a harmless fungus) and they spread viruses as they move from plant to plant. Encourage hoverflies, lacewings and ladybirds and they will eat them voraciously.

Choose resistant varieties. In the case of broad beans, beat the black bean aphid season by planting early under cover. If you do get caught, cut off the tops of the plants where they congregate. Cover with horticultural fleece, though not if plants need to be pollinated. Squash the aphids or cut off infected shoots and drop

into soapy water.

Wash them off the plants with a powerful jet of water, or spray with soft soap or an insecticide soap.

Apple sawflies

These pests spend the winter in the soil and lay their eggs in spring on immature fruits. The resulting maggots, which are white with brown heads, burrow into the fruit, leaving a trail of excrement. By the time they have reached the core, the fruit will fall off the tree. Sometimes the maggots die in the fruit – the apple will grow on to maturity but it will be distorted. Pick up any fallen fruits before the maggots get out and back into the soil. Rake back mulches and cultivate around apple trees to expose the maggots to the birds.

Apple scab

A fungus which shows as black or brown scabs on fruits and leaves. These can spread until the fruits are blackened, distorted and cracked, eventually falling off the tree. Practise good hygiene and remove all affected fruit. Prune back to allow good air circulation. As a last resort, spray with Bordeaux or Burgundy mixture.

Asparagus beetles

The adults are chequered black and yellow and the larvae are dark grey. The adults stay hidden around the plants through winter and emerge in spring to lay their eggs. Both adults and larvae will defoliate asparagus and skin the stems. Be watchful from late spring and remove them. Burn the foliage at the end of the season when you cut it down. Clear away hiding places where they may hibernate. As a last

177

resort, use derris liquid or dust.

Bacterial canker *See canker.*

Beet leaf miner

This shows as large brown patches on the leaves of beetroot and spinach beet. It is caused by the white maggots of the leaf mining fly. There are two generations each summer. Pick off all the affected leaves or squash the pests within the leaves.

Beet leaf spot

A mild fungal disease affecting the beet family. Signs are small round spots with a purplish edge and pale centre. The overwintering fungus is spread by rain, tools or hand, and flourishes in hot and humid weather. Clean up the plants, removing affected leaves. Use fresh seed for the next crop.

Big bud

This is caused by blackcurrant gall mites. They are tiny white grubs that feed and breed inside the flower buds through winter, causing them to swell. They will affect the health of the bush and can spread viruses. Remove and burn all affected buds. If it's very bad you can cut the bush to ground level to start afresh the following year.

Birds

When soft fruit is ripening, birds can strip it with the speed of light. Pigeons are partial to young brassicas and can desecrate a crop. Use netting and bird scarers – anything that flaps in the wind will help. Old CDs tied along lines are effective as they flash as the light catches them. Humming lines will also put them off.

Black bean aphid *See aphids.*

Blackcurrant gall midges

These minute white maggots feed on the tips of young leaves, causing dryness and making them drop off. Choose resistant varieties. Spray the maggots with insecticidal soap.

Blossom end rot

This shows as a tough leathery patch at the 'blossom end', or base, of tomatoes. It may not affect all the fruits. It is caused by dryness at the roots, or from soil that is too acid. Pick off the affected fruits and water the plants well and regularly.

Blossom wilt

An air-borne fungus carried by wind or insects. It can affect apples, pears and all the stone fruits. The spores rest in cankers over the winter and the fungus spreads onto the blossom, killing it and moving onto the leaves. You will see small beige pustules on the affected areas. It may be quite localized at first. It spreads more quickly in damp weather. Prune out infected areas before it spreads, removing cankers.

Bolting

When a plant feels under pressure, it is inclined to panic and flower early.

Botrytis *See grey mould.*

Brown rot

This is caused by various air-borne fungi that penetrate tree fruits (particularly apples) through broken skin. It results in rot and whitish pustules forming. The fruit will either fall off or wither away. Birds often cause the injury pecking at the fruits and can carry it from tree to tree. Rain will spread it also. Remove affected fruits and destroy them.

Prune back any diseased spurs. Net against birds.

Cabbage white butterfly

The caterpillars of the cabbage white are large hairy yellow creatures with black markings. They feed on the outer leaves of brassicas, leaving holes, and can strip a plant with speed. The larvae of the small white cabbage butterfly are velvety and camouflaged green. They eat the hearts. There are two to three generations a year in spring and early autumn. Watch out for them and try to catch them before they burrow in. Pick off the affected leaves. Grow under fine mesh. You can wash them off if you get an infestation with a good dousing of water. The biological control is *Bacillus thuringiensis.*

Cabbage moth

This pest has only one generation a year. Their green or light brown caterpillars eat holes in the leaves of brassicas and burrow into the hearts. They also go for onion leaves. Pick them off before they burrow, or grow under fine netting. The biological control is *Bacillus thuringiensis.*

Cabbage root fly

This is a very serious pest particularly to brassicas, though it can destroy root crops as well, making them inedible. The adults look like small horseflies but it is the offspring of small white maggots that do the damage. The eggs are laid near or on the plants and the pupae overwinter in the soil. Symptoms are wilting and poor growth. The worst damage is likely in late spring but second and third generations can make it a summer-long problem.

Prevention is simple. Put collars of carpet underlay, about 10 cm (4 in) diameter, around the plants individually or plant through fleece. A layer of fine mesh netting placed over the soil immediately after planting or sowing will prevent the pupae burrowing.

Cabbage whitefly

These are sap-feeding insects which attack brassicas. The tiny white-winged adults fly up when disturbed while their scaly brown young stay still on the undersides of leaves. A slight infestation causes little harm but don't let it get out of hand.

Symptoms will be leaves sticky with honeydew and sooty moulds. The insects are around throughout summer and start laying eggs from mid-May onwards. Clear away all brassicas at the end of the season. Douse infected plants with a good jet of water. It is said that fennel and lovage will attract the parasitic wasp *Aphelinus* which will deal with them effectively. As a last resort, spray weekly with insecticidal soap.

Calcium deficiency

This is fairly unusual. It can occur on very acid soils and where there is a lack of water as plants need moisture to take up calcium. It usually shows as poor growth but can result in blossom end rot.

Cankers

These are caused by a group of fungi and bacteria and can be devastating to fruit trees. They are most likely to occur in wet weather in spring or autumn. They enter the fruits from the smallest wound. The first signs are an area of bark sinking inwards and resin may ooze from cracks and fissures.

The entire tree may then start to die. Remove diseased parts, cutting back to healthy tissue, and burn. Improve growing conditions. If the situation is bad, spray with Bordeaux mixture.

Capsid bugs

These small green insects suck sap from the tips of the shoots, particularly of currants and apples. They spread toxic saliva while they are at it. The first sign is multiple small holes. If extreme, the plant will take on a ragged appearance with dying buds and shoots and deformed fruit. Attract birds and remove any fallen leaves where they may lurk. As a last resort, use insecticidal soap.

Carrot fly

The adult females lay their eggs around root crops and the resultant larvae tunnel unseen into carrots, celeriac, parsnips, parsley and celery. There are usually two generations, one in late spring and another in midsummer. The most effective deterrents are either to grow the whole crop under fleece or to erect vertical barriers of fleece, finest mesh, heavy cardboard or sacking at least 60 cm (24 in) high. This will thwart the females as they fly close to the ground and in straight lines.

Sowing in late spring will avoid the first wave and make the second less serious as the population won't have built up. Companion planting with onions is said to confuse both the onion fly and the carrot fly which track by scent. There are disease-resistant cultivars – as the flies don't like the taste but might eat them if there is nothing else, a sacrificial row of ordinary carrots among them

should guarantee success.

Celery fly

These little white maggots eat the leaves of celery plants. Catch them early and pick off and burn the affected leaves.

Celery leaf spot

This disease is caused by a fungus, usually in the seed. It generally appears first as tiny brown spots on the leaves and can spread over the plant rapidly in damp conditions. Cut away any infected parts of the plant. Use fresh disease-resistant seed next time.

Chocolate spot

A fungal disease, of broad beans particularly. Small brown spots appear on the leaves. In wet weather it can become serious. Make sure that broad beans have good rich soil, good air circulation and sharp drainage. Pull out any that are badly damaged. Clear weeds and debris. As a last resort, use copper fungicide.

Clubroot

A serious and widespread fungal disease which particularly affects brassicas and sometimes root vegetables such as turnips and swedes. There is no cure. The roots become distorted, forming an elbow-like 'club' or a series of tuberous swellings, known as 'fingers' or 'toes'. If your brassicas are wilting although they have enough moisture, dig one up and check the roots.

If affected, burn or bin the whole crop without delay before the disease spreads. Avoid using the same soil for brassicas for as long as possible, keeping in mind that clubroot can live in the soil for twenty years.

Take every precaution to avoid it in the first place. If your soil is acid (the most favourable conditions for clubroot), add lime to bring it up to a pH of 7 or more. Rotation is crucial to avoid a build-up of the disease. Keep weeds under control as some common weeds, such as shepherd's purse, are in the brassica family and can harbour clubroot. Don't use fodder radish and mustard green manures for the same reason. Be very strict about cleaning tools, and remember that you can spread it on your boots. Buy transplants from a reliable source if you haven't grown them yourself. Grow disease-resistant plants fast, in the right season for them, and the best possible conditions. Start plants in sterile compost, or if sowing outside, make a bigger hole than usual and fill with clean proprietary compost.

Codling moths

These lay their eggs on the fruit and leaves of apple trees. The resulting pink black-headed caterpillars tunnel into the fruit, often without trace as they tend go in near the stalk. After about four weeks when the fruit is spoilt, they head off to pupate. Pheromone traps, put up from May to July, will catch some and warn you of their presence. As a last resort, derris will kill them if you spray it on before they go into the fruit.

Coral spot

An aptly named fungus that will get into a wound or a dead branch and causes die back. Currants are particularly vulnerable. Prune out all affected stems down to healthy wood and burn them.

Crown rot

An individual or joint attack by fungi and bacteria in the soil. The effect is a rotting off of the crown, where the leaves join the root. Sometimes you can save the plant by cutting off the infected areas back to healthy tissue. Improve growing conditions.

Cucumber mosaic virus

This can affect a wide range of plants, including marrow, courgettes, peppers and spinach, as well as cucumbers. The leaves will develop unnatural yellow patterns and the fruits will be distorted. Burn the plants, taking great care not to spread the infection. Buy resistant-varieties and remove weeds and debris where the spores will overwinter.

Cutworms

These can sever the stem entirely on wide range of young vegetables and will attack strawberries, too. They are the larvae of a group of nocturnal moths which lay thousands of eggs around the stems of plants in summer. The soil-borne caterpillars, which are in shades of brown, yellow and green, and curl into a C-shape, will work their way through a row of vegetables by night. The first signs are plants that have been severed just below the soil level. You will find the caterpillars under the surface of the soil. Clear weeds which the moths like for egg laying and put a collar of carpet underlay around the stems. Turn over the soil for the birds to find them in winter.

Downy mildew

This disease is caused by fungi which penetrate into plant tissue. They live in the soil for up to five years, as well as in plant debris. Discoloured areas appear on the leaf surfaces with corresponding white or pale grey fungal growth on the undersides. If allowed to spread, entire leaves will die. It thrives in damp, warm conditions and is commonly found on a wide range of crops, particularly when young. Remove infected leaves and destroy them. Improve air circulation and clear weeds. Water at the base to avoid spreading it.

Eelworms *See potato cyst eelworm.*

Flea beetles

Small and shiny, these jumping beetles emerge in spring and can fly long distances to find food. Young brassicas are their favourite fare and they leave little holes in leaves and stems. Their larvae feed on the roots. A bad attack will check older plants and can kill seedlings. Protect crops by growing under cloches or fleece. Grow plants as fast as possible in the right season and conditions to get them through the vulnerable period. If you get an infestation, put boards smeared with car grease or slow-drying glue under the plants and shake them. The beetles will leap into the trap. Clear debris round plants. A last resort is derris powder.

Gooseberry sawflies

These are quite visible being at 2.5 cm (1 in) long. They are green caterpillar-like creatures with black spots. They can completely defoliate gooseberry bushes if not checked. Look out for them from spring to autumn. Pick them off from the undersides of leaves before they cause too much damage. In autumn, rake away any mulches and turn over the soil lightly to invite birds to find them.

Grey mould or botrytis

A common disease, particularly in damp summers, causing leaves, flowers and buds to rot. It's a fluffy mould which, when disturbed, releases clouds of spores, infecting everything around it. Avoid over-crowding, and clear any rotting vegetation around plants as it will harbour it. Provide a good air flow. Remove all diseased plants.

Halo blight

A bacterial disease particularly affecting dwarf French and runner beans. The first symptoms are dark spots in the centre of a pale 'halo' on the leaves. This is followed by yellowing between the veins. The disease comes in the seed, and rain spreads it. If you catch it in time, you might save the crop by picking off the leaves. However, next year start again from a fresh source.

Leaf spot

A fungal disease which affects a wide range of plants, including peas and broad beans. The symptoms are grey or brown spots encircled with rings of discoloured tissue. Sometimes they develop tiny black spots. Leaf spot doesn't do a great deal of damage. Pick off and burn affected and fallen leaves. Don't water overhead or handle the plants.

Leaf miners

A cross-section of many different insects and their larvae which burrow around within the leaves of plants. You can detect them by the meandering pattern of damage which eventually makes the leaves go dry and brown. If you hold the leaf up to the light you may spot the culprit. Though not generally too harmful to the plant, the thought of eating them is not very appetizing. Pick off and destroy the affected leaves.

Leaf mould

A disease which is usually confined to indoor tomatoes in high humidity. A greenish fungal growth on the undersides of leaves causes yellow patches on the upper sides and, as it spreads up the plant, leaves shrivel and die. It is very infectious. Choose resistant varieties. Destroy diseased material. Keep well ventilated and don't water from above. Copper fungicide may do the trick.

Leaf spot

A general term for both fungal and bacterial diseases that cause spotting – black spot is a common one. The spots are dead areas and as they spread, leaves drop off. It is generally not very damaging. Remove affected leaves and burn. Make sure the plants have plenty of air circulation and don't water from overhead as this can spread it.

Magnesium deficiency

This is caused by acid soil and by the overuse of high-potash fertil-izers. Magnesium is easily washed out by heavy rain. The symptoms are yellowing edges and the areas between the veins of the older leaves. As the leaves deteriorate, they may go red, purple, yellow or brown. Foliar-feed with Epsom salts (200 g in 10 litres or 8 oz in 2½ gallons with a bit of washing up liquid) fortnightly for immediate effect. Lime the soil to reduce acidity. Avoid potash fertilizer if this is the cause.

Mealy cabbage aphids

These sap-feeding insects cause yellow patches on the upper surfaces of the leaves. Underneath there will be the pale grey aphids. The effect is to distort the shoot tips and can be very damaging to young plants. All brassicas are vulnerable from spring right through to autumn. Pick the aphids off or give them a good shower of water. If there is an infestation, spray with insecticidal soap.

Mice

Sometimes they steal newly planted seedlings without trace and raid your shed. Use cloches to protect plants or trap the mice.

Mildews *See downy mildew and powdery mildew.*

Onion fly

Having spent the winter below ground, onion flies emerge as adults in May. They lay their eggs on and around the host plants – onions in particular, but leeks, shallots and garlic also. The resulting small white maggots cause havoc with the crops. They bore holes into them, eat the roots and cause the plants to rot. Remove any affected plants and destroy. Outwit the flies by rota-tion, plant sets rather than seedlings, and cover with fine net or fleece before the flies arrive.

Onion neck rot

A fungal disease exacerbated by wet weather. The signs of damage don't usually appear until the onions have been in store for a couple of months. They become soft and discoloured. A grey, fluffy, fungal growth develops, particu-larly around the neck of the bulb. The fungus lurks in onion debris and on the soil. Grow your onions by the book – use top-quality sets, allow for plenty of air circulation while they are growing and during storage. Don't store any that are damaged. Remember to practise rotation.

Onion white rot

A fatal disease caused by soil fungus, to which the whole onion family is susceptible. A fluffy white fungus dotted with little black specks spreads over the base of the bulbs and the roots, and the leaves turn yellow and wilt. The black specks are 'sklerotia', or 'fruiting bodies' that will lurk in the soil for up to seven years waiting for the next host. Dispose of the crop and avoid using the same land for the onion family for eight years.

Parsnip canker

This shows as rough brown, red or black patches usually on the shoulder of the roots. It is a fungal infection that enters through a wound. It could be through a tiny hole left by a carrot fly. There isn't a cure but it is a good idea to buy disease-resistant seed.

Pea and bean weevil

If you find U-shaped holes in the edges of leaves of your peas and beans, it will be these tiny grey beetles. The larvae live in the soil and feed on the roots and the adults emerge in June or July. Generally, they don't do too much harm except to young and vulnerable plants. The best defence is to cover with cloches or net when you plant.

Pea moths

These are tiny caterpillars with black heads. They lay eggs on the flowers to hatch out inside the pea pod. Avoid by planting early or late to avoid the breeding time. Cover with fine mesh when in flower. Turn over the soil for the birds to get at them in winter. As a last resort, apply derris liquid a week after flowering and two weeks later.

Peach leaf curl

This is a fungus that attacks the unfurling leaves of peaches and nectarines. It causes the leaves to twist and curl, change colour, develop red blisters and drop off. It is spread by rain and is prevented by covering the plants from later winter to spring. This is done by constructing a wooden frame and hanging clear plastic curtains, with a roof piece, over the entire plant and tucking the ends into the soil. Open up on dry early spring days for pollination. Pick off any affected leaves and burn. As a last resort, use Bordeaux mixture as the leaves emerge.

Pear leaf blister mite

This is more unsightly than harmful. Microscopic gall mites burrow into the leaves, resulting in yellow or pink blotching and blistering. There is no real cure apart from removing affected leaves promptly.

Pear midge

These tiny larvae of a fly or gall midge burrow into young pear fruits which slowly turn black and fall off. The maggots go back into the soil to pupate for the following year. Pick fruits at the first signs and destroy. Spray with derris just before the flowers open up.

Pear scab *See apple scab.*
Plum leaf curling aphids

The green winged aphids feed on the leaf sap of plums and greengages. The symptoms are curled and crinkled leaves in spring; the aphids will be nesting inside. They fly off to pastures new, herbaceous plants usually, after a few weeks and the trees will put out new leaves. They return at the end of summer to lay their eggs ready for the next season. Treat as for aphids, bringing in predators, squashing or dousing them with water, or removing affected leaves. A last resort is derris or insecticidal soap.

Plum moths

These produce little pink and brown caterpillars that feed inside plums and leave their excrement in it. They burrow out to overwinter in fissures in the bark. A pheromone trap in late spring will warn you of their presence and disrupt mating. Spraying in early summer with derris may catch them as they hatch.

Potato blackleg

This disease is caused by soil-borne bacteria. It first shows as stunted leaves and blackened rot at the base of the stem. The parent potato will also be rotting. It enters the potato through a break in the skin and may be isolated to a single potato plant in a crop. It is more likely in wet conditions. Avoid damaging potatoes, particularly when lifting them. Only store tubers with unbroken skin. Buy certified seed potatoes.

Potato common scab

A bacterial disease usually occurring in dry weather and on sandy soils, particularly if newly cultivated. Circular scabby patches appear on the tubers, which can usually be peeled off. Increase the acidity of the soil and the water-holding capacity with well-rotted organic matter. Keep the crop well watered and buy resistant cultivars.

Potato cyst eelworm

This pest is to be avoided at all costs as there is no cure. Each microscopic nematode female can lay 500 eggs, which stay in the ground for ten years or longer waiting for a host plant to arrive before they hatch. On an allotment where much potato growing has taken place over years, eelworm eggs are likely to be lurking in the soil. The larvae feed on the roots. The first symptoms are drying, dying leaves starting from the bottom, followed by poor crops.

If allowed to build up there will be crop failure. Look for varieties with resistance where possible. Avoid bringing the eelworm in on your boots or tools from other parts of the allotment site that may be infected. Keep up the rotation with as big a gap as possible before returning to the original potato patch. Put on lots of well-rotted compost and manure to bring in nematode predators. When the ground is fallow, plant a mustard green manure (*Sinapsis alba*) as it inhibits eelworms.

Potato powdery scab

A fungal disease mostly found on heavy soils where potato crops have been grown over the years. The potatoes form scabby patches which burst to release thousands of spores into the soil. There is nothing for it but to destroy the crop and abandon the site for potato growing for three or four years, only returning to it when the drainage has been improved.

Potato and tomato blight

This shows as brown marks on leaves and stems and a downy white mass of fungal spores on the undersides. The spores wash down into the soil – the tomato fruits and potato tubers develop sunken areas, and tomatoes can also get leathery patches. Other fungi and bacteria join in to induce a fast-spreading highly infectious soft rot.

Remove and destroy any infected leaves. Buy resistant strains and good-quality seed potatoes. Space plants widely for air circulation, and water at ground level. Earth up and mulch potatoes with straw to prevent the spores reaching the tubers. Dig up all potatoes at the end of the season. Any left will infect the next crop.

Powdery mildew

This shows as a whitish powdery growth – typically on the upper sides of the leaves but can be almost anywhere – on a wide variety of plants. It is caused by a group of fungi. If left to develop it can cause yellowing, distortion, dead spots on leaves and leaf drop. In severe cases it can kill. It thrives particularly on young plants in dry soil in humid conditions. Catch it early and remove affected leaves.

Keep the plants watered but avoid spreading the fungi by watering from overhead. Don't overfeed plants with high nitrogen fertilizers as they will produce soft lush growth. Look for cultivars with disease resistance. As a last resort, spray with copper fungicide – Bordeaux mixture or Burgundy mixture.

Raspberry beetles

These pests feed on the flowers and lay their eggs on raspberries, blackberries and the hybrids. The yellow larvae burrow into the fruits, making them dry up and shrivel. You quite often find them in the fruit when you harvest. Expose the ground around the canes for the birds to find the overwintering pupae and cut the canes right back to ground level. You will miss next year's fruit but it is important to get rid of the raspberry beetles.

Raspberry cane spot

A fungus that shows as purplish spots with a white centre on the young stems of raspberries, blackberries and the hybrids. In extreme cases it can split the canes and cause leaf drop. Prune out affected canes as soon as you see it before it spreads.

Raspberry spur blight

A fungus that first appears on the buds of new raspberry and loganberry canes. It shows as deep purple splotches. If left unchecked, it will spread to the canes, turning grey with tiny black spots of 'fruiting bodies' in winter. The result is poor crops. The fungus spreads rapidly in wet or overcrowded conditions or where too much nitrogen has caused soft sappy growth. Prune out diseased canes before the fungus spreads. Thin for the following season. As a last resort, apply Bordeaux mixture when the buds are forming and a couple of weeks later.

Red spider mite

This seems to be increasing in our warmer summers. They are microscopic brown mites, flaring to brilliant orange-red in winter. Traditionally associated with the greenhouse, they sometimes escape in summer. The outdoor sap-feeding fruit tree version is usually kept under control by natural predators where chemical sprays are not used. Their presence is revealed by a silvering of the leaves, followed by a mottled yellowing. They like dry conditions best, so a good squirt of water on a regular basis will help to keep them at bay, with or without the addition of insecticidal soap.

Replant disease

This condition is something of a mystery. The symptoms are unhappy plants. Generally associated with roses, it occurs with fruit trees as well. It happens when you replace a fruit tree with another of the same species in the same spot. If you cannot find a fresh site for new plantings, the only way to prevent it is to dig out the topsoil to a minimum depth of 45 cm (18 in) and put in fresh soil from another part of the plot.

Root aphids

These are trickier customers than normal aphids as they work unseen to weaken plants. Different types live among the roots of lettuce, runner and French beans and Jerusalem artichokes. They are tiny, yellowish and secrete a fluffy wax. Rotate crops and buy aphid-resistant cultivars.

Shot hole

A general term for bacterial and fungal infections that cause holes edged with a brown ring to appear in the leaves. Remove affected leaves and destroy. Keep up air circulation and remove weeds.

Silver leaf

A fungus that enters through wounds, affecting only individual branches at first and causing a slight silvering. Plums are particularly prone. Leaves drop off and branches will die in time. Eventually the whole tree will perish. Prune in summer only as wounds heal more quickly when the tree is growing vigorously. Cut back to healthy wood and burn any infected prunings. Clear away dead timber where the spores lurk.

Slugs

A universal menace. There are many different species, and some live underground and attack roots and burrow into potato tubers. Slugs like warm moist weather and come out to feed at night. They shelter and breed under stones, in amongst piles of leaves, under garden debris, in the soil, and under mulches (the one disadvantage).

Encourage predators, including frogs, toads, birds, hedgehogs, shrews, slow worms and beetles. Cover small plants with cloches. Surround plants with inhospitable sharp or dry mulches – gravel, egg shells, wood chips, soot, ash, or lime. Do torch-light vigils and catch and destroy slugs by dropping them into a salt solution. Using tongs or rubber gloves makes this slightly less repellent. Trap and drown them by sinking plastic pots of beer or milk into the ground, changing the bait from time to time and stopping if you catch beetles.

They will gorge until they die on bran. Scooped-out melon and grapefruit skins make hiding places for them to congregate, as do old planks or wet newspaper – they can then be collected and destroyed. Lay out alternative food sources; they will choose rotting vegetation over fresh, so old lettuce leaves kept moist under cover of a tile will draw them away to where they can be collected.

Snails

These present the same problems as slugs and the same treatments are effective, though frogs won't eat them nor will parasitic nematodes be able to get at them effectively.

Soft rot

A bacterial and fungal disease which results in decay of plant tissues. It affects swedes and turnips, showing as a greyish mushy rot on heavy wet ground. Start again, trying raised beds for better drainage.

Sooty mould

This results from the honeydew excreted by aphids, whitefly and mealy bugs. Though unsightly as leaves get covered with grey to black mould, it is not in itself harmful except that it reduces light and air getting to the leaves. The only way to deal with it is to go after the pests.

Tip burn

This can affect lettuce and chicory, making the leaf edges turn brown. It is usually caused by calcium deficiency due to dry roots or the soil being too acid. Water well and if your soil is acid, lime it before planting lettuce next time.

Tomato blight *See potato and tomato blight.*

Violet root rot

Filaments of violet fungal threads cover the roots, crown and stems of plants. It can affect asparagus, beetroot, carrots, celery, parsnips, potatoes, strawberries, swedes and turnips. The first signs are yellowing and stunting. It is most commonly found in wet, acid soils. Remove and destroy the crop and change the soil conditions before trying again.

Vine weevils

The white grubs live in the soil and feed on plant roots, causing poor growth. The black adults are less harmful. Appearing at night to nibble the outside edges of the leaves, they leave small ragged holes. Most die by winter. Predominantly female, they lay so many hundreds of eggs in the soil through the summer months that it is difficult to eliminate them. A parasitic nematode, either *Heterorhabditis megidis* or *Steinernema carpocapsae*, watered on the soil in spring or late summer is effective.

Viruses

These come in many forms, all incurable. The first signs are loss of vigour and stunting and distortion, followed by strange colour changes and patterns on leaves including mosaic patterns, flecking and mottling. Viruses can be caused by soil-borne nematodes and fungi. More commonly they will be passed from plant to plant by aphids or even gardeners as they move around handling different plants. Try to prevent the spread by strict hygiene and keeping the aphid population at bay. Buy certified virus-free stock where possible. Destroy and burn infected plants as soon as a virus is detected. See cucumber mosaic virus.

Whitefly

These tiny flying insects suck the sap on the undersides of leaves and excrete copious amounts of sticky honeydew. If you shake the plants you can suck them up with portable vacuum cleaner or spray them with insecticidal soap.

Wireworms

The orange click beetle larvae live underground and bore holes into carrots, brassicas, strawberries, lettuce, onions, tomatoes and potatoes. They are mostly found in grassland and the good news is that, as your allotment becomes more cultivated with less grass, they will diminish in number. You can trap them by burying carrots, cabbage or a potato on a stick to attract them away from your crops. Keep the ground free of weeds and dig it over in winter for the birds to find them.

SAFEGUARDING YOUR SITE

ALLOTMENT LEGISLATION

1830 Act to Amend the Laws for the Relief of the Poor

Parishes permitted to set aside up to 50 acres of wasteland for allotments. A second law allowed the same for crown land.

1845 General Enclosure Act

Enclosures only permitted if provision for allotments was made.

1887 Allotments Act

Local authorities must provide allotments where there is demand. They must take into consideration any representations made to them by six voters or ratepayers resident in the area and provide sufficient plots.

1908 The Smallholding and Allotments Act

Endorsed the 1887 Act and imposed further responsibilities on councils. Local authorities now permitted to compulsorily purchase land for the provision of allotments. Allotment sites might be sold if the local authority is of the opinion that they are not needed.

1919 Land Facilities Settlement Act

This deleted reference to the 'labouring poor' and made allotments open to everyone.

1922 Allotments Act

States that 'the expression allotment garden means an allotment not exceeding forty poles in extent which is wholly or mainly cultivated by the occupier for the production of vegetables and fruit crops for consumption by himself and his family.' A minimum of six months notice must be given with compensation for evicted tenants.

1925 Allotments Act

This act established statutory sites, which must not be sold or converted to other uses without ministerial consent. The minister must be satisfied that adequate provision is made for displaced tenants. Local authorities must incorporate allotment provision in town planning.

1950 Allotments Act

Tenants are permitted to keep rabbits and hens. Concessions on rent may be made. A year's notice to quit is required. Local authorities are no longer obliged to provide allotments on demand in populations of under 10,000. Their obligations are to statutory allotments only (these are the 87 per cent owned by the local authorities in England and Wales. Community gardens, temporary and private sites are not covered by these laws).

1969 The Thorpe Report

This was the result of a government-commissioned inquiry into allotments. Recommendations were to upgrade allotments into landscaped leisure gardens on continental lines, with communal buildings and good facilities. It was not acted on by the government but several authorities – most notably Bristol and Birmingham City Council – did create some successful leisure gardens along these lines.

1998 The Select Committee Report 'The Future for Allotments'

This was produced by an all-party committee of MPs. Recommendations were that the law should be overhauled and that the government should take further measures to protect allotment sites. With certain exceptions, temporary sites of thirty years or more should become statutory. The local authority should have to appoint an allotment officer, provide water and fencing, advertise vacant plots on notice boards and consult plot holders prior to sale. When allotments are sold, alternative, near-by statutory sites should be supplied. The law on growing mostly vegetables and fruit for the consumption by the family should be relaxed. Local authorities should promote self-management.

The government did not act on the report but made two recommendations – that local authorities should effectively promote allotment sites before selling them. The Local Government Association should provide best practice guidelines for local authorities.

2001 Growing in the community: a good practice guide for the management of allotments

Along the lines of the Select Committee Report, this is an invaluable, practical guide for anyone involved in regenerating allotments.

ACTION TO TAKE

No plot holder can feel free from the threat of developers. The number of plots has dwindled from 600,000 before the First World War to some 300,000 in England and Wales today. With our housing shortage, hard-pushed councils can be tempted by offers that may run into millions on prime sites. Take every step to safeguard your allotment from being turned into concrete.

Lack of demand is the loophole through which many allotments have slipped. The Smallholdings and Allotments Act of 1908 permits authorities to sell sites if they are of the opinion that the land is not needed for allotments. The typical scenario is for sites to slide downhill while tenants do too little, too late. When sites become neglected, weed-ridden, vandalized and used as rubbish dumps, no one wants to take on a plot. When there are high vacancies, the case can be made that there is no demand.

The single most effective defence against developers is to keep the allotment fully occupied. To attract prospective customers, the site needs to be well kept and run. If it has the support of the local community and environmental value as well, the local authorities will find it very difficult to make an argument to close it down.

Self-management

The best allotment sites are those with good leadership, sparking off enthusiasm and friendship so that everyone pulls together.

Some councils promote allotments, advertise them, improve them, prepare plots for new tenants and run courses for beginners. Others do not. If your site is not thriving, consider taking a more active role – the greater the degree of self-management, the more the allotment holders will assume responsibility and take pride in the site.

Councils offer various levels of independence, usually negotiated when trust has been established through time. It is to their benefit to hand over some of the management as it saves them time and money. A 'partnership group' takes over some of the work. It arranges tenancies, collects the rent and does minor repairs while the council pays for the overheads and deals with any major work. A self-managing group, or association, leases the site, runs it more or less independently and is in a position to apply for grants and funding. NSALG can supply model constitutions and advice.

Filling plots

If you have vacant plots the first step is to publicise them. Put up a notice on the gate and advertise them on the web. Drop leaflets door-to-door, in doctors' surgeries, local libraries and other public places. Take a stand at the local farmer's market or the summer fair. Approach local groups and offer them plots. Many allotment sites have community plots for the disabled, ethnic minorities, refugees, beekeepers, environmental groups, the brownies and cubs, the over-fifties or schools.

Eddie Campbell, the Allotment Liaison Officer for North Birmingham, came up with the idea of running gardening classes for the pupils at the local schools. 'We design the plot, dig it over, discuss what they like to eat, learn about propagation and the kids grow peas and runner beans and all sorts over six to ten weeks. It's an extra curricular activity but they enjoy it so much they turn up every week.'

Zoy Mills, a teacher in agriculture, started the Women's Organic Community Allotment in Walkley, Sheffield, in 2001. Women of all nationalities and ages are invited to join in working the three plots. The orchards provide apples, and the third plot is devoted to growing vegetables and a wide variety of medicinal and culinary herbs. A willow circle will be woven into a shelter. Thanks to a local grant they have a pond backed by a mosaic made by a community artist and a polytunnel to grow exotic vegetables. They are planning to start herbal workshops.

Be seen to be green

Run your allotment organically. Put in wildlife habitats and keep records. If you still have spare plots, or areas that are not suitable for cultivating vegetables, consider putting a nature reserve in the form of a native woodland, a wildflower meadow or a wildlife pond. Get advice from your Local Agenda 21 officer. One of their aims is to optimize biodiversity.

Once a natural wildlife area, two-thirds of the New Chesterton Allotment site in

Cambridge was taken over for housing. In 1999, the allotments were awarded an Agenda 21 grant to make two ponds in an area of semi-flooded woodland and a hazel coppice. Three species of damselfly and five types of dragonfly as well as colonies of frogs and newts have settled in the ponds. Linnets, flocks of goldfinches, meadow pippets, migrant siskins, skylarks, sparrow hawks, kestrels and buzzards have also been seen.

Another good idea for a vacant plot is a communal compost heap. If everyone chips in with their compost you can build a magnificent heap quickly. It will need to be properly organized and planned. Sometimes grants are available.

Get the community behind you

Many a David and Goliath battle has been won, even on private and temporary sites, when the local community is up in arms. Befriend them and share the site, have open days, parties and festivals. Consider making public areas – you may need to apply for a 'change of use' for part of the site. Be careful, however, not to turn the allotment into a community garden as it will not then be protected by the laws governing allotments.

Join up with other sites

Make a website with other local allotments and join in a national web ring so you can back each other. Be prepared to link with neighbouring allotments if they run into trouble.

In 1999 the Cambridge Allotments Network took up the cause of the Whitehill allotments. Part of the site was threatened by a proposal to build a new stadium for Cambridge United Football Club. Dave Fox and Paul Jones from neighbouring allotments joined forces with the Whitehill site. 'We used the Council's processes to state our point of view.' Dave Fox says. 'We explained why allotments are fabulous and this one particularly so. We brought in researched local information, Local Agenda 21 and linked our arguments with their own policies – particularly how they support allotments. You have to talk in their terms. I think the Council expected us to look like country bumpkins when we had a meeting. They seemed surprised when we turned up in suits and ties and gave Power Point presentations.'

Earning money for improvements

With an average rent of £3 per month per plot, allotments are generally strapped for cash. The Allotments Act of 1922 stated that the allotments should be wholly or mainly cultivated by the occupier for the production of vegetables fruit for consumption by himself and his family. In other words, you cannot use the allotment for business. Here the loophole is the word 'mainly'. Check with the management. Most are relaxed about a small amount of trading at farmers' markets or at a local level if the proceeds are for the benefit of the allotment. Many sites have a trading shed and can sell gardening goods at a cheap rate to the public on payment of a nominal joining fee. Generally, the restriction on growing flowers is regarded as plain silly by site managers.

Raising grants

The council may give small grants which can make quite a difference to your site. With a council grant of £300, Kelvinside Allotment, in Glasgow, planted a mixed hedge of hawthorn, prunus, alder, guelder and briar roses – lovely to look at, good for wildlife and excellent defence against vandals.

If you need larger amounts of money, apply for a grant from the many big funding bodies. Get advice on filling in the application as it can be a challenge (see page 189).

LOOKING TO THE FUTURE

Now is the moment to rally. In the 21st century, allotments are seen as models of political correctness. They are nature reserves through towns, producers of fresh local food and recyclers of waste. They are acknowledged to be excellent for health, both for body and soul – a lifeline for many people. As gardening puts everyone on an equal footing, they have unique social potential. With many friends in high places, all we need now is the will to succeed.

USEFUL ADDRESSES

Funding advice

The Allotments Regeneration Initiative (ARI)
54-57 Allison Street
Birmingham B5 5TH
Tel: 0121 643 0402
www.farmgarden.org.uk/ari.
Run partly by NSALG. Grants are given out.

Community Fund
9th Floor, Camelford House
89 Albert Embankment
London SE1 7UF
Tel: 0845 791 9191
www.community-fund.org.uk
Advice on lottery grants. See their booklet 'Before You Apply'.

National Council for Voluntary Services
Tel: 0114 278 6636
www.nacvs.org.uk
Can help with advice on business plans, making a constitution and applying for grants.

Local Council
The Grants Officer and the Local Agenda 21 officer can advise and can sometimes give out grants.

Groundwork Trust
A charitable trust giving advice (and sometimes grants) to help the environment. See phone book for branches.

Other organizations

Henry Doubleday Research Association
HDRA Ryton Organic Gardens
Ryton-on-Dunsmore
Coventry CV8 3LG
Tel: 0204 7630 3517
www.hdra.org.uk
Researches and promotes organic gardening and food.

National Society of Allotment and Leisure Gardeners (NSALG)
O'Dell House, Hunter's Road, Corby, Northants NN 5JE
Tel: 01536 266 576
www.nsalg.demon.co.uk
Advice and help with funding, self-management, threatened allotments. Insurance schemes and bulk seed.

Federation of City Farms and Community Gardens
The Green House, Hereford Street, Bedminster, Bristol BS3 4NA.
Tel: 0117 923 1800
www.farmgarden.org.uk
Promotes community allotments, gardens and city farms.

The Royal Horticultural Society
80 Vincent Square
London SW1P 2PE
Tel: 020 7834 4333
www.rhs.org.uk

The Soil Association
Bristol House, 40-56 Victoria Street, Bristol BS1 6B
Tel: 0117 929 0661
www.soilassociation.org.uk
A membership charity at the heart of the campaign for organic food farming.

Women's Environmental Network
PO Box 30626
London E1 1TZ
Tel: 0207 4819144
www.wen.org.uk
Brings together ethnic minority women to grow their own food. Information and advice on how to adapt a site.

Websites

www.ncare.co.uk/allotmentring/
www.allotments.net
www.weather.telegraph.co.uk
www.kitchengardens.dial.pipex.com/kglist.htm.

Suppliers

HDRA Heritage Seed Library
HDRA, Ryton Organic Gardens
Coventry CV8 3LG
Tel: 024 7630 3517
Email: enquiry@hdra

Association Kokopelli
Ripple Farm, Crundale
Canterbury, Kent CT4 7EB
Tel: 01227 731 815
Rare varieties, good catalogue.

Suffolk Herbs
Tel: 01376 572 456
www.suffolkherbs.com
Organic seed and pest controls.

Vida Verde Seed Collection
14 Southdown Avenue, Lewes, East Sussex, BN7 1EL
www.vidaverde.co.uk
Heirloom and rare vegetables.

Tamar Organics
Woodlands Estate
Gulworthy, Tavistock
Devon PL19 8JE
Tel: 01822 834 887
Seed and garden supplies.

Just Green
Freepost ANG10331
Burnham-on-Crouch
Essex, CMO 8BF
Tel: 0800 389 6002
Biological and other organic pest control and insect habitats.

Brogdale Orchards
Brogdale Road, Faversham
Kent, ME13 8XZ
Tel: 01795 591491
Expert information on English fruit, plant centre and mail order.

INDEX